I0198166

Colonel Disbrowe, M.P.

Vice Chamberlain to Queen Charlotte.

Old Days in Diplomacy

Recollections of a Closed Century

BY THE ELDEST DAUGHTER OF

THE LATE

Sir Edward Cromwell Disbrowe, G.C.G.

EN. EX. MIN. PLEN.

WITH A PREFACE BY

M. Montgomery-Campbell

SANS PEUR ET
SANS REPROCHE

L & N

SECOND EDITION

LONDON

JARROLD & SONS, 10 & 11, WARWICK LANE, E.C

[All Rights Reserved]

1903

Dedication

TO

The Honourable Mrs. Richard Boyle.

(E. V. B.)

To "E. V. B."

My Dear Cousin,

  With your kind permission I dedicate to you these rambling recollections of the daughter of an old Diplomatist.

    Yours very affectionately,

      C. A. A. DISBROWE.

CONTENTS.

PART I.

CONTENTS.

PART II.

PREFACE.

HAVING had the privilege of being of some slight assistance to the authoress in preparing these most interesting reminiscences for the press, I am endeavouring, with her permission, to gather up diverse threads and to dwell on certain points in this preface which could not have been dealt with equally satisfactorily in footnotes.

In the following pages, life at various foreign courts during the first half of the past century is brought before us in a series of realistic sketches, and in addition we are enabled to trace the diplomatic career of Sir Edward Cromwell Disbrowe from its eventful beginning amidst the storm and strife of 1810, to its peaceful ending at the Hague in 1851. To have been entrusted when still a mere youth with missions calculated to tax the powers of the most experienced of men, Sir Edward must have undoubtedly given early proof of very exceptional abilities. Both when attached to Sir Charles Stuart during the Peninsular War, and later, when with Lord Cathcart and the Russian Headquarters, he was constantly the successful bearer of dispatches in circumstances of great danger and difficulty, and often found himself face to face with all the horrors of war. It was thus in Southern Europe during Spain's gallant fight for freedom, and again in Germany, when the young diplomatist crossed the blood-stained field of Leipzic three days after the famous engagement.

After following the allied armies to Paris, he was given the more peaceful post of Secretary of Legation at the Danish Court, yet here also great responsibilities, though of a different character from heretofore, were thrust upon him. Owing to the absence of the Minister, he was called upon to act as *Chargé d'Affaires.* It seemed ever to be his destiny to be rewarded for work well done by fresh demands on his energy and capacity. The State papers relative to the Congresses of Vienna and Aix-la-Chapelle, which are embodied in this volume, give distinct indication of the confidence reposed in him by his various chiefs, by their singling him out to accompany them on occasions of such paramount importance. And this is fully confirmed by graphic touches in the faithful Eggert's letter concerning " my gentleman's " travels and undertakings.

A further proof of the esteem in which Sir Edward—or Mr. Disbrowe, as he then was—was held by his official superiors, was his appointment as Minister Plenipotentiary and Envoy Extraordinary to the Court of St. Petersburg at a time when, as his daughter very justly points out, the slowness of international communication rendered it impossible for intricate questions, necessitating prompt action, to be referred to the authorities at home for their approval and sanction.

Lady Disbrowe's letters and Sir Edward's own
memorandum deal with the remarkable events of
the year 1825, including the conspiracy previous to
the Accession of the Emperor Nicholas, an epoch to
which reference has been made by various subsequent writers as the period which marked, if not the
birth of Nihilism, at least the first decisive mani-
festation of a movement which has since left its
mark on the history of the great Russian Empire.

At the Court of the Netherlands, where he
became so conspicuous a favourite and enjoyed the
personal friendship of King William II., considerable
demands were again made on Sir Edward's tact and
power of reconciliation on his first arrival. This
was owing to the strained relationship which had
existed for some years between England and the
Netherlands by reason of the different attitudes
assumed by the two Courts in reference to the
Belgian revolution. Both the pacific nature of his
influence and his thoughtful guardianship of British
interests showed that he was fully equal to the
occasion. Proof had already been given by the
authorities at the Foreign Office of crediting him
with skill in completing commercial treaties by his
having been sent to Stockholm to negotiate a
reconciliation between the French and Swedish
Governments, in which he had been successful, and
on which occasion he had been instructed to
endeavour if possible to establish commercial
relations with Sweden. In reference to this he
has himself left the following note: " I had the good
fortune to succeed, and obtained the approbation

both of the Foreign Office and the Board of Trade.
I returned to Sweden in 1834 charged to negotiate
a treaty, which circumstances delayed; but before I
left the country all the preliminary difficulties were
got over and nearly so as affected Norway, and for
the completion of the details a Norwegian plenipotentiary followed me to London.   On my arrival
in Holland I was instructed if possible to engage the
Dutch to enter into a commercial treaty, an attempt
that had failed on several occasions.   The result was
the Treaty of Commerce and Navigation, which I
signed in 1837, and which I am happy to be able
to add has been found very beneficial to British
navigation."

During the years spent at the Hague (from 1836
to his death on October 29th, 1851), Sir Edward was
actively employed in the negotiations for the
twenty-four articles by which England, France, and
Austria, guaranteed the Independence of Belgium, as
also the Grand Duchy of Luxemburg and the Duchy
of Limburg to the King of the Netherlands.   He was
still engaged in negotiations connected with the
Dutch navigation laws, when death closed his life
of unremitting effort and usefulness in the service
of his country.   From many letters in my own
possession, I have been enabled to form a clear
picture of the singular beauty of his character in
private life, as a devoted husband and father, a good
son and son-in-law, and faithful and devoted friend.
In the Russian letters, of which it has often been
only possible to produce extracts, it has been
necessary almost entirely to omit the domestic side

for the sake of chronicling public events, and giving
as much space as possible to descriptions of social
life in St. Petersburg and Moscow at a very
interesting period. Had it been possible to introduce
many of the more homely touches contained in these
letters, it would have been seen that his loyal devotion to public duties never caused Sir Edward to
forget his little girls, left at Walton Hall, that he
sent them tender messages in every letter, and that
the question of effecting a reunion with dear ones
at home was ever in his thoughts as in those of his
wife. It was a sore trouble to them both that the
uncertainty of the length of their stay in Russia
made it a question of constant discussion as to
whether their children should be brought to join
them or not. One delightful touch of domesticity
I cannot omit. Writing to his father-in-law, and
speaking of his " own dear babes," Sir Edward adds :
" But I must not talk or write of them, I hardly dare
trust myself. How delighted they seem to have been
with their work-boxes and so delightful also. I am
now looking forward with pleasure to hearing how
they received my little present of combs and brushes
for their dolls. The dressing-case is quite my idea."

Of the impressions made on a wider circle by Sir
Edward's life, the following extract from a Hague
paper, dated November 2nd, 1851, gives a clear
impression. From supplementary evidence it is easy
to gather that it was written in all sincerity, and it
corroborates how truly worthy he was of the respect
and reverence with which his daughters cherish his
memory :—

"The Demise of His Excellency, Sir Edward C. Disbrowe, Envoy Extraordinary and Minister Plenipotentiary of H.M. the Queen of Great Britain, has awakened universal regret. It is not too much to say, that Sir Edward's loss is deeply lamented by many persons out of every rank of society. Respected by all who had the opportunity of observing his walk in life and the Christian training of his household, affable and condescending in general intercourse, he was pre-eminently distinguished for unbounded benevolence.

"The poor man found a benefactor in him, and he was ever ready to lend his support to every charitable purpose and to seek out and alleviate unobtruding sufferers. By such deeds he won many a grateful heart, from whose remembrance his memory will never be effaced.

"In the course of a fifteen years' residence in the Netherlands he had acquired an extensive knowledge of the country and of the customs and disposition of the people, as well as of their institutions, laws, and interests. The impartiality with which he could examine into and appreciate all matters was calculated to secure the attachment, in the highest degree, of every Netherlander who had the privilege of knowing him intimately. In the exalted station which he filled he was ever averse to subterfuge, ever facile in the management of affairs, conciliatory and pacific. It may be truly said of him that so far from ever having been the cause of differences between the two Powers, he always endeavoured to reconcile difficulties and to promote a good understanding.

Such was the character of Sir Edward Cromwell Disbrowe, a desire to do justice to such merit and to give expression to the esteem which this distinguished foreigner enjoyed in this city has induced us to dedicate this tribute to his memory."

It must have been gratifying to a family so loyally devoted to Queen Victoria, that, in addition to sending a steamer to carry home the remains of her faithful servant, Her Majesty wrote a letter of thanks to the King of the Netherlands "for the marks of respect and esteem shown to Sir Edward's memory." From a contemporary letter, I learn that " excepting for the funeral of the late King " (*i.e.* of the Netherlands) " such a procession for pomp and magnificence had never been seen, the authorities and military turning out at every town it passed through." This was when the sad cortége was on its way to embark for England, and whilst meeting the wishes of the King, it could also be more truly termed a spontaneous expression of feeling. The consternation that spread over the whole community and the expressions of sympathy and letters of condolence received, appear to have been most touching. Miss Margaret Kennedy, of whom mention is made on several occasions in the following pages, wrote from the Hague at the time of Sir Edward's death, saying: "All possible honours that earth could give have been given to the mortal remains of our loved brother. The King sent two state carriages, and two others, a regiment of infantry and a squadron of cavalry. All the officers of the Burgher Guard followed on foot, all the *Corps Diplomatique*, and

about forty private carriages. The Prime Minister,
General Wellman, M. de Maltitz, and another held
the pall. The two dear boys went in their carriage
with Sir William de Tuyll and the clergyman.*   At
each town they pass through detachments of cavalry
will come to meet it, and the King has ordered that
at Rotterdam all the authorities shall meet it and
every military and naval honour be rendered to his
honoured remains.   Is it not passing strange that
the 'Lightning' should have been sent, and stranger
still, till lately Commander Petley has had it, and
now again it is a Captain Allen.   Sir William de
Tuyll goes over with it and the boys, God grant them
a safe passage . . .   Every class has shown how
truly he was loved and respected, and the poor
mourn their kindest friend, but we must say as he
himself never ceased repeating during his sufferings :
'Thy Will be done.'"

Strangely indeed, must the arrival of the "Lightning" have recalled the journey to and from Sweden
to Miss Kennedy, who, as will be seen, accompanied
her sister and brother-in-law on their perilous voyages
to and from Sweden, on which occasion she has
been described as having done "everything for
everybody." Lady Wynn, the wife of the British
Minister at Copenhagen, in a letter to Miss
Kennedy's mother† written in October, 1836, in
reference to the trying experiences the family had

* Amongst the many friends who showed practical kindness
and sympathy to the mourners on their sad journey to England,
I find special mention of Sir James Turing.—M.M.C.

† Honble. Mrs. Robert Kennedy.

undergone on the outward voyage, says of Miss Margaret Kennedy: "Sir Edward told me that she had been his greatest comfort. Her decision and courage kept them all together and supported them wonderfully."

Even with the passing of years there must be many yet who remember that bright, witty, loving little woman, with her devotion to children, her gifts for entertaining them, and her ever warm friendship. She passed away in 1878, and was laid to rest in Walton Churchyard.

It will doubtless be observed by some readers of this volume that Sir Edward Cromwell Disbrowe is described as G.C.G., Grand Cross of Guelph, and not as G.C.*H.*, Grand Cross of Hanover. Since the point has been brought under my personal notice, I have remarked that H.R.H. the Duke of Cambridge is the only surviving Grand Cross of the Guelphic Order, and that in various peerages when members of that Order are mentioned they are spoken of respectively as G.C.H., K.C.H., and C.H. I have also found this to be the case on tombstones. Sir Edward Disbrowe laid stress, however, on having G.C.*G.* printed after his name; this being more correct, so his daughter assures me. The latter has in her possession one of the original copies of "The Statutes of the Order of the Guelphs, dedicated to His Excellency Count Münster, Hereditary Marshal of Hanover, Minister of State, Grand Cross of the Order of the Guelphs, and Chancellor of the Order."

It is most likely that amongst those who read these lines there will be the descendants of members

B

of the above-mentioned Order, which could not
be conferred by Queen Victoria, who by reason
of the Salic Law could not succeed to the Kingdom
of Hanover whence the Order originated.

As I pointed out in the beginning, it has been
my sole purpose in writing this preface to give such
supplementary information as I could fairly hope
would be of interest to those who might take up
this volume. I have therefore not attempted to
give a complete outline of Sir Edward Disbrowe's
career, as that would be merely anticipating what
will be dealt with in greater detail in these pages.
Whilst writing of this remarkable man, I cannot,
however, help recording two facts in his life, which
have deeply impressed me. First, I have noticed
from the letters and notes which have passed
through my hands that he can never have been a
very robust man, but that his splendid achievements
were due rather to strenuous effort than to physical
strength. Secondly, in days when the observance of
the Day of Rest seems to be less and less regarded
by the unoccupied, I think it very worthy of note
that this busy diplomatist made a rule during the
whole of his official life of abstaining from travelling and entertaining on Sundays. One who
remembers both Sir Edward and Lady Disbrowe
remarked to me recently that "Sir Edward was a
man of much presence, and his wife a typical *grande
dame* of the old school."

Lady Disbrowe's calm strength of character is
plainly depicted in her eventful life, and her letters
from Russia, some of which find a place in the

first part of this volume, show plainly whence her daughter inherited her facile pen. They are the letters of one who, with great powers of description, had trained herself to observe people and things very closely. Lady Disbrowe's father* described her truly when, on writing home from St. Petersburg, he said : " I do not regret not entering more particularly into the picture of Russian courtly amusements, as your sister's pen is so brilliant and correct in description, and she is none of those sulky islanders who think that nothing is good out of their own country, and think all civilities their due, nor does she overrate what she sees and receives, to depreciate her native lovely island."

This quotation from Mr. Kennedy's pen proves that he had an open mind and broad judgment on matters international. No one is said to have been more amused than himself at an incident which happened during his residence at " La Chartreuse," on the Lake of Thun. Even in those early days (about 1820) it was necessary sometimes to be protected against the intrusion of thoughtless tourists, and Mr. Kennedy had found reason to put up a notice on one of his gates to warn off trespassers. A disappointed Frenchman, who had wished to make acquaintance with the domain and had noticed the prohibition to enter, published an account of his experiences. In these he spoke of the owner of the " Chartreuse " as " *çe farouche insulaire, çe misanthrope ridicule.*"

* Honble. Robert Kennedy.

It was at St. Petersburg that Mr. John Kennedy, only surviving son of the Honble. Robert Kennedy, began his diplomatic career as *attaché* to Lord Strangford. Both Sir Edward and Lady Disbrowe make frequent mention of him in their letters from Russia. He was evidently a young man of considerable promise, bright, intelligent, and affectionate in disposition, and an excellent linguist. His sister, writing to one of their younger sisters, Frances, afterwards Baroness von Weiler, says: "You would laugh to see what an important person our Johnny is, nothing can be done without him. 'Kennedy, you will do that.' 'If Mr. Kennedy calls whilst I am out, give this note.' 'Kennedy, take charge of Mr. Jerningham, and put him in the way of doing things; get him a lodging, servants, masters.' In short, Lord Strangford does nothing without John."

Again from Moscow, at the time of the Coronation of the Emperor Nicholas, she writes: "Poor dear John was nearly knocked up in trying to get everything ready for us. You have no idea of his activity and the information he gains and gives. I do not know what we should have done without him. He found a house, carriage, servants, and linen ; no easy achievement, I assure you."

And Sir Edward Disbrowe in a letter to Mr. John Kennedy's father, says: "He is really the most *impayable* Secretary, to do him justice, that ever was."

Mr. John Kennedy was subsequently at Naples and had been just appointed to Washington, when

death overtook him.   He left a widow and four little
sons. The eldest is now Sir John Kennedy, K.C.M.G.,
and H.M.'s Minister at Bucharest. The second, well
known as a sailor, an author, and a sportsman, is
Admiral Sir William Kennedy, K.C.B.   The third
son, Mr. E. B. Kennedy, was one of the pioneers of
Queensland, on which he has written on sundry
occasions, his last book being "The Black Police of
Queensland," published by Messrs. Murray.   He is
known to many friends, especially in Norway, as an
excellent shot and a most experienced fisherman.
The youngest son is Mr. Gilbert G. Kennedy, the
stipendiary magistrate at Marlborough Street Police
Court.

I would only refer to three more persons who
figure in these pages.   Of two only brief mention is
made, namely of the two short-lived sons of Sir
Edward and Lady Disbrowe.   Their pictures with
their attractive boyish faces have been familiar to me
from my early childhood, and amongst family letters
of by-gone days, I find most touching references to
the ways in which they met their deaths.   Edward,
the elder son, who gave his life for his country at
Inkermann, is spoken of as "good and beautiful," and
appears to have been deeply regretted by a very wide
circle of friends.   The "letters of condolence and
sympathy" are described as "still pouring in" in the
following December.   The date of Inkermann was
November 5th.   Old acquaintances at the Hague
vied with those at home in the expressions of their
regret, and the Duchesses of Cambridge and
Gloucester and the Duke of Saxe-Weimar's family

were amongst the earliest to condole, their example being followed by the Royal House of the Netherlands.

The regret for the younger son, who died in Canada in June, 1858, after a few days' illness, was equally poignant. I have before me a most touching description of this young soldier's funeral, written by Colonel Arthur Taylor, R.A., the senior officer present, telling how "the whole of the officers in Montreal, regimental and staff of all denominations, attended, and the whole of the men of Lieut. Disbrowe's own regiment," where he was a "great favourite." He goes on to say that as the procession wound up the mountain side to the picturesque cemetery above Montreal, he found himself for a while beside "the Town Major, a fine-looking white-haired old man, formerly in the 42nd, with which regiment he never missed a battle and was constantly Sergeant-Major to the Duke at Paris. 'Ah, Colonel,' he said in his strange Hieland tongue, 'this hour, this day forty-three years ago, there was death enough where I stood in the corner at Quatre Bras, all our officers almost shot down and lieutenants in charge of the regiment.' And there walked the soldier of fifty years' service with his snowy locks but frame still erect at my side, and a silver ladder of dangers escaped on his breast ; and before us was carried the soldier boy, safe from his one campaign, but called away by that inscrutable decree, which man can only bow to in trust and faith."

I cannot close this preface without some allusion to the one to whom we are indebted for the publication of this delightful record of "Old Days in Diplomacy," namely the authoress herself. To those who have known her in earlier life, or in the last quarter of a century in her Derbyshire home, any words of mine are unnecessary. To them, her never failing energy and kindliness, her strong individuality, and her delightfully frank opinions on matters in Church and State—though they may or may not coincide with their own—are all endeared, as part of herself. But this volume will reach a wider circle, who may seek for the woman behind the writer, and will study with interest the effects both of heredity and environment. They will notice the vivacity and gift of narrating for which perhaps an ancestress of Navarre blood is responsible, and the pluck and spirit, which I venture to believe are a legacy through her mother from Scotland's Royal House. The same touch of kinship may account for her rejoicing at her forebear Major-General Disbrowe not having signed the death warrant of the martyred King; nor can an observant reader fail to trace the strong religious faith, a goodly heritage from Puritan progenitors, to whom also the tone of her opinions on matters ecclesiastical may be traced. Environment on the other hand may be answerable for the interest taken in the Hanoverian Dynasty by one in whom such conflicting influences combine.

Pleasant evenings spent at Marlborough House in days long past, when Queen Adelaide joined the party, have been described to me, and I have been shown the quaint little basket which the Queen-Dowager had taught her nieces' friends to make.

It needed neither heredity nor environment but just the attraction of personal character to draw her with deepest and most loyal attachment to Queen Victoria. In notes which she has entrusted to me, I notice how she delights in every recollection of "THE QUEEN." One little paragraph relative to various balls at Buckingham Palace tells how she was privileged to dance with the Duke of Saxe-Weimar as the "Queen's *vis-à-vis*," probably in the year 1850; another speaks of a gracious smile received on being named to Her Majesty by the Duke of Cambridge as the sister of "young Disbrowe who fell at Inkermann;" and again, she tells with evident delight how Dumas Père, when asked why he hurried off to the Tuileries to see Queen Victoria, after having refused to go to see the Empress of the French, said: "*Je vais voir la femme s'il y avait beaucoup de femmes comme elle je leur pardonnerai d'être reines.*"

It is general nowadays to accord the first Napoleon a gentler verdict than is given him in these pages. It must be remembered that the writer was born when he had not long ceased to trouble Europe, and not many years had elapsed since little children had been frightened into obedience by the foolish speech that if they were not good "Boney" would come to fetch them. In reference to Napoleon I., the authoress has expressed to me a great desire to vindicate the character and conduct of Sir Hudson Lowe, and those of us who may not feel prepared fully to accept the vindication will at least read it with interest as one more of many recent attempts to throw a new light on some figure in history hitherto regarded by most people from a different stand-point.

The authoress of "Old Days in Diplomacy" is interested in records of longevity, and has called my attention to the fact that she knew of three lives covering a period including part of Charles II.'s reign, and more than forty years of Queen Victoria's. The daughter of Dr. John Taylor, of St. Martin's-in-the-Fields, was married in 1693, to the Rev. Charles Jones, Rector of Plumstead, Kent. Seventy-one years after her marriage—1764—she was still living. Her great-nephew, Colonel Disbrowe—of whom a portrait and short record are to be found in this volume, and who was born in 1754, and died in 1818—remembered her well. His last surviving daughter, born 1796, and dying in 1882, at Kensington Palace, where she had lived since 1820, could bear witness to the correctness of this statement. The authoress herself, is in this also bearing out the traditions of her race. To myself and others she speaks most humbly of this volume, which is so full of interesting matter, and says: "Please say they are only the rambling recollections of an octogenarian." For myself, I can only reply, "Would that the world held many such octogenarians, for it would have reason indeed to be proud of them, and with them might hope soon to grow young again."

M. MONTGOMERY-CAMPBELL.

April, 1903.

Sir Edward Cromwell Disbrowe. G.C.G.

En. Ex. Min. Plen.

OLD DAYS
IN DIPLOMACY.

PART I.

CHAPTER I.

EARLY MISSIONS OF SIR EDWARD CROMWELL
DISBROWE, G.C.G.

To meet the wishes of many friends I put down
some recollections of olden days. My father, Sir
Edward Cromwell Disbrowe (born 1790), was the
eldest son of Colonel Disbrowe, M.P. for Windsor,
of Walton Hall, Derbyshire, Vice-Chamberlain to
Queen Charlotte ; his mother being Lady Charlotte
Hobart, daughter of the third Earl of Buckinghamshire.

My father was educated at Eton and Christchurch,
entered the Diplomatic Service in 1810, and served
in it until his death at the Hague in 1851.   He left
England on the 10th of June 1810, to join Sir Charles
Stuart, afterwards Lord Stuart de Rothsay, then our
Minister at Lisbon, landing on the 10th of July, and
being almost immediately sent off to the Headquarters of Sir Arthur Wellesley and the Marquis of
Wellesley, between Badajoz and Almeida.   He
returned to Lisbon for a very short time, but was sent

again to Headquarters until after the battle of
Busaco. All the information I have about those
early days is contained in a letter written to me after
his death by his valued Swiss servant, Franz Eggert,
who accompanied him in his wanderings.

My father was attached to the Mission at Lisbon
until 1813. His next appointment was with the
Headquarters of the Russian Army at Reichenbach
under Lord Cathcart, the Special Ambassador. It
was at Reichenbach that the plans for the battle of
Leipsic were made. My father crossed the blood-
stained field three days after the battle, and used to
shudder with horror when describing the scenes he
witnessed with the dead and dying still lying there.
He and his servant were in a drosky, both with loaded
pistols at full cock. I conclude that he was on the
way to St. Petersburg, to which Mission he accompanied Lord Cathcart.

It must have been either at Reichenbach or on his
way to St. Petersburg that he met with a most curious
experience. He had been sent with a message to a
distant division of the army, and on his return found
that the Headquarters had moved, leaving him orders
to follow with the archives, but not a penny wherewith to execute the order and find a conveyance for
his valuable burden. He did not know how to get a
cheque cashed, and felt at his wits' end. Eggert,
however, came to the rescue, telling him of a horse
fair that was being held in a neighbouring town,
where a cheque would be accepted. So off went
master and man and bought four horses, each leading
two, and sold them for cash by the roadside, thus

obtaining money to enable the archives to be carried
to their destination.

My father was attached to Lord Cathcart's Mission
until 1814, and then named Secretary of Legation to
Copenhagen, where part of the time he was also
Chargé d'Affaires. He was accredited to that
Mission from June 1814, to April 1820. Whilst he
was at Copenhagen, his father, Colonel Disbrowe,
wrote to him, saying: "We are all much alarmed at
the news from France. Bonaparte has got on foot
again, and I fear all Europe will again be disturbed
by his ambition."

On August 15th the same correspondent says:
"Bonaparte is on board the 'Northumberland' to go
to St. Helena. Sir G. Cockburn is the Commander.
Colonel Lowe is to be Governor of the Island and
have charge of Bonaparte's person; and he will not
let him escape."

Poor Sir Hudson Lowe was judged far too severely,
for if he was a hard master, we must remember that
he had charge of one of the most clever and most
unscrupulous of men. I am glad to find that Fitchett
in his admirable work, "How England saved Europe,"
stands up for him and recognises his difficulties.
Indeed, I think the whole civilised world owes a debt
of gratitude to that much-abused man for undertaking and having faithfully carried out such an onerous
task. Lady Lowe was widow of the eldest son of
Sir John Johnson, of Mount Johnson, Montreal,
Canada; a man well known for his influence over the
North American Indians, and a staunch Royalist.
His son had shared his mother's captivity when

prisoner in the hands of the opposing tribes just
before the revolt of 1776.

While still belonging to the Legation at Copenhagen, my father obtained leave of absence "to
attend the Earl of Castlereagh as his Secretary at
the Congress of Aix-la-Chapelle." The King of
Prussia and the Emperors of Austria and Russia
met at Aix on September 29th, 1818. The Congress
was also attended by their Ministers and the English
Plenipotentiaries, and on November 4th, 1818, a note
was addressed by them to the Duc de Richelieu,
stating their determination "to put an end to the
Military Occupation of the French Territories."
France accepted the offer, and a convention for the
withdrawal of the British troops was signed on the
9th of October, and the Congress separated November 21st, 1818.

My father's next appointment was that of
Secretary of Legation in Switzerland, and I gather
from an official letter that he had leave to choose his
place of residence. Zurich was named as a town in
which he might live, and he went there in 1820.

In Switzerland the faithful Eggert picked up a
wife, and friends settled that my father was sure to
follow his example. This he did, for it was there
he met my mother, the eldest daughter of the
Honble. Robert Kennedy, son of the eleventh Earl
of Cassillis and brother of the first Marquis of
Ailsa. He was married at Thun, in October 1821,
and I was born at Berne the following year. From
the time of leaving Berne, late in 1822, my parents
resided in England, my father taking his seat in the

House of Commons as member for New Windsor until 1825. It was the only time, in their married life, that they lived in their own home at Walton Hall, going up to London for the session.

The rest of this chapter and the following shall be devoted to letters describing the events connected with those early missions, including a very quaint letter from Eggert, which gives so vivid a picture of the times, that I have ventured to reproduce it in its original simplicity. Before transcribing from the letters immediately connected with my father's doings, or written by him, I would recall the fact that his father, Colonel Disbrowe, as Vice-Chamberlain to Queen Charlotte, occupied a highly responsible position at Court, the more so, because the Queen was compelled to take a leading part in state affairs, owing to the prolonged illness of King George III.

I was brought up to venerate the memory of the good old King, and believe him to have been a man of more character than is often supposed, and that it was the horrors of the Reign of Terror and the American War which undermined his mental condition. I used to like to hear how, when at Windsor, he would arrive quite early in the morning at the house of my grandfather, who was also his equerry, to make the latter walk out with him, and how, finding him in bed, would tell his three sons to fetch a jug of water, and give him a *"cold pig!"* I have a great number of letters written in an absolutely friendly style by Queen Charlotte to my grandfather as well as from the Princesses. Princess Sophia calls him " the Father Confessor of the unfortunate sister-hood." I here reproduce a letter from Queen Charlotte to my grandfather, which is in my possession, and have kept faithfully to the old-fashioned wording and spelling.

From Queen Charlotte to Colonel Disbrowe, her Vice-Chamberlain.

" The Queen sends Colonell Disbrow a Picture of the King's which She had Copied lately & seems to be just the Size fit for His Small Habitation at Windsor & as She knows His Principle so well, that Man & Wife ought not to be Separated, She adds that of Herself & if He Traces any ligness in it, He will always discover a Sincere Wellwisher to Himself and Family in this Resemblance."

Windsor
the 12th August.
    1809

These pictures hang in my drawing-room. Lady Eastlake pronounced the Queen's picture to be an original Gainsborough and the King's a copy, and so did old Mr. Richard Lowe, the lithographer, who told me he was a nephew of Gainsborough. A member of the Royal Academy to whom I showed them, declared that both were copies, as he did also of a picture in my possession of " Eleanor, Countess of Buckinghamshire, wife of the 4th Earl, and eldest daughter of the first Lord Auckland," spoken of by contemporaries as " Pitt's only love." The lady in question married the brother of my grandmother,

The Queen sends Colonell Disbrow a Picture
of the King's which She had Copyed lately
& seems to be just the Size fit for His Small
Habitation at Windsor & as She Knows His
Prenceple so well, that Man & Wife ought
not to be Separated. She adds that of Herself
& of the Traces any linness in it, He will
always discover a Sincere Wellwisher to Himself
& Family in this Resemblances

Windsor
the 12th August.
     1809

Lady Charlotte Disbrowe, *née* Hobart. The second wife of the fourth Lord Buckinghamshire was step-grandmother to the present Marquis of Ripon. I always believed the picture to be by Hoppner.

I think the following letter from amongst relics of my grandfather, addressed to Queen Charlotte by Washington's successor, cannot fail to be of interest to many persons in view of a similar mode of address by the President of the United States to Queen Victoria on the occasion of Her Majesty's first Jubilee, having been the subject of much comment. The mode of address is intended to convey the assurance of deepest respect, and the evidence of the letter quoted proves precedent.

To our Good Friend The Queen of Great Britain.

MADAM, OUR GOOD FRIEND,

"I have named James Monroe, Minister Pleni-potentiary of the United States of America to your royal consort. My knowledge of his good qualities gives me full confidence that he will so conduct himself as to merit your esteem. I pray therefore that you yield entire credence to the assurances which he will bear to you of our friendship, and that God may always have you, Madam, our good friend, in His holy keeping.

Written at the City of Washington the twentieth day of April in the year of our Lord one thousand eight hundred and nine."

(Signed)   TH. JEFFERSON.

By the President,

JAMES MADISON, Secretary of State.

C

This letter is the more valuable because of the great interest which has centred round the name of the Minister, whom it was its purpose to introduce, and also by reason of the antagonism created by the Monroe Doctrine.

I pass on to letters connected with my father's early career. One addressed by my grandfather to John Wilson Croker, Esq., at the Admiralty, and dated July 3rd, 1810, is to announce that his eldest son—*i.e.* my father—"is going to Portugal and will set off on Friday next for Plymouth." It goes on to make various inquiries about the sailing of men-of-war and packets.

The opening pages of Eggert's letter deal with the Portuguese experiences. I give it in all its original freshness, only correcting the punctuation, etc., sufficiently to make it intelligible to general readers.

Franz Eggert's Letter. Written after my father's death.

"The way How I came to be noticed by your grand Papa the late Colonel Disbrowe, General Vilette in whose service I was, was recalled from his Station as Comander in Chief from Malta, and appointed to the same Rank over the Island of Jamaica, where he Died and six more Genls. that had come with us from the Mediterian Sea with the yellow fever. Genrl. V. had been in former times A.D.C. to H.R.H. the late Duke of Kent, and before leaving England for the West Indies, we

stopped some time at Castlebrowhill the Residence
of His R. Highness. In 1808 I came back without
a Master, and through the kindness of his late R.
Highness and Major General Cartwright I was
recommended to Major Price, Equerry to Queen
Charlotte. During which time I had occasion to
show my feeble abilities at Several Dinners and
fêtes in Particular at the Jubilee at Frogmore, in
honour of King George the 3rd. and Queen
Charlotte, Here I was noticed by H.M.'s Vice
Chamberlain Col. Disbrowe, your Grand Papa. In
1810 my gentleman was on a visit at Mongwell nr
Wallingford in Oxfordshire, at Dr. Barington's
Bishop of Durham, when I received a Letter from
the Major Duomo of Count Münster from Windsor
Lodge, asking me if I liked to go to Portugal with
Col. Disbrowe's eldest son, as he had spoken to
Count Münster about me. I was highly glad I
had seen your Papa sometimes at the Equerry's
table, and as I spoke the Languages I was engaged
through Count Münster in the month of June 1816
to your Papa. He was yet at Oxford, and on the
10th. of July we left England in the 'Grampus,'
where I nearly got into a Scrape with the Captain.
Old Lady Grey at Portsmouth had given me
several Methodist Pamplets to Disturb amongst the
Sailors, we arrived safe at Mr. Stuart's at Lisbon,
and soon were sent off to the Headquarters of Sir
Arthur Wellesley and to the Marquis of Romana
between Badajoz and Almeida, also at] Cintra. We
hardly been back at Lisbon when sent off again
to the Headquarters, and remained till after the

battle of Busaco. At Coimbra we were billetted in
the Franciscan Convent and my gentleman bought
a grey Horse of an officer, and here I lost him for
5 days.   The Drums beat the trumpets sounded,
Colonel Arbuthnot gave me an order for Post
Horses and a Pak of Letters, but the Postmaster
had escaped with horses and mules out of one gate,
while the French where Fighting with the German
Hussars at the other.   The confusion was Grate,
and so I thought best *sauve qui peut* out of Coimbra.
I passed a peasant with two mules, put our Sadle-
bags, and 2 Cloaks across them and off I started.
Amidst the Confusion I got in the middle of a
Column of Infantry and the sick and wounded, but
Genl. Wilson who commanded them knowing me
yet from Malta, told me to leave the Military Road
and go to Pombal.   Not far from the town, I fell
in with Capt. Allen, he told me that my master
was not taken prisoner at Coimbra.   At a village
before Lorie (?) I found my master again.   He was
with the Marquis of Worcester, Lord March, Capt.
Allen etc.   I was very Glad having been separated
5 days.   He bought from an Atteleri Officer an
Irish *mad* (?) Horse for me to ride to Lisbon.   My
Gentm. took the Letters that I brought from Col.
Arbuthnot and went on, I followed next day.   My
Gent's Camel of a Horse would pass no Bridge
without having his Eyes binded up.   My Gentm.
was very glad that I brought the Horse safe to
Lisbon, where he sold him greatly to advantage.
When the army was in the Lines I was sent up
twice to the Headquarters.   At the Instalation of

Marshall Sir Charles Beresford, I went with Mr.
Stuart to Maffra and acted as his head man. We
might have been 15 or 16 months away, when
returning home with Dispatches, and as my master
was at this time of age, I had the Good Luck to
travel with him in several Countries, visiting some
of the noblest Families in England. When at the
Honble. W. Sneyd's at Keele Hall, there came
Dispatch, that he was appointed attaché to go with
Mr. Sydenham, W. Addington etc. to Spanish South
America, and soon after embarked for Cadiz where
we arrived just as the French were bombarding
from Porto Santa Mariage. As the Spanish junta
did not come to an arangement our Mission was
broke up, and my Gentm. returned to Lisbon.
Here he caught a severe cold and was laid up for
two months when he was well enough Sir Charles
Stuart sent him home with Dispatches in the
Government Packet ' Prince Eugene,' Capt. Peters,
and we were nearly shipwreckt on the Cliff cald
' Deadman's Point.' I bought some fine preserved
Fruit for the young Ladies.

My Gentm. was appointed attaché to the Earl of
Cathcart in June 1813. We left London and
Embarkt at Harwich for Gothenbourg, in a
government Paket, and came in a Collision. At
Gothenburg he bought the Caleche of Mr. Toad
at the London Inn, went to Istadt, and Embarked
on board a Bomb vessel for the Insel Rügen and
arrived with ammunition etc. for Prince Bernadotte
at Stralsund. At Neu Strelitz we Breakfasted at
the Post, the People were so Glad to see an

Englishman again that they wld take no Payment
for the Breakfast.   My Gentm. made the Postmaster's wife and daughter a Present, to each a
Long Jaconet Checkt Neckhandkerchif which
made great joy.   In Berlin we learned that the
Headquarters were at Francfurt on the Oder.
Arrived there we found no Headquarters.   We
changed money, bought Powder, loaded the Pistols,
and set out in search of the Emperor's Headquarters,
for there were 3 even 4.   The Emperor of Russia,
the King of Prussia, and Gnl. Katuroff and the
Prussian Genrl.   In the night we came within
Sight and Call of the French Bivouaque Fires, and
were obliged to leave the Post road and take the
left through the wood.   The Postilion not knowing
the Right Road drove into the thicket.   At last
the Cariage upset to the left ; at this affair my
Gentm. had a narrow Escape, for on seeing the
French Bivouaque fires he Desired the loaded Pistols
to be taken out of the Case and put one in Each
Poket of the Cariage and when the Cariage upset,
the Pistol fell out of his side Poket and struk him
just in the right temple.   Thank God it did not
go off, God knows what wd have become of me in
this Critical situation.   By getting up the Cariage
Caused rather a Little noise, and our Lamp crashed
to atoms.   All at onced there appeared a Piket of
Cosaks.   Being night, they were full of brutish
Politeness.   Thanks to my Star, I could just speak
Enough Polish and a little Russian to tell them it
was the ' Aglitsha Pastanik,' if not they would
have been too free and friendly with the Contents

of the Cariage. They just had been forraggin a
Cow and some Geese. At Daybrake, we arrived
at the Station where there was also a Party of
Prussian Cavallery, whose officer told us that the
Headquarters had all Changed. The Emperor of
Russia was at Peterswalden, but all his staff and
our ambassador at Reichenbach and so we arrived
safe at Lord Cathcart's. My Gentm. bought two
Pony's Harness and a Coachman, from Col. Hudson,
and During the Armistice he went to see all the
strong Places in the quarter of Breslau. Breslau
was neutral. There we found a bank that gave
us money on London, Mr. French the Bishop of
Dublin's son Profittet of the occasion and went
everywhere with us to view, Glogau, Glatz, Silber-
berg, etc., at Glatz my Gentm. had supped and
was noting down his journey, when the Innkeeper
brought the book for Travelers to Put Down their
name and Rank, when my Gentm. shouted out
' Zounds, Dont bother me now. Eggert, you write
Down, say I am Drum Major.' I did as I was
bid—my Gentm. wore the uniform of a Major of
the local Staffordshire Militia, which Queen
Charlotte had granted him but next morning when
the Horses were Put to, such a Crowd of People
asembled before the Inn, when we Enquired the
Reason of this the Landlord said, *Die Leute wollen
den Englischen Regiments tambour sehen., der mit
seiner Eigenen Equipage Reist.* Good fun for my
master. The Armistice was now at an End. The
Horses he sold to Capt. Dowson, General Stewart's
A.D.C. General Stewart was Minister to the King

of Prussia. During the stay I had the Honor to speak twice to the Emperor Alexander, he came on horseback and stoped at the garden-fence, hollowed me and ask if Ld. Cathcart was at home in good English, in the Evening My Gentm. told me, that if ever it shd happen again I was to Ignore him, and only title him ' Sir.' The Headquarters broke up. My Gentm. and Mr. Veare Ld C's Privat Secretary Started the next Day for Prague on the Road between Chemnitz and Podiband. We overtook the King of Prussia whose Cariage had broke Down, my Gentm. jumped out and went toward the King and offered him our Swedish Calèche. All the Dispatch boxes were put into Mr. Veare's little Cariage, and I remained with all the Rest of Luggage on the Road until a Bohemian *Leiterwagen* came to take me up. The King asked me what Cuntryman I was, when I told him, he told me to remain always faithfull to his Friends the English. At last the *Leiterwagen* arived and I followed the night and next Day. At noon I arived at Prague we were billetted in the Palace of Wallerstein and remained till a short time before the Battle of Leipzig. During this time I went to see several operations at Teplitz, Carlsbad, as likewise the surrender of Vandame. Count Truchsess A.D. Camp to the King of Prussia Came in the name of His Majesty to thank my Gentm. for the loan of the Cariage and handed me two *Dubble Friedrichs D'or*—but a wink from my master and I Declind of accepting the donation, although my bones ached me for a week after from the shaking of the wagon. My Gentm. left his Calèche at the Language Master's, and we went with Mr. Veare. We already heard the news of the Battel of Leipzig and arived when they took Prince Poniatousky out of the river. The Head-quarters went off soon after, we followd next Day in a Post Chaise with a quantity of Dispatch boxes. I bribed a Prussian Grenadier to let me get into a bake house to get two Rolls for my Master's breakfast and I pd a Rix Dollar for a Small Comiss Brodt from a marketvendor. We arived safe at Weimar. One of Ld Cathcart's best horses Died, the Emperor made him a present of a much finer one. Each Side the road lay Dead Soldiers of all nations and arms of Every Description. They carried one man that was not quite Dead. We stopped. He had been laying in the field 3 days. My Gentm. ordered me to Pour some Cognac into his mouth, when he opend his Eyes, and Praised God and my Master. He belonged to the Polish Lancers. . . . From Weimar we were obliged to leave the Gt. Military Road and go to Rudolstadt, here my Gentm. went with Mr. Gordon, relation of Ld Aberdeen, to have a Sight of Erfurt. I was to get on by the first Conveyance to Meiningen, but no horse no cart or Carriage could be got for any money. I had already waited from morning till 3 p.m. when Mr. Daniel King's Messenger arrived from Prague. Mr. Daniel had Dispatches for Ld. Cathcart and so we kept Each other Company in waiting, he had been Butler to Ld Bathurst, he did speak neither French nor German, but good English.

From the road from Leipzig there came a Prussian
train of 3 waggons, Escorted by 2 officers and about
20 Grenadiers, one of the officers I recolected from
a Billiard Room at Reichenbach. I begged him
to give us a lift, he gave us leave to put the Effects
on but that we were to walk. Poor Mr. Daniel
had been well fed and was rather corpulent could
not keep Pace with us, so at last the Officers had
Compassion and we loaded him up on a Wagon.
At night we Bivouaqued in a field round a good
fire. Next day toward 11 o'clock we arived at
Meiningen and found my Gentm. Soon after came
Mr. Valentine, Ld C.'s Valet a Scotchman and
told me his Lordship wanted to see me.

Lord Cathcart asked me if I was Mr. Disbrowe's
servant what Country I was what Languages I did
speak, I told him none Perfect, but that I could
make myself understood in Several. He smiled
and asked from where I brought the Messenger, if
I had been with General Villette in Malta etc. etc.,
at last he said in Good Italian '*andate da Monsieur
Penny, Capo di Cucina e fatte una buona Colazione.*'
Here I bought from a Cosak two Horses one with
Saddle, one I paid for 11 Ducats. At night Headquarters broke up, and there I was mounted on the
top of the Saddle Bags outside the Little Horse like
a Sancho Panza. On the road to Aschaffenburg,
I was so near Dying with a Pain in my Side that
I could not get on My good Master jumped off his
Horse and tyed me his Silk Handkerchieff round
my waist, and we arived at Aschaffenburg late with
a Good appetite and no money. I sold my watch.

Next Day we arrived at Frankfurt, the Horses
fetched more than they had Cost. We Biletted at
a Jew's, very good quarters. My Gentm. made
several Excursions to see the French pass the Rhine.
All at onced he came back very ill and remained
so six weeks, he was attended by a Dr. from the
Emperor's Staff to whom he gave a Handsom Gold
Snuff Box. When he recoverd we took rooms at
an Hotel.

On the 12th of January 1814 we left Frankfort
for St. Petersburg. At Königsgrätz the Postmaster
told us it wld be quite impossible to go Direct to
Königsberg as the Snow was too Deep, 9 Days had
no Cariage Comunication been that way, and so
we were obliged to go round to Krackau. Although
with 4 Horses, we went on but Slowly tolerable
good Inn at Krackau—the Landlord was a towns-
man of mine, would have nothing for Lodgings nor
meat. He gave us 2 bottels of Hungarian wine
for on the road. We were soon obbliged to put
the Cariage on a Sledge and arived safe at
Warschau. The Postmasters and Innkeepers were
almost all Jews, and very filthy, so that I in general
made the Dinner of smokd salmon, smokd goose,
eggs, and Pancakes. The road was so incumberd
with frozen snow and Bulky that we upset 3 times
on one Station. My Gentm. got impatient and left
the lower part of the Cariage taking only the Body.
He soon left the Body of the Cariage also and got
a Kibitsky long and large Enough for him to lie
in like a Cradle, with 2 hoops at the top, a Russian
Matt over them, straw inside, a Blanket and Cloak

to Cover him.—I got a sort of baking throu* on
a Sledge, all of wood no Iron, so that I was Swung
from one side of the road to the other and upset
very often I remained behind. At one station near
Lifland, a ragged Postilion, had a Sword at the side,
my Gtm. ask if there were any fear of wolves.
'Oh no,' said he, he was intitled to wear a Sword
as he was a Baron. Good fun for my Gentm. At
one of the Places where I served up his little Dinner
my good Master said, 'Eggert sit Down and take
your Dinner.' He poured me out a glass of Hungary
wine and said, 'Let us Drink my Father's health it
is his birthday.' *Dolce ricordo.* At Riga the Postmaster told us he wld give us 4 Horses as ordered
by the Imperial Padro-gigna but could not give two
Postilions, as all able men where gone with the army,
so that I was my own Coachman.   We dined at
the 'Stadt London,' Drew money at the 'Staddel'
and set out for St. Petersburg. Sometime I arrived
half an hour behind my Gentm. being upset in the
snow, and before I get all my Hordes and Bagage
into my throw (trough), he had nearly arrived at the
next Station. I was at last so frosen with Day and
night Drivins that I was ready to Drop. At Narva
my Gentm. agreed with a Victoria who tok us in
one night and a Day to St. Petersburg where we
arived the 6th. February 1814 at 7 in the evening
having lost an English Cariage in the Russian
Snow. I could not attend my Master for several
Days the Baltik wind had frose my whole left side,

* Trough.

Ear, nose hand and foot. . . . In the middle of the Summer arived the King's Messenger Mr. Hayes with my Master's appointment as Secretary of Legation to the Court of Denmark. My Gentm. had a very comfortable little Cariage made at Petersburg, and we left Petersburg for London, Berlin, Hanover, Deventer. At the Hague the Cariage remaind with Mr. St. George who was attaché there, the Ambassador was at Brussels. We arrived safe at Windsor Stoped near two months there, Set out for Copenhagen, Mr. Foster soon after our arival got leave of Absence and my Master was *Chargé d'Affaires.* The first winter he had the misfortune breaking a bone in his leg and was laid up a long time. Mr. Foster had married Miss Albinia Hobart. When he returnd my Gentm. got leave, he had bought another chariot, Embarkd in a boat a Cross the Brülle was nearly Lost, got safe to Yarmouth, and back to London. We returned to Copenhagen, embarked at Harwich and arived safe at Cuxhaven, it was late in November the road bad to Hamburg, my Gentm. chose to go by water, embarked on an Elbe boat called the 'Blankenase,' putting two Planks a Cross to get the Cariage on, the River was coverd over with a thick fog, a Swedish Brig Coming Down with the Stream run against the Diky of the Cariage and was near upsetting us all. We arrived at Hamburg in the middle of the night, half starved with hunger and Cold. Next morning set out for Copenhagen, the Cariage was heavy loaded, we had many things for Mr. Foster, Miss Hobart and Baroness Nicolai, the Russian Minister's

wife. We travelled always Day and Night, it was
a smart post. The road was Slipery, the foremost
Horse fell on its nose and never got up alive. My
Gentm. said, 'this is a bad omen.'—After we had left
Resinsburg the Right Side hind Spring of the Cariage
broke. Soon after our arival Mr. and Mrs. Foster
left to Pay a visit to His Mother the Duchess of
Devonshire, At Rome. He tok our Russian Cariage
with him. My Gentm. was *Chargé d'Affaires* and
kept a good Establishment. In the Sumer of 1818
my Gentm. was sent for to join Lord Castlereagh
at the Congress at Aix-la-Chapelle, we soon left
and went via Hamburg and Hanover and stayed
two Days at the Duke of Cambridge's. At Cassel
we went to see the Famous Wilhelmshöhe. Passed
the Rhine at Coblentz, slept at Bonn, at Cöln, bought
Eau de Cologne for Queen Charlotte, which she never
got for she Died before we arived. At Aachen my
Gentm. was invited to all the festivals that were
given in honor of the Sovereign. Lady Cathcart
had her two white fine Bull Dogs with her, one of
them Caught hold of the Emperor Alexander while
he was shaking hands with her Ladyship. When the
Congress was over we left for England. While at
Aachen my Gentm. had a Gt. deal to Do, he sometime sit up near the whole night translating. We
embarked at Calais. At Dover we arived rather
late and set off immediately for Downing Street.
On the road beyond Canterbury by the lights of
our Cariage Lamps, I could see two men on horseback coming full speed towards us. I had just my
hand on the Pistols, when my Master hollowed out

'Eggert the Pistols.' Both of us thought they were
highwaymen. One Cald out my name, it was
Tom, Capt. Disbrowe's Servant. He brought the
melancholy news of my Gtm.'s father.—We went
as fast as ever the Horses could go leaving the
Dispatches at Downing Street and Direct to
Windsor not having taken any nourishment since
Calais. My Good Master was very much afflicted.
—Mr. Sharman, myself, Mr. Crook the butler of the
late Col., who my Gentm. had given the nickname
of Elephant, because he was very stout and Blew his
breath so loud, we accompanied the body to Walton,
and assisted to put it into the Family Vault. About
this time Miss Disbrowe, now Lady Taylor, got
married, Col. Taylor Recevd the Knighthood the
Day of his mariage. Soon after we left England
and made for Copenhagen, for the last time. We
arived safe at Copenhagen and stayd till 1819 when
my gentleman got apointed *Chargé d'Affaires* to
Switzerland. In England I had the pleasure to go
with My Gentm. to all his Estates at Highamferris
and bought a Dog Moggi of a renowned Poacher, my
Master bought a Beautiful littel Mare of his Agent,
and while we were at Sir Thom. Kiniston Powl,*
orders arived to be off for Switzerland. In London
my Master bought another horse named Jewel
Engaged Thomas Colt as Groom, Plate and Glass
took from England, Porcelain bought at Paris, at
Epernay my Gentn. regaled us with a bottel of
Champaine. July 1820 the Guns at Lucerne fired

* Sir Thomas Kynaston Powell.

a salute to welcome my Master's arival at the Swiss
Diet. We took a small house out of town, M. de
Virgole the Spanish and M. de Tailerant* the French
Minister each side of us. In a fortnight after the
Groom and Horses arived as also the Goods, then
we showed these Gentm. an English Set out.
Admidts the fêtes Mr. Basset, Kg's Messenger
arived, with Dispatches and my Gtm. soon left
Lucerne, across the Lake and Mountains for Milan
on the affairs of Queen Caroline. Then he set off
for Lausanne and Geneva and gave me Orders to
go to Bern and get a house, which I did, at M.
Bay's *entre le Port*, a very comfortable one much
to the satisfaction of my Gtn. as also a tolerable
honest Cook. Soon after he got acquainted with
the Honble. Mr. Kennedy. I also was sent off to
Besançon to go and meet Miss Louisa and Miss
Hariett Disbrowe to bring them to Bern, also our
Little Dog Moggi who knowd me directly, after a
long time absent. I was sent off to Zurich to get
Lodgings for the time During the Diet, I was
fortunate enough to get a House with a beautiful
view over the Lake. My Gentm. made often
Excursions across the mountain to Thun.† I had
not much to do so I took a wife, when my Gentm.
gave me £10, and the first time he had seen her
he told me I had choosed a little wife, thinks I
to myself what can one get for £10? We returnd

---

* Talleyrand (?).

† Honble. Robert Kennedy was living at the "Chartreuse,"
on the Lake of Thun.

to Bern and 11 Days after my Gentm. got himself married, and now the fêtes began and happy we were all. Later the Coachman had a night and a Day the Horse ready saddled to take the news of Miss Charlotte's* birth to Mr. Kennedy at Thun, under whose window lay a long Pole, if he came by night to knock at the bedroom window, and to give the news. For it the coachman got from Mr. Kennedy a 20 frc. Piece. In the autumn we left for England. In the Tuilleries Garden I had the Pleasure of cariing Miss Charlotte Disbrowe about. At Kensington was the first *pied à terre*. After we took a House in Welbeck Street where I received from the Littel Miss Disbrowe 'Mordant's Improved Penholder' with a box of cut quills for a Christmas box. These here lines I write with the keepsake of those times. Your Papa took a House in Somerset Street, Portman Sqr. The 11th. of August 1824 you arived with your Papa and Mama at your Estate Walton Hall, Derbyshire, they after an absence of 26 years.

In 1825 Your Papa was appointed to Russia and I went with the Honble. T. A. Foster to Turin. In 1846 in the month of March I entered onced more into your Papa's Service at the Hague. In November I was allowed to go to my Present *Riposo del Viagiatore* with time to reflect '*das Leben ein Traum*.'

Most Honord Miss Disbrowe, my wife joins with me in thanking you and all those belonging to your

* The Authoress.

D

Dear family many many times for all kindness you have bestowed on us."

Your Obedient Servant,
FRANCIS EGGERT.

CHAPTER II.

THIS chapter is devoted to official records of the Congresses of Vienna and Aix-la-Chapelle and to letters from my father written during the early missions and wanderings of which Eggert gives so original a description, with the addition of a letter from Major-General the Honble. William Stewart, which appears to me to be well worth preserving. This distinguished officer was the second son of the fourth Earl of Galloway, and born in 1772. He married the daughter of the Honble. John Douglas in 1804, and died in 1827. The Duke of Wellington, in his dispatch on the battle of Albuera—fought May 16th, 1811—says: "Major-General the Honble. W. Stewart most particularly distinguished himself and conduced much to the honour of the day. He received two contusions, but would not quit the field."

ALMANDRALEJO,
May 27th, 1811.

"Many thanks, my dear sir, for your most kind letter of the 19th, which followed me to this place, where I brought my Division a few days ago. The very obliging manner in which you offer me your aid, under the idea that I was a patient with many of my brave comrades in arms at this place, shall never be forgotten by me.

I had the good fortune to escape severe blows on the 16th, in a manner not a little surprising, for the scene of general destruction has very rarely been exceeded ; two-thirds of officers are *hors de combat* in two of my three Brigades. I received a rather sharp shot at the commencement of the affair, which shot away my eyeglass and laid my clothes open to the collar-bone, and at close of the day I received a spent ball on the instep which obliged me for nearly an hour to leave the Field. Excepting a little lameness I am nearly recovered.

Our situation was rather a critical one, but I trust that all things considered we acquitted ourselves well. Our Spanish friends fought well and I owe the preservation of my Division to their support, for the enemy's columns were so heavy as although not to have defeated us, yet such as would have at last killed us off. My third brigade (Highland) was reduced from 1600 to little more than 500 in desperate fighting on the same spot, but to their glory showed no symptoms of retreat. One of its regiments, the 57th, came out of action under the 11th in command, his ten seniors being *hors de combat*, a rare case, I believe. We, however, gained our point, and by such occasional strong measures the Peninsula is, I apprehend, to be saved. If Napoleon will but engage in a Northern war we may look for

the accomplishment of all our wishes in this part of
Europe. I otherwise fear not so soon, and I wish
that our good friends in England would not be quite
so sanguine as they appear by the last papers to be
on the subject.

Dear sir, with many thanks for your late kind
attention,

Very faithfully yours,

W. STUART.

P.S.—The 4th Division, including General Allen's
Light Infantry and all our cavalry, are forming the
covering army in this part of Estremadura, while
Lord Wellington is carrying on the siege of Badajoz
with the 3rd, 7th, and Portuguese Divisions."

This is followed by a letter, also from the Peninsula,
from my father, but bearing no date :—

From Mr. Disbrowe to Colonel Disbrowe, M.P.

" MY DEAR FATHER,
                We yesterday recd. intelligence of the
sailing of an expedition from Cadiz consisting of 600
Guards, etc., amounting to 1000 British and between
6 and 7000 Spaniards under the command of ——.
Skenet, who defended Sanfa, commands the British.
We have no official intelligence from Lord Wellington
later than the 10th, but we are informed of his having
reached San Ildefonso on his march from Segovia,
which town was entered by General D'Urban, and our
advanced guard on the 3rd ; the Garrison of Madrid
is in a great measure composed of Juranentados,
whose attachment to the Government of Joseph is

only to be relied on as long as his Party is successful ;
in fact they are deserting very fast to the
Empecinado, who is in the neighbourhood of
Madrid. On the Eastern Coast, Suchet has still
a very large force, but his attention is so divided
between Catalonia and Valencia that unless he
abandons some material point he cannot in any
great degree influence the success of Lord Wellington,
whose successful arms report has carried to Madrid.
This, however, wants confirmation. Soult's chief
attention seems lately to have been directed against
Ballesteros, who will probably find it necessary to
retire into the kingdom of Murcia. Hill, after
retiring to Almandralejo in order to prevent Drouet
from turning his flank, waited until Officer had defiled
to the Partido di Serene, and again advanced his
Headquarters to Lafra. If this Expedition from
Cadiz should join him it will make his force a very
considerable Corps. In the North the Siege of
Astoya is still carried on. I am not informed whether
George has left Cadiz or whether he remains. Sir
H. Sullivan sets out for the Army to-morrow. My
leg is better, but I am still rather lame. Stuart is
very well and sends his best regards.

If you can ask it, will you get me leave to wear
the Windsor Uniform while abroad? as a military
Coat is not quite the thing for a civilian here.

Best love to all at home."

Your most Affecate. Son,
E. C. D.

The next three letters were written during my

father's multifarious journeys whilst attached to
Lord Cathcart. The first gives his impressions
regarding the arrest of a certain Mr. Temple as a
spy, and is addressed to Lord Kinnaird.

REICHENBACH,
July 17th, 1813.

"DEAR KINNAIRD,
I have now heard the other side of Mr.
Temple's story and I do think be he who he will,
that he made his appearance under such suspicious
circumstances as fully justified his being detained.
He represented himself to Lord Cathcart as an
American, and produced a passport stating him to be
an inhabitant and a native of Boston in America,
and consequently an American subject. This passport
was countersigned by the American Consul at
Hamburg. He next stated himself to be an
Englishman and a British subject, although born
in America. Lord Cathcart then told him that he
could not exactly make out what he was, but as
he represented himself to be only travelling for his
amusement, he would recommend his going to
Colburg, to which Mr. Temple assented, and his
lordship offered to procure him passports. Now
the answer to the statement Mr. Temple made to
you (that he was arrested at the particular desire of
Lord Cathcart, who told him there was an
opportunity of going to Colburg that night with
a Russian (or Prussian), and that this man was
secretly instructed to arrest him and carry him
away to Silderburg) is very satisfactorily accounted

for. Lord Cathcart had been promised by the
Prussian authority that passports to proceed to
Colburg should be given to Mr. Temple on his
arriving at a certain village (I believe Görlitz),
where Lord Cathcart was to send him immediately.
Mr. Temple was at that time considered as a
prisoner, and was accordingly forwarded by my
Lord Cathcart under charge of a *feldjäger* to the
place where the Prussian authorities then were,
about two German miles, with a request that he might
receive his passports and be at liberty to proceed to
Colburg. The Guard sent with him by Lord
Cathcart was necessary to ensure his arrival, as
without that or proper passports, he could not have
proceeded. The Prussian Government, however,
stated that since acceding to his lordship's
request they had received such strong corroborative
evidence in confirmation of their former suspicions
of this man that they deemed it necessary to
detain him.

From that moment it became a question between
the British Minister to the Court of Prussia and
the Government of that country. Lord Cathcart
had asked for passports not in the character of a
British authority, but merely stated privately that
he saw no reason for suspecting the man, though he
did not exactly know who he was, and recommended
them to send him away, Mr. Temple being *willing to
go.*

How far the evidence corroborative of the
suspicious circumstances under which he made
his appearance will justify his continued detention

under those aggravated hardships, which he has
suffered in Silderburg, as I have not seen it, I shall
not offer an opinion ; but the very circumstance of
his coming *into a camp* from the enemy's outposts
in a time of active warfare, calling himself an
Englishman yet travelling with American passports,
a country with which we are at war, countersigned
by the American Consul at Hamburg where we had
a resident Minister, would, I must confess in my
opinion fully justify his detention until he had
undergone the strictest examination. He was not
arrested under the suspicion that he was not the Mr.
Temple the author, but because he arrived with
this army under very suspicious circumstances.
I must, however, fully acquit my Lord Cathcart,
under whose cognisance it was not after he was
arrested by the Prussian authorities. As he has
proved himself to be an American by his passports,
and states himself to have been born in that country,
proof of his being a British subject must be brought
before the Prussian authorities can admit of his
being claimed in that character by a British Minister,
and I think he has brought the whole mischief on
himself by choosing to travel with foreign passports.
I understand he is a native of *Boston*, and not of
Canada, as I think he stated to you.

Pray excuse the trouble I give in thus entering at
full length with this subject. Remember me to Mr.
Hobhouse, and tell him I delivered his letter safe to
Mr. Baillie, who arrived here the day after my
return."

Yours truly,

E. C. DISBROWE.

A second letter from Reichenbach addressed to a friend gives much information regarding the movements of the allied armies, their hopes and fears, and the general plan of campaign.

REICHENBACH,
August 3rd, 1813.

"MY DEAREST FRIEND,

I have received your letter of the 9th of July, as also one from Henry and one from Douglas, by the two couriers which have arrived since bringing papers, etc. Up to the 21st I have not received anything.

The armistice expires in seven days with a notice of six more, so that we expect to move on or about the 14th. I have not heard any talk of the renewal of it.

Bonaparte, after having been beyond Mayence, was expected about this day at Dresden. Of the exact strength of the corps assembled in that quarter I am ignorant, but the Grand Army in Saxony cannot be less than 250,000 men. A corps under the command of Marshal Augereau, which was assembled at Würtzburg, has marched to the South of France in consequence of Lord Wn's. victory.*

The Corps of Beauharnais, which was destined to threaten Austria on the side of Lintz in conjunction with the Corps of Augereau, will thus be reduced to act singly.

I have not seen very late returns of the strength of that corps, but as the greatest exertions have been

---

* Lord Wellington's victory.

and still are made to increase it, I conclude it will
not fall much short of 90,000 almost entirely new
troops.

Little doubts are now entertained of Austria
joining the Allies. An Austrian General has lately
been accredited to this Army, and arrived about a
week ago. The Russian and Prussian Army in
Silesia, by the most reasonable estimates, amounts to
from 170,000 to 200,000 men in the highest spirits,
with a numerous and well-appointed train of
Artillery, under the command of General Bauley
de Jolly, whose reputation, if it does not shine
conspicuous as an enterprising successful General,
may at least claim the merit of prudence. You may
remember that he commanded at the commencement
of the last campaign. At the period when the French
crossed the Niemen, the Russian Army was extended
along their own frontier from the Baltic almost to
Moldavia by following his own plan of constantly
retreating in spite of the murmurs of the Generals
and the Army, who cried out for a general action
to stop the French in their career. He collected the
Army and formed that junction with Bragation
which enabled Marshal Kutusow to carry into effect
the opposite plan of which he was the great advocate,
namely, that of stopping the French by a general
action. The inefficacy of this plan, even after that
junction, was proved by the event of the battle of
Borodino, a measure to which the Marshal was
pledged, having gained the command of the Army
by becoming the great advocate of the *fighting
faction.*

We therefore certainly possess in General Baulay
an officer proved to be capable of steadily following
a plan formed on the best of his own judgment, a
point of no little importance in an Army like the
Russian, where the supreme command must always
be obtained by petty intrigue and Court interest, and
where consequently the General must come into
command in a manner pledged to a certain line of
conduct by which he hopes to merit the approbation
and to meet with the support of a certain faction at
Court and among the generals and officers under his
own command, and whose decisions are therefore not
free from the guidance of public opinion.

I shall now give a short comparison of the
formation of a Russian and French Army, and
endeavour to deduce a fact on which the success
of the war must much depend. The great difference consists in that the French Army have
a very large proportion of light infantry,
accustomed to act on their own intelligence
individually, and who are more aware of their
danger and therefore less able to stand close
fighting, being trained to avoid dangers ; whereas
the Russians have superior physical powers, added
to the fact of the men being perfect automatons,
unaccustomed to act upon their own intelligence,
and therefore less conscious of the dangers they are
incurring, and have been found, in the various actions
of Prussian Eylau, Pultava, Borodino, etc., etc., and
Bautzen to be superior in that kind of fighting.*

* For the same reason you may defeat but cannot annihi-
late an army thus constituted.

No dread need be entertained of the result of an action brought to the test of the bayonet, but the want of light infantry to pursue a flying enemy will, I fear, prevent their following up any victory so as to render it decisive. As to the probability of bringing on such an action, the superiority of French artillery renders it less likely, and where each side brings from 600 to 700 pieces of artillery into the field it must reduce the battle to an action of that arm ; on the other hand, a campaign in the fastnesses of Silesia and in the mountains of Bohemia offers probabilities of such an event.

Having said thus much of the Grand Army, I shall proceed to say a few words on the two flank armies (supposing Austria to join us), and a general sketch of what seems to be the most probable outline of campaign. This army in Silesia, which, I think, we may safely call 190,000 men, by becoming an army of appui and observation, can retire under cover of Silderburg, Gratz, and Neisse, drawing her supplies through Bohemia from that country and from Poland, by which line she will more effectually defend the line of the order than by retiring behind that river, for the French will never dare to push on into Poland leaving such an army unbroken in their rear.

Should Bonaparte determine on following this army into Silesia, the Austrians, whose force which was extended from Budweis to Egra, are now collected in the neighbourhood of Laun and in front of Budein. The number with the last reinforcements is supposed to amount to upwards of 120,000 men, and would effectually cut off his communications with Dresden ; while the Prince Royal, whose corps is assembling at Imenbreitzen, between Wittenberg and Berlin, would have the option of joining the Austrians at Dresden or of crossing the Elbe and moving into Westphalia. The Corps of Davoust is marching up the Elbe from Hamburg to Dresden.

The Prince Royal of Sweden's army is composed of about 36,000 Swedes ; Count Walmoden's, 10,000 German Legion ; Genl. Bülow's, Count Warazon, and Genl. Chemicheff, Russians ; which, with some Prussians, amount to about 50,000, giving a total of about 90,000. Nothing can exceed the enthusiasm shown by all classes in Prussia, and no doubt is entertained that similar sentiments will be manifested throughout the north of Germany on the first occasion.

It is therefore hard to suppose that Bonaparte will advance beyond his present position, and we receive constant accounts of the works he is constructing at Seiquite, having assembled a corps of 45,000 men in the rear of his position. Should he come to the resolution of awaiting the Allies there, there seems to be a safer method than that of an attack in the front—namely, a flank movement through the Passes of Mittenau into Bohemia, when, by crossing the Elbe at Brandeis, and forming a junction with the Austrians, his flank is most effectually turned. This movement might be executed very easily even should we retire to Sildeburg by the roads of Nachod and of Brunnen, thus turning the source of the Elbe. Of the last plan I have heard little said, so that if it is intended to act upon it the greatest secrecy is observed, but I cannot help thinking it very probable.

We have seen Bonaparte escape most wonderfully, but I believe he is now in a greater scrape than ever, and if the Allies are true to themselves and to one another, unless some excessive blunder is committed, I do not see how he can redeem his fortunes, pressed as he is on all sides at the moment when it was of the most consequence to him to have a formidable army here. He has found it necessary to detach first the Corps of Augerau, and subsequently two divisions from the army in Silesia, under the command of Ney, to act in Spain.

As this is probably the last courier we shall send until hostilities are commenced, I have entered into such details as I thought most interesting."

The last letter from my father in connection with the movements of the Allies which I am in a position to quote was written from Russia to my grandfather, and reads as follows :—

St. Petersburg,
Feb., 1814.

" My dear Father,
    Our latest news from the Army is the 28th Jan. I do not like to hear of holding a Congress. Now is the time to destroy the monster, now or never. The very meeting of Plenipotens. and the accession of England to that measure, coupled with the arrival of Lord Castlereagh, is worth 100,000

men to Bonaparte. Besides, I do not understand
Monsieur going to Headquarters, and Louis the 18th
to Holland and the Duc d'Angoulême being
received with Lord Wellington's Army, if we are to
treat with Bonaparte. I wish I could see one bold,
decided step taken in favour of the Bourbons, for
without it we shall meet with no effectual concur-
rence and assistance from the French people.

If the Allies are afraid to do that, let them send
the family out of the territory over which their
influence extends ; anything is, and must be,
preferable to half measures.

Circumstances have done more for the good cause
than men. Timidity and irresolution may yet ruin
us. One bold measure, one hard blow well put in,
and the business is done. Give my best love to all
at home, and

Believe me ever your most affectionate son,

E. C. D.

I am here quite out of the way of all sorts of
news, so pray let me hear pretty frequently from
all of you."

The following official declaration shows how the
Powers looked upon Bonaparte.

"VIENNE, *le* 13 *de Mars*, 1815.
Déclaration du Congrès relative à
Napolèon Bonaparte.

DÉCLARATION.

Les Puissances qui ont signé le Traité de Paris,

réunies en Congrès á Vienne, informées de l'évasion de Napoléon Bonaparte et de son entrée à main armée en France, doivent á leur propre dignité et à l'intérêt de l'ordre social une déclaration solennelle des sentimens que cet événement leur a fait éprouver.

En rompant ainsi la Convention qui l'avoit établi à l'île d'Elbe, Bonaparte détruit le seul titre légal auquel son existence se trouvoit attacheé. En reparôissant en France, avec des projets de troubles et de bouleversemens, il s'est privé lui-même de la protection des lois, et a manifesté, à la face de l'univers, qu'il ne sauroit y avoir ni paix ni trêve avec lui.

Les Puissances déclarent, en conséquence, que Napoléon Bonaparte s'est placé hors des relations civiles et sociales, et que, comme ennemi et per-turbateur du repos du monde, il s'est livré à la vindicte publique.

Elles déclarent, en même temps, que fermement résolues de maintenir intact le Traité de Paris du 30 Mai 1814 et les dispositions sanctionnées par ce Traité, et celles qu'elles ont arrêtées vu qu'elles arrêteront encore pour le compléter et le consolider, elles emplôiront tous leur moyens et réuniront tous leurs efforts pour que la paix générale, objet des voeux de l'Europe et but constant de leurs travaux, ne soient pas troublée de nouveau, et pour la garantir de tout attentat qui menaçeroit de replonger les peuples dans les désordres et les malheurs des révolutions.

Et quoiqu'intimement persuadés, que la France entière, se ralliant autour de son Souverain légitime,

E

fera incessamment rentrer dans le néant cette dernière tentative d'un délire criminel et impuissant, tous les Souverains de l'Europe, animés des mêmes sentimens et guidés par les mêmes principes, déclarent, que si, contre tout calcul, il pouvoit résulter de cet événement un danger réel quelconque. Ils seroient prêts à donner au Roi de France et à la nation française, ou à tout autre Gouvernment attaqué, dès que la demande en seroit formée, les secours nécessaires pour rétablir la tranquillité publique, et à faire cause commune contre tous ceux qui entre-prendroient de la compromettre.

La présente déclaration, insérée au Protocole du Congrès réuni à Vienne dans la séance du 13 Mars 1815, sera rendue publique.

Fait et certifié véritable par les Plenipotentiaires des huit Puissances signataires du Traité de Paris. À Vienne le 13 Mars 1815.

Suivent les Signatures dans l'ordre alphabétique des Cours :—

Autriche.	{	Le Prince de Metternich. Le Baron de Wessenberg.	Portugal.	{	Le Cte de Palmella. Saldanha. Lobo.
Espagne.	{	P. Gomez Labrador.	Prusse.	{	Le Prince de Hardenberg Le Baron de Humboldt.
France.	{	Le Prince de Talleyrand. Le Duc de Dalberg. La-tour-du-pin. Le Cte Alexis de Noailles.	Russie.	{	Le Cte de Rasoumowsky. Le Cte de Stackelberg. Le Cte de Nesselrode.
Grande Bretagne.	{	Wellington. Clancarty. Cathcart. Stewart.	Suéde.	{	Loewenheim.

Contemporary official copies of this document and of the following, relative to the Congress of Aix-la-Chapelle, are in my possession, and I reproduce them with the permission of the Foreign Office.

"*Copie imprimée au nombre de* 100 *exemplaires pour le seul usage des cabinets.*

CONVENTION.

Conclué à Aix-la-Chapelle, le neuf Octobre, 1818, entre S.M. le Roi de France d'une part et chacune des quatre Cours d'Autriche, de la Grande-Bretagne, de Prusse, et de Russie d'autre part.

Au Nom de la Très-Sainte et Indivisible Trinite.

Leurs Majestés l'Empereur d'Autriche, le Roi de Prusse et l'Empereur de toutes les Russies s'étant rendus à Aix-la-Chapelle, et Leurs Majestés le Roi de France et de Navarre et le Roi du Royaume uni de la Grande-Bretagne et d'Irlande y ayant envoyé leur plénipotentiaires, les ministres des cinq cours se sont réunis en conférence, et le plénipotentiaire françois ayant fait connoître que, d'aprés l'état de la France et l'exécution fidéle du traité du vingt novembre mil-huit-cent-quinze, sa Majesté Très-Chrétienne désiroit, que l'occupation militaire, stipulée par l'article cinq du même traité, cessât le plus promptement possible, les ministres des cours d'Autriche, de la Grande-Bretagne, de Prusse et de Russie, après avoir, de concert avec le dit plénipotentiaire de France, mûrement examiné tout ce qui

pouvoit influer sur une décision aussi importante,
ont déclaré, que leurs souverains admettoient le
principe de l'évacuation du territoire françois à la
fin de la troisième année de l'occupation, et voulant
consigner cette résolution dans une convention
formelle et assurer en même-tems l'exécution
définitive du dit traité du vingt novembre mil-
huit-cent-quinze, Leurs Majestés etc. d'une part et
le Roi de France d'autre part ont nommé à cet effet
leurs plénipotentiaires respectifs etc.

Lesquels après s'être réciproquement communiqué
leurs pleins pouvoirs, trouvés en bonne et due forme,
sont convenus des articles suivans.

Article Premier.

Les troupes, composant l'armée d'occupation,
seront retirées du territoire de France le trente
novembre prochain on plutôt si faire se peut.

Article Second.

Les places et forts que les sus-dites troupes
occupent, seront remis aux commissaires nommés
à cet effet par sa Majesté Très-Chrétienne dans
l'état où ils se trouvoient au moment de l'occupation,
conformément à l'article neuf de la convention
conclue en exécution de l'article cinq du traité du
vingt novembre mil-huit-cent-quinze.

Article Troisième.

La somme destinée à pourvoir à la solde, l'équipe-
ment et l'habillement des troupes de l'armée

d'occupation, sera payée dans tous les cas jusqu'au trente novembre sur le même pied qu'elle l'a été depuis le premier décembre mil-huit-cent-dix-sept.

ARTICLE QUATRIÈME.

Tous les comptes entre la France et les puissances alliées ayant été réglés et arrêtés, la somme a payer par la France pour compléter l'exécution de l'article quatre du traité du vingt novembre mil-huit-cent-quinze, est définitivement fixée à deux-cent soixante-cinq millions de francs.

ARTICLE CINQUIÈME.

Sur cette somme celle de cent millions valeur effective sera acquittée en inscriptions de rentes sur le grand-livre de la dette publique de France, portant jouissance du vingt-deux septembre mil-huit-cent-dix-huit. Les dites inscriptions seront reçues au cours du lundi, cinq octobre mil-huit-cent-dix-huit.

ARTICLE SIXIÈME.

Les cent-soixante-cinq millions restans seront acquittés par neuvième de mois, à partir du six janvier prochain, au moyen de traités sur les maisons Hope et compe. et Baring frères et compe., lesquelles de même que les inscriptions de rente mentionnées à l'article ci-dessus, seront délivrées aux commissaires des cours d'Autriche, de la Grande-Bretagne, de Prusse et de Russie par le trésor royal de France à l'époque de l'évacuation complette et définitive du territoire françois.

Article Septième.

A la même époque les commissaires des dites Cours remittront au trésor royal de France les six engagemens non encore acquittés, qui seront restés entre leurs mains, sur les quinze engagemens délivrés, conformément à l'article second de la convention conclue pour l'exécution de l'article quatre du traité du vingt novembre mil-huit-cent-quinze. Les mêmes commissaires remettront en même-tems l'inscription de sept millions de rente, créée en vertu de l'article huit de la sus-dite convention.

Article Huitième.

La présente convention sera ratificé et les ratifications en seront échangées à Aix-la-Chapelle, dans le délai de quinze jours ou plutôt si faire se peut.

En foi de quoi les plénipotentiaires respectifs l'ont signée et y ont apposé le cachet de leurs armes.

Fait à Aix-la-Chapelle, le neuf octobre de l'an de grâce mil-hùit-cent-dix-huit.

CHAPTER III.

AT THE COURT OF ST. PETERSBURG.

IN 1825, at the age of thirty-five, my father was offered a most tempting and flattering appointment. It was to go as Minister Plenipotentiary to the Court of St. Petersburg during the absence of the Ambassador.

Plenipotentiary had then a far fuller meaning than in these telegraphic days. Full powers had to be exercised according to the discretion of the Minister, as much valuable time, and consequently influence, would have been lost while waiting for tardy orders from the Foreign Office.

My parents always considered the time they spent in Russia as the most interesting of their diplomatic experiences.

On the 8th of April my father started for Russia, travelling overland by Calais, Brussels, and Königsberg, reaching St. Petersburg in four days from Berlin. My mother followed in June by sea, accompanied by her father and brother, on board the "Richard Reynolds," a sailing vessel. Her first letters are taken up with descriptions of her presentation to the Emperor and Empress, the

Grand Duke Nicholas and his beautiful wife, daughter of the King of Prussia and of Queen Louisa, who had suffered so cruelly at the hands of Bonaparte. My mother also mentions the Grand Duke and Grand Duchess Michael, the latter being a daughter of Prince Paul of Würtemburg.

Lord Strangford was appointed Ambassador very shortly after my father was sent out as Minister Plenipotentiary. Even before my mother's arrival the latter wrote: "Here I am at once Minister Plenipotentiary, and I retain my rank, even when an Ambassador is present; it is expensive, but the post is an important one, and consequently more likely to lead to a good mission—at least, if I am to continue in the career, and that point is worth consideration. If the Court goes to Moscow, I shall remain here during the winter as is usual, and receive my £15 per diem."

I do not gather when Lord Strangford arrived, but on the 12th of October (N.S.) my mother says: "Lady Strangford produced a young man on Saturday, and is wonderfully well." That young man was the well known Percy Smythe, the Oriental scholar and the last Viscount Strangford.

The description of my parents' experiences at the Russian Court shall be given in extracts from their letters, as well as those of my grandfather and my uncle, John Kennedy, who began his too brief diplomatic career at St. Petersburg. His life, which was one full of promise, was cut short at the age of thirty-six, by his dying after a short illness at Brighton, where he had gone with his wife and young

family previous to sailing for America to take up a
fresh appointment at our Legation at Washington.
The letters from St. Petersburg begin, as will be seen,
with the announcement of my father's arrival at St.
Petersburg.

*From Mr. Disbrowe.**

ST. PETERSBURG,
March 27th, 1825.
April 8th.

"MY DEAREST LOVE,—I arrived here yesterday
morning, about half-past eleven, very well, but
rather tired ; the roads latterly being most dreadful,
full of drifts of snow, but no possibility of using a
sledge from its great irregularity. . . ."

From Mr. Disbrowe.

ST. PETERSBURG, $\frac{5}{17}$ *April*, 1825.

" I have passed this morning very unprofitably, it
must be admitted—namely, in paying my visits of
ceremony to the Prince and Princess of Orange, and
the Grand Dukes Michael and Nicholas, of each of
whom I have had a separate audience.   There
remains only the reigning Empress, who is not yet
well enough to receive, and the two Grand Duchesses
who are confined.   The Emperor is gone to Warsaw
this day . . . . The Neva opened yesterday about
one o'clock.   The bridge was carried away by the ice

* These letters and extracts are selected from my book,
" Original Letters from Russia, 1825-28," published for private
circulation in 1878.

as usual, and there exists no communication as yet between the different parts of the City.   The effects of the last inundation are everywhere visible ; the water was five feet deep in the entrance to this house, but we are too high to be in any danger . . . . I live in the Maison Lanskoi, Great Moskoi, near the Moska."

From Mr. Disbrowe.

" Now, as to this city, and the life I lead here ; it is very much altered.   All the great open houses that I knew before, where we dined *table ouverte* once a week, are *fermées sans exception.*   The last two years have swept off the Golovins, and others whose names you will hear, and recollect hereafter.   Of my old acquaintances, I find the Duchess of Serra Capria* ; he died a year and a half ago.   It was the most splendid house here.   She lives in a corner, and receives about thirty of her old acquaintances and friends—vastly stupid—and she has invited me ; her daughter, Madame Apraxin, a young, very amiable woman, dead.   Princess Breloffsky's† house closed on account of the death of one daughter, the other, Princess Zeneide Volkonsky, settled at Moscow. The Golovins as I said above, dead and gone ; the two families of Galitzin gone.   Princess Kourakin gone mad, her house closed.   My acquaintances therefore who remain are Count and Countess Litta who still receive, and Nesselrode, the Secretary of State for Foreign Affairs, but his wife is absent.   I ought not to forget Princess Volkonsky, a very

* Capriola (?).   † Beloschky.

pleasant woman, whom I have known this long time, and Madame Bètancourt.

Of the Diplomatic, La Ferronaye tells me he thinks he will bring his wife back next winter ; I hope he may. Madame de Lebzeltern, the Austrian's wife, is clever, and can be pleasant. Madame de Ludolf, the Neapolitan, and Madame Guerriero the Portuguese, all receive; the Countess Laval also, as well as Countess Maistre, and one or two others occasionally. There are the theatres ; I have not been to any of them, so I cannot speak of them.   I am looking out for another house on the English Quai for June, or so soon as I hear Strangford is coming. Adieu once more, my dearest love, at least for the moment, as my *chasseur* announces my carriage and four to be at the door to convey me to dinner at La Ferronaye's, who will not forgive me if I keep him waiting ; *petit convert*, does not that sound magnificent ? "

From the Honble. Robert Kennedy.

(Extract, London post-mark, 29*th July,* 1825).
Petersburgh, in a good house in a good long street, Monday is all I know.

" I wish I had something worth telling you, all is worth seeing. Our evening drive yesterday was delightful ; the crowds of folk, the beautiful country houses on the borders of the Neva, and the small rivers, which are many and run parallel, are all enlivened by these handsome buildings and those of a grander scale belonging to the Emperor.   The palaces are magnificent, and the Greek Church

Cazan filled with French Eagles taken from them in their disastrous retreat from Moscow.

We are to be shown up to her Majesty the Empress, but the day is uncertain. John goes in a sort of a uniform of Disbrowe's. This is only to ensure tickets for the great *fête* of St. Somebody, and then we shall turn our horses towards Moscow. Lord Bloomfield will be of the party. Sir Alexander Malet is the *attaché;* he is a very nice, pleasant young man. There are a great many military manœuvres going forward, and if I can stick on a saddle, I will try to get one peep at them. Visiting is poor Anne's occupation daily and *eveningly.* Only think, she paid (D. said so) 200 this morning before she got up, and so did I, and so did John. Only think of poor Anne's astonishment. Just before dinner was announced, she exclaimed: 'What a prodigious appetite I have,' and lo! we saw on the table one small plate of raisins, one of apples, ditto of oranges, and some sweetmeats. I was ready to cry. So this was Russ! Luckily my olfactory nerve was most agreeably assailed, and I jumped for joy.

No meat, no vegetables appear on the table, so you know nothing of what is to come. We are not yet reconciled to this way of living, but it familiarises, and the dinner is shorter. We drive about behind four horses and go like the ——. The city is nearly empty, and all the great folks who can get away are out of town, and the windows are covered with whitening to prevent the sun spoiling the furniture—an excellent plan. The city is made up of enormous houses and magnificent palaces, but still there is an air of *tristesse*, different from the bustle of a commercial town."

From Mrs. Disbrowe.

ST. PETERSBURG, $\frac{13}{25}$ *July*, 1825.

"Yesterday I had a day of it. Got up at six to accompany the gentlemen to Czarskosèlo, where they were presented to the Imperial Family, and where I was to spend the day with a Madame Longuinoff whom I had never seen.

Well, a good shaking of twenty-two versts brought us safe to the Palace. I found my way to my friend, and my *beaux* went to dress and to prepare for their honours. Madame Longuinoff is 'Secrétaire des Commandements de S. M. L'Impératrice Mère.' And as, in this splendid country, everyone attached to the Court is lodged by it, as well as their family, I found my friends in their pavilion, a little wooden house, near the palace, where they contrive to stow themselves and their children. Yesterday they were in a peculiar bustle, for every corner was in requisition for people from a distance to attend the ceremony (and of course having their friends) for dressing-rooms, and how they contrived to deck themselves out in such places as they did, I do not know. However, I hear that at the Peterhoff *fête* many people dress in their carriages, ladies as well as gentlemen, so I expect to learn lessons of contrivance in this country. There were lodgings prepared for all the gentlemen who were to be presented and carriages to attend them. Everything seems to have been on a most splendid scale; and Lord Bloomfield who was so long with our King, says he never saw anything so magnificent as the arrangements at Court here. At Peterhoff, the *corps diplomatique*, as well as the strangers invited, will be lodged, boarded, and *carriaged* during the three days of the *fête*. The children here seem brought up as in France, eat of everything, and are as sallow as possible. Most of the boys are dressed in shirts made of print or coloured stuff bound in gold or silk galloon. These shirts have long sleeves, and reach to the ankles, close up to the neck, and open at the side, only confined round the wrist. Most of the servants are slaves, and Madame Longuinoff told me that as the children of those who have once been taken into the service of the house are never sent to the fields again, the nobles must find some employment for them, otherwise they would be idle, for they are bound to support them whether they are good or bad. Her mother has established different sorts of trades in her house for these dependants; some make *blonde*, others embroider. On Sundays and *fête* days (150 per an.) they work for their own profit, but the other days for their masters. In some families the slaves are very comfortable, but in others, she owns, they were treated worse than brutes. Fortunes here are not estimated by money, but by the number of peasants the owner has. When any great work is to be undertaken the nobles must supply so many men to work, or sometimes the Crown lends them; sometimes these slaves can purchase their freedom or their liberty for a certain time. I believe this is chiefly

the case with the merchants, who are enormously
rich, and form quite a distinct class here.   The
women are very finely dressed in this class—I mean
handsomely so—and the only peculiarity of their
costume is a frightful silk cap, which fits tight to the
head, has no sort of trimming, and is the most
unbecoming thing imaginable.   I stood by some of
these women yesterday, who had diamond and pearl
ear-rings, cashmere shawls, worked gowns, such as
any lady would be glad to own, and yet the whole
spoilt by these horrible skull caps in the most showy
colours.   I am very much diverted by finding the
Russian costume of our quadrille at Naples is the
dress of all the wet nurses here ; we ought to have
had open caps, the closed ones denote married
women.   Amongst the peasants it is considered the
greatest disgrace that can befall a married woman
that a man should see her hair, and if by accident
her husband should enter the room when she was
combing her hair, her first care would be to cover her
head, even should she have no other resource than
putting her petticoats over her head.

Sposo sent off a messenger last week.   I do not
know when you will receive the treasures with which
he is charged.   Do not imagine that the horse's head
in the drosky is bent and try to straighten it, for it
is a representation of the *furieux* here, or *attelage à la
Pègase*, the most extraordinary invention of eleven
years' standing that ever came into any imagination,
but very picturesque.   The horse goes prancing and
dancing with his neck bent back, as if he was looking
after the driver, or attempting to tear himself away ;

he is placed outside the shafts, is of no other use
than mere show. I believe horses are trained to this
position from their birth, and I fear very cruel means
must be used before they can acquire this attitude ;
it is rather alarming at first sight, but *les furieux sont
bien doux* in reality.

Madame Longuinoff told me yesterday that many
Russian ladies spend £400 or £500 a year upon their
dress, and that these are *moderate ;* the *elégantes* spend
a great deal more. Then again the Princess Sophie
Volkonsky said four gowns carried her through last
winter, but I fear she is no rule, as she chooses to be
very independent and has ideas of her own, dares to
walk about without a servant, to drive with only one
pair of horses, will not go to court—in short, ' *on la
trove très singuliere.*' Her daughter, Princess Aline,
is one of the nicest girls, I understand, very accomplished and well brought up, but she sometimes
suffers from her mother's oddities. Madame
Lebzeltern, *née* Countess Laval, is a Russian, but
married to the Austrian Minister here ; she speaks
English like a native, is a great musician, and I
mean to like her. Her father is a Frenchman, her
mother an enormously rich Russian. We dined there
the other day, had a splendid feast, and the ice was
served in dishes of the same material ; they looked
like cut glass, were fluted, and of a pretty shape.
I hear they may be easily made."

Finished $\frac{15}{17}$

From Mrs. Disbrowe.

ST. PETERSBURG, $\frac{4\ August}{23\ July}$ 1825.

" It is near eight o'clock ; we have just done dinner, having returned from Peterhoff. Lord Bloomfield and Sposo are deep in diplomacy in one room ; Lord Castlereagh, Messrs. Bloomfield and Kennedy and Sir Alexander Malet relating juvenile feats and planning further mischief in a second room ; and your humble servant in a third, just within hearing of all their voices. Now to try and describe the wonder and beauty of the Peterhoff *fête*, no easy task, I assure you ; but I will try and be very accurate, and leave the flourishes to your imagination.

On Tuesday, August 2 (N.S.), we set out for Peterhoff in the following order : Mrs. Parker* and Mrs. Disbrowe in the green chariot, Mr. Pickard on the box, drawn by four horses abreast driven by a post coachman, whose proximity was evidently denoted by strenuous calls upon the olfactory nerves.

Messrs. Kennedy and Disbrowe, attended by the *chasseur*, were in a coach of extensive dimensions, drawn by six horses, four in the shafts and two leaders. About eight we reached our *Palais au Jardin Anglais*, found very spacious apartments prepared for us, and then accompanied by M. and Madame Ludolf we went to the Parade at the Palace. We went in a carriage called a *ligne*, which holds eight, and is just like two sofas placed back to back on wheels ; these are allowed to drive through all the

* The lady's maid.

F

gardens, the wheels being so broad that they do not cut up the walks. The Emperor supplied us with these, with house, board, servants—in short, nothing can exceed the handsome manner in which the *corps diplomatique* is treated; in no country are they so *fêté*.

5th. An English post just in . . . . Well, now I will try an account of the *fête*. I left all the *corps diplomatique* assembled *au Palais du Jardin Anglais.* Our apartments were very spacious, plenty of glasses, but not otherwise overstocked with furniture. As Russian servants give their masters no concern, no preparations were made for ours beyond space. However, Parker never thinks of making a difficulty, and contrived to pass two nights on a sofa without sheets, and with only cloaks for covering. She is always good-humoured, and I must not forget to mention that she dressed my hair beautifully for the whole day—presentation, dinner, and ball. I was delighted with my presentation. La Comtesse Litta ushered me into a room and then left me with L.M. Impériales. The Emperor (Alexander) kissed my hand; and I pretended to salute his cheek, *à la Russe.* The Empress Elizabeth* would not allow me to kiss her hand, but embraced me, and they were both so gracious, so affable, that I was quite sorry to be sent away. The Empress-Mother came into the room where I was placed, and stood talking to me some time; she is a wonderful person for her

* Daughter of the Margravine Amèlie of Baden, *née* Princess of Hesse Darmstadt.

age, as erect as a young girl, and a very fine figure.
They were all quite kind to me, and I wish my
presentation was still to come, though I was dreadfully frightened before it took place.   My gown was
made here, very simple, of *tulle* over white satin, with
a long train, which I managed wonderfully well, and
had not one tumble.   Count Salahoub, an M.C. of
the Court, was deputed to take charge of the
diplomats, to instruct us in our parts, and see that
every attention was paid to us.   We sat down (about
fifty) to dinner at three, a most splendid repast.   At
seven the Emperor's carriages came to take us to the
bal masqué.   The gentlemen wore dominoes of
various descriptions.   Our three had black lace ones ;
the most comical things possible.   Ornamental they
could hardly be called, and their texture certainly
prevented their being useful.   One hundred and
thirty thousand were stated to be assembled.   The
Empress told Mr. Disbrowe that upwards of 4,000
carriages came to Peterhoff that day, and the
Emperor had 4,000 horses of his own employed in
the services of the Court.   Of course lodgings for
such a concourse was out of the question, and it was
a most extraordinary sight to see the bivouacs ;
carriages of all sorts and descriptions converted into
dressing and sleeping-rooms.   In one you might see
a fair lady adorning herself, in another a party at
dinner ; here a group of white-haired, scared looking
Finns ; there some neat German colonists, Tartars,
Calmuks, Jews ; horses, carts, men, women, and
children covered the ground, and formed altogether
the strangest assemblage it is possible to conceive.

People of every class were admitted to the palace ;
and it was a striking spectacle to see courtly dames
in gold and jewels, Emperor, Grand Dukes and
Duchesses, Princes and Counts, whirling through
crowds of rustics ; men with long beards, women with
russet gowns, who gazed with respectful astonishment, and though in close contact with those
grandees, showed no symptoms of rudeness, and
were as quiet and unpresuming as if they had been
bred to palaces and balls. They stood close to the
Imperial party; there was no pushing or shoving,
no noise ; it really was wonderful. I should think
that such a *fête* could only be given in Russia, where
the people are so docile and orderly.

6th. Papa and John set out with the Bloomfields
and M. de Kielmansegge at five, for Moscow. I shall
have the happiness of seeing them again. They go
by Sweden to England."

From Mrs. Disbrowe.

St. Petersburg,
4 *September*, 1825.

"Our little trip into Finland succeeded famously.
We set off accompanied by General Dornberg, the
Hanoverian Minister, a most agreeable elderly
person. Our *attelage* beat anything I ever saw
during the whole course of my travels. Four little
atoms of horses abreast, driven by our own coachman, and two leaders with flowing manes ridden
by a postillion, generally in his shirt, though
sometimes we were favoured with a coat of sheepskin,

the wool inside.   We went at an amazing pace, and
always full gallop up-hill, which discomposed Parker's
and my nerves at first most amazingly ; however, we
met with no accident.   The greater part of Finland
seems composed of granite.   The roads were as hard
and smooth as tables, the only difficulty was to wind
safely between the enormous masses of rock through
which the road was cut.   We were disappointed with
the cataract of Imalta, yet it certainly is a fine sight
to see a broad river forcing its way through a narrow
passage of steep rocks.

Our visit to Baron Nicolai at Mon Repos, close to
Wyborg, was very pleasant.   His garden is one of the
lions of the country ;   it is on the sea-shore, and
abounds in masses of granite, which offers plenty of
scope for varying the scenery, and he has taken
wonderful advantage of it by ornamenting it with
temples, towers, shrubberies, pillars, etc., etc. On one
promontory he has built a gothic castle, dedicated
to the memory of his parents, and had permission
to have the ground consecrated and made it a
family burial place.   His father and mother and
two children are already interred there, and the
vault for his wife, who died at Copenhagen about a
year and a half ago, is nearly finished.   Such an
arrangement would make me melancholy.

Baron Nicolai has three dear little boys, the eldest
is six, the youngest four years old, and they speak
English, German, French, and Russian with perfect
ease.

We came to our new house on Friday (how
unlucky !).   It is comfortable, neither so large nor so

elegant as the last, but in a much better situation, in point of view being on the Quai Anglais, on the beautiful Neva, which now affords a constantly varying active scene of vessels and boats, and in the winter is to amuse us with horse-races, skating, *montagne-russes*, and various other entertainments on the ice. The English church is only three doors from us. Yesterday morning we went to a Russian breakfast, which Princess Sophie Volkonsky gave. First came a dish made of salmon, gruel and pastry, next cakes of flour, not unlike pancakes, then two sorts of mushrooms. Here they eat sorts that are considered poisonous in England ; and then we had sweetmeats of the *marmure*, a wild raspberry that grows in Finland, very highly flavoured, and a taste not unlike quinces.

The races the other day were very pretty. The only uncommon part was a race ten times round the course, or twenty versts (three versts make two English miles), between eight Kosack horses mounted by little boys."

From Mrs. Disbrowe.

St. Petersburg, $\frac{5}{17}$ *Sept.*, 1825.

" Since writing last Tuesday's budget we have done nothing but see sights. We spent one whole day in the gardens and palaces of the Czarskosèlo and Paulowski ; but what are called gardens here are pleasure grounds, ornamented with temples, bridges, monuments to the dead and obelisks to the living, lakes, towers, ships, grottoes, hermitages, etc.,

etc., and flowers, close to the house. The palaces contain gilded halls, beautiful paintings, variety of furniture, silk, satin, and tapestry hangings ; in short, it is impossible to describe them. I expected to find abundance of malachite, but greatly did I deceive myself; it is very scarce and very dear, and what, with me, greatly lessens its merit, though in reality it enhances its value, is that it is never made up in solid blocks as marble is, but the vase, or table, is first made in some other material as a foundation, and then a coating of malachite is laid on in little pieces, almost like Mosaic, just merely *plineered* (I do not know how to spell that word). A small slab not bigger than a folded letter costs several pounds sterling, so do not expect me to bring you back an inch of it. Princess Sophie Volkonsky took care of us at Czarskosèlo, and dedicated the whole day to our amusement. Yesterday we went in a body— Middletons, Guerieros, etc.—to see the gold and silver plate, china and glass, given to the Grand Duke Michael,* with a new palace, by the Emperor ; very handsome, but nothing extraordinary. Afterwards we went to see a golden peacock turn his head and spread his tail, a silver owl roll his goggle eyes, and a gold cock crow ; an immense useless piece of mechanism, made in England, of all places in the world, and sent as a present to the Empress Catherine."

* The Grand Duke Michael gave Mr. Kennedy a box con taining fifty specimens of the various woods employed in building the hall.—M.M.C.

In a letter of October the 29th, my mother mentions her father's departure from St. Petersburg in wintry weather. She dreads the long cold journey for him and describes it as being first to Abo, thence by boat to Stockholm, which may take from two to six days. From Stockholm the route lay by Copenhagen. Altogether five weeks were to be spent *en route.* The same letter refers to a visti to M. Nariskin's house, where there were beautiful pictures, including a St. John by Domenichino.

CHAPTER IV.

DEATH OF THE EMPEROR ALEXANDER.

ON the 27th of November (O.S.) came the un-expected news of the death of the Emperor Alexander at Taganrog, in the Crimea. He died of typhus fever after six days' illness. Alexander I. was certainly a prominent figure in European history in the first decennials of the nineteenth century. A tone time a determined opponent of Napoleon Bonaparte, then in 1807 completely dazzled and led by him, and brought to conclude the Treaty of Tilsit after the famous interview on the raft on the Niemen.

Tilsit's secret treaties, how they were betrayed ; who contrived to witness the *tête-à-tête* have been the subject of endless surmises. Though subsequent events have proved to me that the identity is sufficiently established, I omit the name of the English knight, who, being on board the raft dis-guised as a Russian peasant, saw both Emperors sign and seal the treaty. The witness escaped to Portsmouth, and gave notice of what he had seen and heard. One of the articles of the treaty was that the Danish fleet was to be given up to

Napoleon.   An expedition was therefore sent at
once from England to take possession of the fleet
in question, and Copenhagen was bombarded.

But to return to events at St. Petersburg. My
mother's letter showed what an unexpected blow
the Emperor's death was to the whole nation.

From Mrs. Disbrowe.

St. Petersburg, 30 *November*, 1825.

"We began this week in grand style ; a ball at
M. de la Ferronaye's.   I chaperoned Aline
Volkonsky, and stayed until half-past three.   It
was very pleasant, a very brilliant assembly, and
went off with great spirit.

The Count de la Ferronaye wishes he could get
an ukase for banishing the cotillon, but I suspect
he will not succeed, it is such a favourite dance here.
It sometimes lasts two hours, and is, I think, mighty
dull when danced every night. They had a new
figure, blinding the gentleman and then making him
choose a lady ; but as it was done by throwing a
shawl over their heads, it spoiled too many toupées,
and therefore did not succeed.

Our acquaintance, Count Apraxin, was terribly
annoyed at it.   They say he rouges and paints his
eyebrows and mustachios.   My charge looked
extremely well, though she would wear her old
black gown. She had pink marabouts in her hair,
and her mother's emeralds and diamonds on. You
have no idea how much the girls dress here, and
put on such mixtures : yellow gowns trimmed with

sky blue or red flowers, blue gowns over pink slips, etc., always with jewels. My next favourite to Aline Volkonsky is Alexandrine Alopeus, daughter of the Russian Minister at Berlin, but now passing a winter at St. Petersburg. Madame Alopeus* is an old friend and flame of Sposo's ; she must have been angelic, and is still one of the handsomest women I ever saw. Countess Modène and her daughters are great favourites ; they are excellent people, and the Comtesse quite famed for her goodness."

27 Nov. O.S.
9 Dec. N.S. 1825.

P.S.—Little did I think to add such a P.S. The most melancholy event has taken place. The Emperor is dead. Only six days ill ; of typhus fever. It is an event of the utmost importance, not only to poor Russia, but to the whole civilised world. The poor Empress Elizabeth had the melancholy consolation of being with him during the whole time, and of performing the last sad duties of a wife. She has known little of the happiness of one, poor thing, but he had returned to her latterly, and they were united at the last. She closed his eyes, gave him the cross to kiss, at Taganrog. The poor old Empress learnt it this morning, and dropped as if shot on reading the news. They thought she was gone also, for as she is laced from head to foot, she turned quite black directly. The Grand Duke Constantine succeeds."

* Remarried to Prince Lapoukin.

Extraits des Lettres du Prince Volkonsky, relatifs à la maladie et la mort de l'Empereur Alexandre I.

Le $\frac{15}{27}$ Novembre.

" Je n'ai ni la force ni la tête assez à moi pour vous rendre ce qui se passe en moi. Nous sommes tous menaçés d'un malheur terrible par la maladie de l'Empereur, qui est devenu très grave et même dangereuse depuis quelques jours. La fièvre qu'il avait prise dans son voyage en Crimée, a changé en fièvre bilieuse enflammatoire, pour comble de malheur il a refusé tous les secours d' l'art après la potion de Rhubarbe qui l'a degouté. La maladie ayant commencé à empirer, les Médecins ne savaient quel parti prendre. Je me suis décidé à leur conseiller en Chrétien de lui proposer la Communion, et d'engager le Confesseur à lui faire une exhortation pour ne pas refuser les remèdes. J'ai fait cette proposition en presence de l'Empereur, qui l'accepta et recut les Saints Sacremens. Le Prêtre lui a très bien parlé. Après cela il s'est décidé a se faire appliquer les Sangsues et a prendre tous les autres remèdes nécessaires, qui ont produit beaucoup d'effet, et qui ont calmé la chàleur pendant quelques heures ; mais plus tard elle revient, et continue depuis avec tenacité malgré les sinapismes que l'on avoit appliqués à plusieurs reprises. Mon attachment pour l'Empereur connu pour juger de l'ètat où je me trouve. Je ne le quitte pas ni le jour ni la nuit aussi suis-je à bas ; pourvue seulement que le Tout Puissant veuille nous sauver du grand

malheur qui nous menace, car il n'y a que Lui Qui
le puisse.

La pauvre Imperatrice malgré sa chètive santé
ne le quitte pas.   Dieu donne qu'elle âit assez de
force pour supporter le malheur qui nous menace !
. . . . . ."

Le $\frac{18}{30}$ *Novembre à 4 hrs. du soir.*

"La Lueur du mieux d'hier, de la santé de
l'Empereur a passé comme un nuage.   Vers le soir
la fièvre a redoublé de manière qu'a plusieurs
reprises il a manqué de mourir.   Cette nuit dernière
a été terrible, la matinèe d'aujourd'hui a été aussi
mauvaise, vers midi il a commencé à reprendre des
forces, et se soutient jusqu' à ce moment.   J'attends
la nuit avec une frayeur inexprimable.   Dieu donne
qu'il ait assez de forces pour la supporter."

Le 19 *Novembre.*
1 *Decembre.*

"C'en est fait !   Le coup fatal nous a frappés ce
matin à 10 heures 50 minutes, l'Empereur Alexandre à cessé de vivre après une agonie de 11
heures de suite.   L'Impératrice ne l'a pas quitté
un seul instant, c'est elle qui lui a fermé les yeux
et la bouche.   Que Dieu lui donne des forces pour
soutenir ce malheur inouï !   Quant à moi je suis
extenué de fatigues de Corps et de l'âme.   Je suis
inconsolable de la perte que je viens de faire !
Outre qu'il étoit mon Souverain, il étoit encore,
j'ose le dire, un Ami qui pour moi n'est plus à
remplaçer."

Lettres de l'Impératrice Elizabeth à l'Impératrice Mère à Petersbourg.

TAGANROG *du* $\frac{17}{29}$ *Novembre.*

"CHÈRE MAMAN,—Je n'ai pas été en état de vous écrire par la poste d'hier. Aujourd'hui, grâce en soit rendue mille et mille fois a l'Être Suprème il y a du mieux très décidé dans l'état de l'Empereur de cet Ange de bien veillance au milieu de ses maux, Pour qui, sur qui, Dieu manifestrait Il Son Infinie miséricorde si ce n'était sur lui ? Ah ! Mon Dieu ! quels cruels moments j'ai passés ! Et vous, Chère Maman, je me figure vos inquiétudes. Vous recevrez le Bulletin ; vous avez vu à quoi nous en étions reduits hier, cette nuit encore ! Mais Wylie aujourd'hui dit lui même que l'état de notre cher malade est satisfaisant, il est faible à l'excés. Chère Maman, je vous avoue que je n'ai pas ma tête, et ne puis pas vous en dire d'avantage. Priez avec nous, avec 50 millions d'hommes, que Dieu daigne achever la guèrison de notre bien-aimé malade ! "

19 *or* 20 *Novembre,* 1825.

" J'ai tout perdu, l'ange n'est plus, il sourit mort à moi, comme il a fait vivant. Il ne me reste que vous, Maman, avec laquelle je souhaite venir pleurer et être présente à l'enterrement. Je resterai auprès du mort, et je suivrai autant que mes forces le permettront."

Le 21 *Novembre.*

" Notre cher défunt a repris son air de bien

veillance, son sourire me prove qu'il est heureux, et qu'il voit des choses plus belles qu'ici bas ; ma seule consolation dans cette perte irréparable est, que je ne lui survivrai pas longtemps, j'ai l'espoir de me rèunir bientôt à lui."

From Mrs. Disbrowe.

St. Petersburg, $\frac{2}{14}$ *Dec.*, 1825.

"Do not set me down as affected, dear folks, if I write in a melancholy mood. It is impossible to be otherwise in the midst of the general gloom that now prevails amongst these people.

Never was a monarch so mourned ; but it is not as their Emperor that they deplore him, it is as a common friend. Every individual weeps as for the loss of their dearest, best friend. He was loved for himself; was so affable, so benevolent, interesting himself about his lowliest subjects ; entered into the concerns of all around him in the most affectionate manner ; and in short completely identified himself with his people. Mr. Law (the English chaplain) gave us a most impressive sermon on Sunday, and passed a beautiful eulogium on the late monarch. The church was hung in black, and it was altogether extremely affecting. The only signs of life that the Emperor showed during the few last days was taking the Empress's hand frequently and putting it to his heart and lips. He did this about half-an-hour before his death. He received the Communion on the 12/24, and then said : ' I never felt so happy before ; do with me as you like.' His best friend—Prince Pierre Volkonsky—and the Empress never left him. After he died the Empress washed his hands, placed his feet together, and then threw herself on his body. I should think her cup of misery is now filled. She is wonderfully calm, and has had no particular attack since the sad event. The Empress-Mother is also very resigned. This is the fifth child she has lost, but of course this is the hardest blow of all. On the 17th there had been a slight amelioration of the fever. A courier was dispatched with the good news. Upon receiving it the poor old Empress immediately ordered a *Te Deum* to be celebrated. The ceremony was just begun when the fatal news arrived. The Grand Duke Nicholas repaired to the chapel, stopped the service, and made signs to the priest to take the cross to the Empress, saying to her : ' My mother, look on that sign of suffering, and be resigned to the greatest misfortune you can meet on earth ; the Emperor is dead !' She took the cross, clasped it to her breast, and dropped down as if she also was dead ; and it was some time ere she recovered. The Grand Duke Nicholas was the first to swear allegiance to the Emperor Constantine. Constantine is Viceroy of Poland. It is uncertain when he will arrive, perhaps not this week. It is supposed he went to Taganrog upon hearing of his brother's illness. The mourning will last a year. The first part will be dreadfully dismal. The order is not yet announced, and so I do not know exactly what it is to be, except that gowns are to be common black flannel, quite frightful. I hear the length of the trains is to be fixed, and the quality of the stuff according to rank.

Princesses Sophie and Aline set off for Taganrog to join Prince Pierre Volkonsky on Saturday. He writes : ' *C'en est fait ; l'Empereur n'est plus, ma carrière est finie ; j'ai servi cet Ange, je ne pourrais servir un autre Souverain. Dieu sait je l'ai servi comme Ami non seulement comme mon Empereur.*'

The Empress-Mother expresses great gratification at the way in which the English have solemnized the Emperor's death, and says : ' *Remerciez ces bons Anglais pour moi.*' Since the sad news the towns have been entirely deserted, a remarkable trait of the grief of the people."

From Mrs. Disbrowe.

St. Petersburg, $\frac{14}{26}$ *December*, 1825.

To the Honble. R. Kennedy.

" Long live the Emperor Nicholas ! Ignoramuses that we were to suppose that Constantine meant to govern us. We were fifteen days in this pleasing error. Everyone took the oath of allegiance to him. All expected his arrival with impatience, but he will have nothing to do with the crown, and so to-day his brother is declared. Lord Strangford says this ought to be called the Imperial year ; two Emperors of Brazil, two of Russia. Constantine may say what he will ; but he certainly is an **ex.** He got into a great passion when told he was

G

Emperor; asked if they thought him a man to be frightened into making a declaration, or that he did not willingly resign the crown for himself and children, when he signed a document to that effect on his marrying Princess Lowitz! This resignation was formally drawn up and signed by the late Emperor Paul; one copy deposited here with the Empress-Mother and Council, and one at Moscow with the Senate and Metropolitan. In spite of this document he was proclaimed in both places as soon as the death of the Emperor Alexander was known, and all the troops and people took the oaths, and the Grand Duke Nicholas was the first to swear allegiance to him.

Messrs. Heckeren and Kielmansegge have arrived, and at their instigation I took off my mourning to go to see the ceremonies at the Cazan Church and hear the *Te Deum*. I had got to the top of the stairs, when, lo and behold! appeared Sir Daniel Bayley* with a tremendously long face, to tell us not to stir, for one of the regiments had refused to take the oath to Nicholas, bayonetted two of their officers and a general; say that Constantine is shut up in Petersburg, and that they will have no other Emperor but him. They are now this very minute drawn up in square, on the Place d'Isaac, have loaded with ball, and Heaven knows what will follow! The Chevalier Guards took the oaths to Nicholas very quietly, and are assembling to quell this insubordination. The general is killed, but I

* English Consul.

believe the officers are only wounded. . . . . . .
Half-past three. I have been walking on the Quay.
The revolt is in the same state ; frequent cheers
are heard, but they will not receive the Emperor's
aides-de-camp. It is said that even all the people
declare for Constantine, but indeed I think the
Government has been much to blame for trifling so
long with the people, trying to keep them in
ignorance of everything, and thus allowing them to
become suspicious. It is said that General Milaradovitch (Military Governor of the town) is wounded
in the side. Troops are marching up from all sides
to surround the rebels. They hardly deserve that
name, poor misguided people. They (the Imperials)
have just found among them they will retreat down
this way most likely, poor creatures !

Half-past nine. It was dreadful to hear the firing.
Every round went to my heart. I do not know
particulars for certain, except that at this moment
all is quiet, and some say the mutineers have
retreated across the river and dispersed. They were
the Mocofsky Regiment, joined by a battalion of
the Fin Regiment. Do you remember our listening
to their band at the camp ? More spectators than
soldiers have been killed, about a hundred they say.
There are no hopes of General Milaradovitch and
a wounded officer who was carried to Count Laval's.
Both the bridges close to our house were guarded,
and the principal firing was down the back line, and
all communication between this cut off. Every
approach to the Place d'Isaac was prevented.

16/28 *December.* The poor soldiers seem to have

been entirely misled by their officers, and soon returned to duty. They have received a general pardon ; but of course a similar clemency could not be extended to those who conducted them and excited them to revolt, and a great many officers are arrested ; I am told upwards of thirty.

We are all in colours again during three days to cheer the accession of the Emperor Nicholas and his charming Empress Alexandrine, daughter of the King of Prussia. I grieve that he had such a melancholy inauguration on Monday ; he was very much affected, and the Empress wept the whole afternoon. It put an end to all rejoicings ; no illuminations nor public ceremonies. However, I trust that all is at an end, and everything will go on quietly. I went out in a *traineau* for the first time to-day. The town presented a curious spectacle. The traces of the sad event on Monday were horrid : pools of blood on the snow, and spattered up against the houses ; the Senate House dreadfully battered. The whole took place on the Place d'Isaac. Poor General Milaradovitch still lingers. He had escaped without a wound from forty-seven battles, but fell by the hand of an assassin at last. He was shot *à bout portant.* Only think how horrid ! He was robbed of his watch and star as they carried him home dying."

From Mrs. Disbrowe.

21 *December,* 1825.
2 *January,* 1826.

" We talk of and think of nothing but the unhappy

event of Monday. Each day adds new names to the list of conspirators, and almost every family trembles lest some members of its own may not be implicated. It is a most unfortunate business, and brings great distress into the nation.

The Emperor Nicholas has a melancholy commencement to his reign, but he has a fine opportunity of showing his talents, and considers himself happy in being the instrument of bringing the deep-laid conspiracy to light, and of saving his country from all the horrors that would have ensued had a discovery been delayed. Papa will be very sorry to hear that the Lavals are brought into distress by their son-in-law, Prince Troubetskoy, being one of the leading men in this affair. After the events of Monday he went to Count Lebzeltern, and without giving him the least suspicion of his connection with the revolt, asked leave to pass the night in his house, under pretext that Count Laval's was all in confusion in consequence of some soldiers having taken refuge in it. This was placing Count Lebzeltern in a most unpleasant situation, being a foreign Minister, and brother-in-law of the Prince. You may judge of his feelings when he was called up in the night and told that an officer was come to arrest his brother. Of course he could make no opposition, and Prince Troubetskoy has made the most important revelations. It is a frightful business, and though all is quiet for the present, many families are in the deepest distress, and there is still cause for alarm. The soldiers were told to cry 'Constantine and Constitutiaze,' or some such Russian word for con-

stitution.   They asked the meaning of this, and were
told : ' Oh, it's the name of Constantine's wife.' This
sounds like a good story ; but from all one hears
of the deception practised upon the soldiers' simplicity, it is not at all impossible or improbable that
this really happened. Some of the traits of the
soldiers are quite affecting, and it has been so clearly
proved that it was only by deceiving them that they
were induced to revolt, and that they all evinced
the deepest sorrow and repentance as soon as they
perceived the real state of things, and that Constantine's name was only a pretext to their own
views, that all have been pardoned. I long to hear
how you spent your Christmas.   Mine is yet to
come, but I do not expect a merry one. To try
to be amused, I have invited myself to two children's
parties on Christmas Eve, one at Madame Ludolf's,
which, by-the-bye, begins with a meagre dinner, and
the other at Madame de Gise's. They are to have
a tree lighted up in the German way."

23 *December*, 1825.
4 *January*, 1826.

" Charming to have two years at a time ! "

From the same.

St. Petersburg, $\frac{5}{17}$ *January*, 1826.

" We all look so dismal in our black cloth gowns,

high with falling collars hemmed in white according to our rank; weepers of the same width, black
caps; and last night we rehearsed the points, or
schneps, a pointed black band across the forehead,
hiding almost all the hair; it should be quite hid,
but modern coquetry steals out a curl or two. To-
morrow there is to be a very extraordinary ceremony,
and certainly very unseasonable, 'the blessing of the
waters.' The whole court in general attends, but
I suppose this year the ladies will not appear. The
Emperor must, and all his attendants and priests—
without hats, fifteen degrees below freezing-point,
imaginez, in the open air on the river. A hole is
cut in the ice, and formerly the devout used to
plunge into the water and bring their children to
be dipped. It has happened that the shivering
priests let the unfortunate little creatures slip
through their icy fingers under the ice. '*Mais quel
bonheur l'enfant alloit tout droit au paradis*,' was
the consoling reflection for the superstitious.

The sentence on the conspirators is not yet
passed; it is expected next week. It is supposed
that a few will be shot, although there is no existing
law to condemn them to death; others to be
branded, their ears and noses slit, and sent to
Siberia. How horrible! The wife of one is a
charming young woman just going to be confined
of her first child. She came from Moscow to spend
the New Year with her husband, not knowing that
he was arrested or anything of what had happened.
Her only brother, her husband, and brother-in-law
are implicated, and her mother is lying paralysed

in mind and body.   What a complication of misery !
It is said that a standard for the conspirators was
found in Madame L.'s wardrobe, worked by her
own hand."

CHAPTER V.

SIR EDWARD'S MEMORANDUM OF THE CONSPIRACY OF 1825.

WE are still in a volcano here, and the question is far from being set at rest. The causes of the evil lie too deep to be settled by a handful of inexperienced officers on one side, or by the death—however merited—of a few of them on the other. It is not the work of a few obscure individuals; it is a contest for power between the crown and the nobility in a nation in which a third class does not exist.

To understand the true state of the empire, we must go back to Peter I. He subdued a nobility, who had previously domineered over the crown, by firmness and terrified them by his cruelties. Catherine II. managed them with consummate skill and terrified them whilst she overawed them. Paul was their victim. In the time of Alexander they expected to have reigned. Though young he escaped from them, and by great exertions and attention to business was at one period master of his empire. Circumstances, however, made him the great man he subsequently became. Imbued with liberal principles himself, the germ of which was sown in his mind by

La Harpe, he wished in 1814 to prepare his own
empire for receiving those seeds by sowing them in
Poland.   Many of his officers, vain at the success of
the Russian arms, and thinking they were seconding
their Imperial Master's views and flattering his
prejudices, more or less openly professed themselves
amateurs of constitutional establishments. Amongst
this class are to be found the principal nobility and
those most eminent for rank, talent, and opulence.

To these revolutionary principles, and to a previously
formed party among the nobility—descendants of
those who before the time of Peter I. had ruled
Russia in ruling its Sovereign — Alexander gave
consistency by lending his name.   Frightened at the
abyss which he thus prepared for himself, he changed
his views to the destruction of a party to which he
had himself given the strength and force to resist
him.   He resolved to humble—he succeeded in
irritating.   He would have formed a third class out
of the crown peasantry and merchants.   He established guilds or distinctive classes of merchants,
in the first of which nobility were allowed to enter,
and to which class the rights and distinctions of
nobility were granted.   He continued more strictly
and extended to a longer period the time during
which all persons entering the military service
remained in the rank of corporal.   He increased the
taxes on the landowners ; he lent money on mortgage
to a spendthrift nobility. The Government is said
to have encouraged underhand the emigration and
excesses of the peasantry for the purpose of ruining
the nobles.   It certainly took no effectual means to

repress them, either by marching troops or otherwise. He then increased the mortgage by adding to the principal the interest they could not discharge, and is said, under the name of Government, the Lombard, and other institutions under his own control, to have possessed a tenth of the landed property. This estimate will include the proportions foreclosed. In acting thus he has, without calling despotism to his aid, sensibly diminished the power of the nobility; but by pushing the point too far has rendered some of them the fit tools of any desperate undertaking. A general discontent has prevailed in the interior among the peasantry (for four or five years), opposed by new local restrictions on their trade, their prejudices shocked by cutting their beards, and other absurd regulations for establishing military colonies ; and an attempt to incorporate the civil and military character has given matter enough for the discontented to work on, and it was evident (indeed Alexander knew it) that the period of an explosion was fast approaching. The accession of Nicholas caused, most fortunately, that explosion to take place prematurely. A haughty nobility could ill brook the sway of the administration which Alexander had formed, whilst an increasing indolence, preserving however the outward form of attention to business, prevented him from seeing as plainly the real state of his empire as his peculiar situation required. They—the nobility—complained of the influence of foreigners, that a German commissary was Minister of Finance ; that foreign affairs were entrusted to a Greek, and a descendant of a Livonian born on board a British ship in the

Tagus; a Livonian baron, Ambassador in London;
a Corsican adventurer at Paris; a Finn at Berlin;
and many minor appointments; an Englishman in
command on the Black Sea; a German on the Baltic,
whilst his brother was Minister of Marine; an Italian,
Governor-General at Riga; a Würtemberg here, a
Wittgenstein and a Tartar in command of the First
and Second Army, etc. To this flame the uninter-
rupted communication by travelling Russians with
the Carbonari of Italy and France served as a
continual aliment. The first explosion took place
here. That it was not a local discontent, the affair of
the Government of Kiew, the arrests at Tabzein,* the
troubles near the Caucasus, the dread of the line of
conduct to be adopted by Yermolow, plainly evinced.
The officers misled, but failed in seducing the troops.
The soldiers, irritated at the deception passed on
them, and soothed and flattered by their Imperial
master, will most probably in the approaching conflict
side with him. Nicholas might have punished the
mutinous officers with death, and might, perhaps, by
yielding something to their views, have conciliated
the great families, and have governed peaceably. He
might also have been ultimately enslaved by them,
wisely or not I do not pretend to determine. He
has shown them the bayonet, and by the bayonet he
must in future govern them.

Individuals belonging to 150 different noble families
are under arrest, and the suspense in which every
person is kept by the silence maintained as to their

* Touthlim (?).

future fate, acting on the hopes and fears of so numerous a class, renders the situation of the empire more critical every day.

I have said that by the bayonet he must in future govern, but of course this power must have its limits ; how to define those limits is difficult. With the nobility he is in a state of open warfare. He relies, for reason given above, on his troops. A prompt and exemplary punishment would have subdued the officers. It has been delayed too long, and we must bear in mind that the officers of that army are the nobility, and if the contest goes on, a standing army may become a corps of Strelitz.

The affair of the Tschernigow Regiment in the Government of Kiew would have been much more formidable had its chief leaders not been previously arrested. Colonel Moraview Apostel, who commanded the rebels, proclaimed Constantine, the same as they did here the 14th, but, once out of the town, he threw off the mask and declared the Sclavonian Republic. He was joined by peasants to whom he promised liberty, and made a considerable resistance, but, of course, unsupported, he could but fall. I have divided the question into plot and conspiracy—plot, the act of a few to make a revolution that something good perhaps might grow out of evil ; by conspiracy I mean to designate that union of the nobility and others to effect an alteration in the Government and adapt the laws to present times, or rather to their own ideas, many entertaining the wish rather than the hope of effecting it, and undetermined as to the period of execution, dispersed throughout the empire, and having no very definite bond of union.

The object of those in the South—I *believe* I rather
hazard the statement in making *it yet*—was a limited
monarchy, limited by such restraints as these army
gentlemen should think fit to propose ; that of Kiew,
republicanism ; that of the North, or Petersburg, the
destruction of the Imperial family and of all government, in order to establish one in their own fashion.
It was led and organized, I hardly need say, by
inexperienced hot-headed young men, without
principle, and without common-sense to guide
them, and failed.

I have just read a very able article in the *Journal
des Débats*, reasoning on what has taken place here.
(It is to be found under date of the 13th, 14th, and
15th of January.) The necessity that existed for
Constantine to accept the crown and then abdicate
was fully felt by every one but Constantine. His
conduct was extraordinary, but consistent. He was
requested to accept, even if he was determined to
abdicate. He answered (the letter was addressed to
the President of the Council) by a flat refusal ; that
if they chose to proclaim him in spite of his
renunciation and found themselves in trouble in consequence, the fault was theirs, and all the inconvenience
likely to result they might answer for ; *that he never
changed his determination when once taken.* " *Ton
ami vile et basse ne peut pas concevoir qu'on renonce,*"
etc.

The Grand Duke Michael, on his way to Warsaw,
never got further than the Peipus See, at Nenals.
He there received orders from Constantine to proceed
no further with any mission with which he might be

charged. *Le mot de l'enigme* is to be found in the ruling passion of Constantine's mind, "obstinacy." The reasons which induced him to abdicate are lost sight of. He said the word, and having done so, he would see Russia deluged in blood, all his partisans, if he has any—a fact I question—hanged, drawn and quartered ; he will not change.

One law is entirely overlooked in the article of the *Journal des Débats*, which materially changes the state of the question—the law of Peter I., made for a particular purpose, but invariably acted on since, by which the reigning Emperor appoints his successor. Alexander appointed Nicholas. The oath is usually taken to the successor, who is called Czarovitch Grand Duke, a title given conventionally to Constantine, but without reason, as he never was sworn to as heir to the throne, any more than Nicholas, and this created a case of difficulty in itself.

But observe the two proclamations : all Russians are called on to swear fealty to the Emperor Constantine and the heir whom he shall appoint ; secondly, to Nicholas and the Grand Duke Alexander, the son of Nicholas, as heir and successor. They have also forgotten to notice the fact that the Princess of Lowitz is a Catholic,* which must for ever exclude her and her offspring from the throne.

Before I conclude with one word on poor Alexander I. (who has done more for Russia than any three Sovereigns she ever possessed), I will call to your memory the character given of him in 1805,

* Roman Catholic.

after Austerlitz, a character of pusillanimity in the hour of danger, a want of proper confidence in himself and in his own and his empire's resources. This opinion of him had its weight up to 1812. And at the epoch of the French invasion, the dread of his not proving himself up to the mark in that momentous crisis induced those about him to prevent him from joining the army, until the retreat from Moscow had in fact decided the question. We know that *in success* he showed himself valiant, magnanimous, and moderate. I fear, however, the details of his last illness, and I believe I have seen them ALL, will show that he died at the moment when his admirers would most have desired it. He knew of the conspiracy for a long period. He received at Taganrog accounts which showed that the period of explosion was approaching and designated some of the leaders, whose arrest he ordered, dreading however the approach of that crisis, incapable of meeting the storm with the necessary vigour. He died as much of a broken spirit as of any disease with which he was attacked, and this is my full conviction. The Emperor Nicholas has shown during these trials a spirit becoming his high situation, but he is without experience, influenced by his mother, and guided by those around him. If he carries his empire through this storm he is a really great man. He has a good hard-headed fighting second in the Grand Duke Michael.

From Mrs. Disbrowe.

$$Jan. \frac{10}{22}, 1825.$$

" When one thinks of the present state of Russia, or rather of the probable future, it is enough to make one's heart ache. These disturbances near Kief have been dreadful. The soldiers committed frightful excesses, just such as would have been practised had the affair of the 14th either succeeded then or have been deferred till the plot was riper. It was one of the plans to give the soldiers three days' pillage of St. Petersburg. Indeed, we cannot be too thankful for our providential escape. Individuals of most of the first families and talents of the country were engaged in the conspiracy, not exactly that of the 14th, but to establish a free constitution in this empire. Government has the upper hand of them, God alone knows how long they may be able to sustain it."

Another letter written some days later in a lighter strain speaks of "a great importation of foreign princes," which include the Prince of Orange, Prince William of Prussia, afterwards Kaiser Wilhelm I., Archduke Ferdinand of Austria, and an "old friend, Prince Paul of Mecklenburg-Schwerin." Then once more stress is laid on the troublous state of affairs.

" Poor Russia is in a most critical state, and the Emperor will have a most difficult task to guide the helm amidst all the trouble that threatens his empire. Discontent and the seeds of rebellion are deeply seminated throughout the realm ; he may smother the

H

fire but I fear he will not be able to extinguish it."

The brother of my parents' friends, the Volkonsky's, was deeply implicated in the conspiracy, a young man of great ability, whose mother filled a high position at Court, and who, far from believing any of her own children could be disloyal, had been " loud and severe in her denunciation of the conspirators."

My mother also alludes to an Englishman of the name of Sherborne,* who found out the plot at Kief, and sent word of it to the Emperor Alexander. He was to be " handsomely rewarded," and have the word " Faithful " added to his name in Russia.

* Sherwood (?).—M.M.C.

CHAPTER VI.

CONCERNING THE DUKE OF WELLINGTON.

From Mrs. Disbrowe.

St. Petersburg, $\frac{2}{14}$ *February*, 1826.

" The expected arrival of the Duke of Wellington
gives immense satisfaction here; the compliment is
duly appreciated. It is very curious that he should
be the only Russian Field Marshal, so of course he
commands the whole army; how it will puzzle him
if they give in the returns in Russ. All sorts of
honours are destined for him. He is to be lodged by
the Court at the house where old Mr. Gourieff lived
and died, on the Great Quay; an officer and *feldjäger*
will be sent to meet him at the frontier, and what is
best of all, a magnificent sable *pelisse*, or perhaps
two, each worth 6,000 roubles. I hope the Duchess
will get at least a trimming on his return, I mean a *fur*
one, for I believe she has had enough of other sorts
from his Grace. A new *attaché* is also coming out,
an ' Honble. Jerningham,' Lord Stafford's son. I wish
I knew whether he is an eldest son, he would be a
prize here. Lady Strangford has been very unwell

indeed, from having taken cold, but is again almost recovered.

I went to see the preparations in the Cazan Church, but they were not finished; I daresay the effect will be good, though it does not promise much yet. The fine granite pillars are twisted round with silver and black alternately, the hangings in black velvet with silver fringe, the windows closed by silver crosses on black velvet; the *catafalque* looks like a Chinese temple supported by green pillars. I hear the preparations in the fortress are much handsomer. The procession will be some versts in extent, and it is said the Empresses with the two first classes mean to follow the corpse on foot from the Cazan to the fortress, but I should think the Dowager incapable of such a walk. The 14th is the day fixed upon for the funeral. On Sunday next the Imperial family retire to Tszarskozelo, and every house will be closed until after the ceremony.

There was a most splendid dinner given to the Duke yesterday by the French Ambassador; upward of fifty people, the whole Corps, and some of the principal Russians. Madame de la Ferronaye was 'armed' out by Lord Strangford and the Duke of Wellington. Was not that a monopoly? Poor Lady Strangford was unable to come, she has been seriously ill. I hear the Duke of Wellington is so bored with the daily parades he is obliged to attend that he means to curtail his stay considerably. His journey hither was quite a triumphal progress; military honours awaited him in every town; *fêtes* were prepared, but these he only attended at Berlin.

He arrived here on the 20th day from his departure, having slept every night on the road during six or seven hours, remained one day at Weimar, and three at Berlin. Was not that expeditious? Amongst other presents prepared for him are a pair of Toula pistols set in diamonds, value £6,000 sterling. Every honour is paid him, but I suspect he gets annoyed. You will hardly credit it, but I am writing before nine o'clock, as to my great surprise I find Sir Alexander* sets off at 10 a.m. instead of at midnight."

From Mr. John Kennedy.

ST. PETERSBURG,   27 *February*, 1826.
                 11 *March*,

"MY DEAR FATHER,—The Duke of Wellington, as you may easily conceive, is made much of here, and in daily attendance upon some member of the Imperial family. The Russians are not accustomed to see a Commander-in-Chief walking about without his uniform, and their ideas of military grandeur had led them to expect a full dress upon every occasion. M. de la Ferronaye gave him a splendid dinner on Monday, when the Countess offered one arm to the Duke, and one to Lord Strangford, who otherwise must have taken precedence.   Count Blome gave his on Thursday, Lord S. gives one to-night, and M. de Lebzeltern to-morrow.   They cannot complain of want of good living, however well grounded may be the complaints of dulness.   His Grace's suite is composed of Lord Fitzroy Somerset,† who puts me

* Sir Alexander Malet.   † Afterwards Lord Raglan.

in mind in outward appearance (particularly having lost an arm) of Captain Tyler, and whose manner is extremely unaffected, I mean without the least military pretension, and well calculated to please his constant master and companion ; Captain Cathcart, Lords Fincastle and Douglas, and Mr. Bligh, are old acquaintances of yours at Geneva. The last are all pleasant, gentlemanly men, but it is impossible for them to enliven the general monotony, which falls doubly heavily on them, being here for so short a time, and having left such gay residences as London and Paris. After the funeral we may expect a change. The ceremonies begin at Sarskoë Selo on Sunday, here on the Wednesday, and will continue about ten days. They will be imposing, but the churches of the Cazan where the body lies in state, and of the fortress where the tomb will be, are too small to contain a vast multitude, particularly as the crowded preparations occupy a third of the former and two-thirds of the latter, originally small."

From Mrs. Disbrowe.

Written either late in February or early in March, 1825.

"On Saturday the corpse is to arrive at the Cazan Church. We ladies of the *Corps Diplomatique* are especially invited ; it will be a most fatiguing affair. At nine o'clock we are to be at the church and stand until the ceremony is over. My great fear is the cold, for we can have no wrappings of course, and we shall be some time under the colonnade. Our dress to be worn is warm; the two great veils on the head will be comfortable, and the flannel train may serve as a cloak whilst we wait. The whole corps assemble at the French Ambassador's, and we proceed from thence with an escort of cavalry. Great injunctions are given about our houses being properly secured and watched, and every precaution taken to prevent disturbances. Sixty thousand troops and pieces of loaded artillery are ready in case of need, but I trust all will pass off quietly, as most, and I believe all, of the ill-intentioned are safe in custody. Lady Strangford is still confined to the house. She has been laid up ever since the Duke came, and has not seen him once. I told you of her insisting on receiving company one evening when she was so ill that she could hardly stand. It ended by her retiring and leaving me to do the honours . . . . Baron Palmerstjerna desires to be particularly remembered to papa, and so does M. de Ludolf. Count Lebzeltern is recalled. M. de Bombelles comes here as *Chargé d'Affaires.* Open your ears to hear that his Grace the Duke of Wellington honours us to-morrow with his company at dinner, and comes without being invited, which is the best part."

(A P.S. found loose, written before March $\frac{8}{20}$).

"The body arrives to-morrow and is to be buried the Monday following.

Captain L. Horton has been adding to British laurels by saving all the merchant ships from a great fire at Cronstadt, supposed to be on purpose to

revenge some inquiries the Emperor ordered to be
made about naval stores, in which it was discovered
that the *rats* had eaten equipment for twelve sail of
the line, brass cannon, iron bedsteads and all. This
assertion was actually made."

From Mr. John Kennedy.

St. Petersburg, $\frac{8}{20}$ *March,* 1826.

"Last Saturday we attended the ceremony of the
entrance of the body of the late Emperor into the
Cazan Church. We were previously assembled in
the church and remained there from half-past ten
until three, excepting during the time we braved the
cold and frost and a thick snow-storm on the steps,
watching the procession. The '*Herault de Joie,*'
in·complete golden armour, formed a striking contrast
to the gloomy colour of the black cloth and large
chapeaux rabattus, the same as worn by our coal
heavers in London. The different armorials of the
different provinces and dependent states of Russia
were on shields overhanging each side of a horse,
one horse for each representation, and *appliqués* on
black cloth which, covering the animal entirely,
extended two yards beyond him, and was supported
by two train-bearers.

The funeral car was gold, surmounted by a lofty
catafalque. The coffin, when removed into the church
and carried up the steps of the *catafalque* prepared
for it, and which represented a small temple, tastefully arranged, proved too heavy for the *aides-de-
camp,* and was borne by about twenty old soldiers.

The Empress-Mother came in just before, not having been able to follow on foot according to her intention. The Emperor and Empress followed immediately, then the Field-Marshal Duke of Wellington, and the principal officer with the regalia. The church had, when lighted up, a much finer appearance than we had expected, but everybody suffered excessively from cold, having generally supposed that, notwithstanding the total want of stoves, the crowd would make it oppressive, whereas the crowd were not allowed to enter. The poor soldiers on duty suffered from seven in the morning all the evils of a freezing inaction, and one actually let drop his bayonet, which struck Prince Sapieha on the chin and cut it. Perfect quiet and decorum prevailed amongst those who witnessed the procession, as everybody could not, and indeed few could, break through the strong guard placed at every avenue leading into those streets through which it should pass. The body has been declared too disfigured to be opened to public view, but during certain hours of the day everybody may walk round the coffin, going in at one door and passing out at another."

From the same, probably written

$\frac{8}{20}$ *March,* 1826.

"Jerningham, our new *attaché*, seems a quiet, gentlemanly fellow; if I am obliged to change my quarters, I may arrange with him. Disbrowe is in great spirits, and can now make up his mind to wait

here a month or two longer.   His brother's appointment and his own pleasing letters have made him
quite happy.

We had no disturbances lately, owing to the
vigilance of the police.   The Emperor treats
anonymous letters with silent contempt, and we
suppose the chief conspirators, and I am afraid
Princess V's. brother, have been condemned to a
public death."

From Mrs. Disbrowe.

"MY DEAR FRANCES,—John has written you an
account of the funeral, I suppose.   You must know
that it is rather a sore subject with me.   I am sorry
I did not go to the burial itself, but remained with
the rest of the ladies, merely to see the procession
itself pass over the *Champ de Mars* from Prince
Hohenlohe's windows.   I was most desirous to have
gone, but Mr. Disbrowe now says he thought I was
joking when I expressed this wish ; and therefore, as
he had no inclination to go himself, he did not
encourage my plan ; and another thing I hesitated
about was being the only diplomatic lady at the
church, and was fearful the others might have taken
it as a censure upon them.   I saw the coffin at
Tszarskoselo and three times in the Cazan Church ;
but the bustle, crowd, pageantry, and cold entirely
took off my attention, preventing my feeling that I
was attending the funeral of the Emperor I had so
much liked.

The Imperial family went to the church twice
every day whilst the body was in the Cazan.   They

knelt round the coffin during the prayers, and kissed
it both on their arrival and departure. It was
astonishing to see how firmly and actively the old
Empress walked up and down the *catafalque.* The
Empress Alexandrine seemed much more feeble.
At Tszarskoselo the hat and sword the Emperor
wore last were laid on the coffin, and I was much
more affected at seeing them than anything else.
Here the crowns of Cazan, Tauride, and the Imperial
crown and sceptre, and all the Orders Alexander ever
held were placed on cushions and stands on the
catafalque. The aides-de-camp who accompanied
the body from Taganrog look quite worn out; and
yet they say the burial is quite a second loss to them;
they had become attached and so accustomed to
watching the body. They kept watch alternately,
night and day, and always stood on the bier when it
travelled. Ilia, the coachman, who had driven the
Emperor for upwards of twenty years, obtained
permission to conduct the funeral car from Taganrog
to the grave. He was a very interesting person.
I could distinguish his grey bushy beard, which,
according to etiquette, ought to have been cut off;
but he cried three days about it, and was so miserable,
that he was allowed to keep it. It is said that the
circumstance of his conducting the bier tended more
than anything to tranquillise the people about the
real death of the Emperor, for it had been reported
that he was not dead, but imprisoned, and that the
funeral was an imposition, but when they saw Ilia,
they were convinced that he would not have been
deceived, and sure that he would not have been

prevailed on to drive aught but the body of his late master. The Emperor was buried on the 14th, just the twenty-fifth anniversary of his accession and of the death of his father, the Emperor Paul and exactly a century since the death of Peter the Great.

I must tell you a fine sentence of the Emperor Nicholas, and then leave great folks. He has received many anonymous letters telling him his life is in danger, etc., etc., and some one advised him to attend to them. ‘*Non, on veut me faire tyran ou poltron ; je ne saurais être ni l'un ni l'autre.*’

Yesterday I went to Sir James Wylie's rooms in the palace, to see a most beautiful parade of 30,000 men. We were extremely well placed, just behind the Emperor, Princes, Guards, etc., and saw everything to the greatest advantage. They defiled just before us, or the Emperor, I do not know exactly which. One luckless wight was just saluting the Emperor when a clumsy drum-major struck his horse and nearly upset him ; and only fancy the scene, carried off the fine flowing *tail* with which the steed was adorned, and exposed a most shabby stump with which nature had blessed him. The rider never suspected what had happened, and went on with his work to our infinite amusement. The Emperor laughed too. The Emperor has given the Duke of Wellington a regiment to be called by his name.

4th April, 1826. The Duke goes on Thursday. I am sorry for it. I shall quite miss Lord Fitzroy Somerset and Mr. Bligh. I have been actively

engaged in their service in procuring for them models
of the Russian carriages, and have at this moment no
less than two chariots and four, two calèches with
four horses abreast, four droshkys and six *traineaux*
on my table for them.   They are like those I sent to
my babies, but seem to please grown up children
extremely.   The Duc de Raguse is to be the
Extraordinary Ambassador from France.   I hear he
is making splendid preparations, and at one ball each
lady is to be presented with a fan and *bouquet de
fleurs artificielles* from Baton's.   M. de Pont Carré is
already gone to Moscow to get all things ready for
M. de la Ferronaye.   Poor Lady Strangford has only
been able to dine at table once since the Duke of
Wellington came; it was last Saturday, and she
looked just like a ghost.   Only think of Mr. Bligh's
good luck, he shot the bear at the hunt the other
day.   He waited until it came within twenty yards of
him, and then brought him down with the first barrel.
When he was down General Sabloukoff banged two
barrels into him, under pretence of finishing him, but
in reality to have a claim to the booty.   Mr. Bligh
gets the skin.   What a feather in his cap!"

$\frac{9}{21}$ *April*, 1828.

"All silent still about the inhabitants of the
fortress; some say nothing will be decided these six
weeks, others that the business will drag on till the
Coronation, and that then the advantage will be
taken of its being *un moment de grâce*, and pardon be
extended to many.   Arrests still go on, however;

some have already been *let out*, others slightly
implicated, sent off to the Caucasus, or some other
fortress for a few months; all the guilty part of
Moscofsky regiment are marched off to the
Caucasus.

27th. I hope you have observed the honourable
mention made of Sir Alexander's arrival in the
French papers. '*Le Chevalier Mulet chargé de
dépêches.*' I wonder if they made the *calembour* on
purpose.

If you hear that the Duke of Wellington has
ordered 15,000 picture frames, you need not believe
it, and unless you like the marvellous; also that he
lost eight hundred thousand roubles at play is equally
worthy of credit. Here both are sworn to as facts.
I verily believe he never touched a card whilst
here."

CHAPTER VII.

DEATH OF LADY STRANGFORD. ARRIVAL OF THE DUKE OF DEVONSHIRE.

From Mrs. Disbrowe.

ST. PETERSBURG, $\frac{4\ May,}{22\ April,}$ 1826.

" NOW to begin my Easter history, for like the rest of the Russian world, we have thought it necessary to make this quite an epoch, to be beguiling ourselves with the illusion that we are particularly happy and superlatively amused.

I must date from last Saturday at midnight, when, accompanied by John and my Sposo, I went to the Imperial Chapel, in full puff, and had the exquisite satisfaction of seeing Nicholas I. slobber some hundreds of old and young, tall and short, thin and thick, ugly and handsome dutiful servants of the male kind. Such a ceremony! It began with the Archimandrite, and terminated with Count Salahoub, *Maitre des Ceremonies,* of whom papa no doubt has a tender recollection. The Empresses were not present. The young one was ill, and the Dowager did not like to appear in public, so that the scene was not so splendid as it usually is. The maids of honour who did attend were, generally speaking, old and ugly. The Emperor kissed about 700 on both cheeks, and it really was a most extraordinary spectacle to see these people come up to him in regular files, or rather strings, to receive the accolade ; and how thoroughly his Imperial Majesty rubbed and wiped and rubbed his mouth again, which had been in such constant exercise for about two hours and a half. It was over about three o'clock ; but our expedition did not end here, for on quitting the palace we observed a tremendous fire, and, supposing it to be at no great distance, we thought to take a look at it, but after proceeding about four versts we gave up the plan. The Emperor however went, as is the custom on such occasions, and did not get home until six o'clock. Twelve brick houses were burnt, about an equal number of wooden ones, and many horses perished. It began about ten o'clock, when almost every person was in the churches, and no assistance could be procured for some time. Owing to Halker's discretion I saw no genuine celebration of Easter Sunday. He prevented the *esvoscheks* (coachmen) and *d'vornecks* from presenting me their offerings in person, so I received the eggs in a very humdrum way, and paid ten roubles for each. I forgot to say that the Emperor kisses the Archdeacons and Deacons three times in token of the Trinity, one on each cheek, and the third on the chin. I hear he did not shave for the two preceding days, in order to ward off as much contact as possible.

No orders for going to Moscow ; no official

announcement of the Duke of Devonshire's Embassy. Very tiresome, disagreeable, and affronting. I do not feel at all as if we should go to the Coronation, and perhaps after all there may be none for some time, for the Empress Elizabeth is very ill. We are all in colours this week, and look extremely well. Lady Strangford was presented on Wednesday, and really looked quite young and beautiful, so much so that everyone was quite astonished. Mr. Charles dressed her head to perfection, and Madame Turin made her gown exquisitely. If I go to the Coronation, what train shall I have ? It is too late to embroider in gold or silver. Sir Alexander Malet writes as if he were going to Walton, so I hope he will. Mr. Disbrowe and I actually paid nine-and-twenty visits on Easter Monday. Are not you overcome at the very idea ? "

From Mrs. Disbrowe.

St. Petersburg, $\frac{13}{25}$ *May*, 1826.

" Having no home news to furnish, I will begin by foreign, though it is of a melancholy nature— the death of the poor Empress Elizabeth at Beleff on the 4th of May. This event has long been expected, nor can anyone regret its having taken place. She considered herself a burden to all around her, and felt as if her affection blighted every object on which she bestowed it. She has been rapidly declining ever since she left Taganrog, but seemed extremely desirous to reach Colonga (280 versts from Moscow), where the Dowager Empress was waiting

I

to meet her. But this wish was not to be gratified, she only reached Beleff, within eighty versts of her destination, and then felt she could proceed no further. She dined that day with her suite at a half-way house, but left the table immediately after the soup. Her eyes were already dim, she was become so deaf that she did not hear a violent thunderstorm that took place, and her voice was scarcely audible. She wrote to the Empress-Mother, slept two or three hours, woke about four o'clock, complained of being uncomfortable, but desired that the physician might not be called if he was asleep, and then seemed to doze again, but it was to awake in another world ; her gentle spirit had fled, her sorrows and sufferings were over, and we humbly trust that she is now happier than it was permitted her to be on earth. An express had been sent to the Empress-Mother, but she arrived three hours too late. By this event we all again are thrown into deep mourning, and must attend another funeral.
. . . . . The Coronation and its *fêtes* are of course suspended, and all the Extraordinary Ambassadors come or coming are likely to have a much longer stay than they expected. There is no way of amusing them ; theatres, dancing, and any apparent entertainment is forbidden. We ladies return to our weepers, veils, and *cloth* gowns.

Poor Lady Strangford is again seriously ill ; not in danger, I hope, but very, very ill."

From Mrs. Disbrowe.

"You must have been much shocked at the

melancholy event Mr. Disbrowe announced to you by the last post, for though you did not personally know poor Lady Strangford, yet our connection with her must have created an interest about her in your mind, and I am sure you feel for the five little children. Lord Strangford has been in a dreadful state ever since her danger was apparent; hardly left her room, and has neither been to bed nor tasted food since. The funeral is now going on. She is buried about six versts from here. It was her own wish, expressed to me in her former illness, that she should be buried in this country, as privately as possible. Lord Strangford had already given orders for the body to be embalmed, but of course complied with her desire as soon as I made it known to him. I was the last person to whom she spoke.

Poor Lord Strangford will hasten his departure as much as possible. He says: ' Let me only get out of this country and nothing shall induce me to return to it.' Poor man ! he has had nothing but annoyance, both public and private, ever since he came into it. . . . .

Mr. Disbrowe and John went down to the 'Gloucester' yesterday to endeavour to arrange about Lord Strangford's departure, and next week is fixed on. I hear the Duke has some intention of giving us a *fête* on board the 'Gloucester.' It will be very pleasant, no doubt, but a very long affair, as she lies below Cronstadt.

Our Extraordinary not being a military character, he does not receive the honours paid to the French and the Swede, who are both Field Marshals ; and

as he arrived the last, he must follow them upon all
occasions, which is unlucky, for I do not doubt his
being worth such.   His suite consists of Lord
Morpeth, Messrs. Townshend (Mr. Cholmondeley's
brother-in-law), Fane, Dundas, Cavendish, Lord F.
Leveson Gower, Lord Wriothesley Russell, Lord
William Montague not yet arrived; very splendid
in point of rank, and all promising young men."

June $\frac{21}{9}$, 1826.

"The party to the ship yesterday went off
famously.   Our house was the *rendez-vous*.   We
were about fifty-five persons, all the beauty of St.
Petersburg.   There was Countess Zavadovsky,
Countess Salahoub, Princess Catische Dolgorouky,
Madame Narischkin *née* Potocka, Countesses
Nesselrode, Ribeaupierre, the De la Ferronayes,
Middletons, Ludolfs, ourselves; in short, a very
select, agreeable party.   At half-past one some
embarked on the Duke's barge, others on a Russian
steamer.   At the bar we all got on board an English
steamboat and boiled down to the 'Gloucester,'
who received us with yards manned, colours flying,
and a salute of fifteen guns.

Just as we got on board a sudden squall came
on, but it soon blew over and became fair.   A table
for eighty was laid out upon the poop, and a
sumptuous dinner was soon served up.   The Russian
ladies particularly requested there might be no
dancing, and so did their duty.   There is no dis-
puting a captain's order on board, so of course when

he called for a valse both musicians and foreign
dancers obeyed it, and it went on merrily, the St.
Petersbourgeois seeming very contented to look on.
It was Lady Granville's birthday, and so we all
went in colours ; the Russians as if to a ball in
white silk gowns.

The day and night were beautiful, and almost
equally light."

From Mrs. Disbrowe.

ST. PETERSBURG, $\frac{13}{25}$ *July*, 1826.

"Captain Clifford was extremely anxious to show
us the 'Herald,' so I consented against my self-
approval to go on Sunday, and after church we set
off.   The Middletons, Princess Aline Volkonsky,
and several of the Duke of Devonshire's suite—just
the pleasantest of them, of course, that comprises
my favourites—Lord Morpeth and Mr. Townshend,
but I also like the others very much.

We dined on board.   It is the most beautiful
bijou of a ship I ever saw, the cabins elegantly fitted
up, and everything very handsome.   I wish we were
to return in her in October.   At nine we set off in
great glee.   Some impromptu charades were acted
in capital style, and it was admirable how well they
dressed themselves in our cloaks, and *one* solitary
cocked hat.   I never saw better, even when greater
preparations had been made.   Marriage was one
word.   One act: Marie Stuart and Rizzio's assassination just as he was singing to her.   Two acts :
Different ages in procession, and the whole a most

interesting *noces*, the parson admirably dressed with
a black cloak, and a whole sheet of brown paper
for bands. This same sheet of brown paper trans-
formed him into a magpie when Charpie was performed, and he hopped about with great effect.
About eleven o'clock it became very dark with a
thick fog, and the disagreeable discovery was made
that we had lost our way. Nothing was to be done
but to put out the steam and cast anchor. The
ladies went into the cabin; the young ones slept
soundly, but Mrs. Middleton and I were not so
easily composed, so we talked. The gentlemen
arranged themselves on the deck with the cushions
off the benches and a solitary carpet bag, which had
performed the part of a throne in the beginning of
the evening. All sorts of tricks were put in practise
to obtain these accommodations, and there was a
plentiful quantity of laughing. What made it more
piquant was that the Englishmen were to set off
at seven next morning for Moscow. Not one had
packed up, and they had all come on this party
against the Duke's wish, who was 'sure they would
not be back in time.' At two o'clock it was again
daylight; at five o'clock we reached home. A
fishing boat told us what direction to take.

I have just heard that this morning at three
o'clock five of the conspirators were hanged near
the fortress; but as they were not accustomed to
this mode of punishment, three of the unfortunate
men fell from the ropes. The next class of
criminals who had also been sentenced to death
had their punishment commuted to perpetual exile.

They appeared on the scaffold, had their swords broken over their heads, the epaulettes torn off by the executioner, their uniforms burnt, the dress of the commonest criminals put on them, and then were sent off in carts to Siberia.

Ryleieff Rahousky (who shot Milaradovitch), Postel,* Serge Mouravieff, Apostel, and Bostayieff. Rumine † are the names of those executed.

If the utmost rigour of the law is put in force, the fate of the exiles will be dreadful. They will be sent to the mines, never see the light of day ; and such is the severity of the work that it is said they never live above five years. Poor Princess Sophie, I know, flatters herself that after a few years her brother, Prince Serge (who is amongst those who were condemned to death, but who is sent to Siberia), may be pardoned through the intercession and in consideration of the long services of her mother, and of her husband, Prince Pierre, who was the greatest friend of the Emperor Alexander, and who is in favour with the present Emperor. He is to be *Ministre des Appanages et Ministre de la Cour*. Princess Troubetschkoi (daughter of Count Laval) is determined to follow her husband into exile, but I should doubt her obtaining permission to do so, as he has only escaped death by the promise to spare his life which the Emperor gave him. It is said that the court was most unwilling to give weight to the Emperor's promise."

* Bestel (?).   † Bestougoff (?).

CHAPTER VIII.

MOSCOW AND THE CORONATION.

From Mrs. Disbrowe.

St. Petersburg, $\frac{30}{18}$ *July.*

"The great question is at last decided. We go to
Moscow, and moreover go in a great hurry. Two days
given me to make my preparations, and on Tuesday
night we are to be off. It was only settled last night,
and we had company to dinner. To-day is Sunday ;
nothing advanced, and Tuesday is a great *fête* day.
However, kind Madame Bobrinski gives me a dress
she had worked for herself, and no doubt Madame
Turin will do her best for me. I am very glad we are
going, but I fear the journey will fatigue my Sposo a
good deal. He is not strong yet, but you know when
there is work to do he thinks of nothing else. John
will procure us a lodging, and we intend to be
frequently invited out to dinner. The greatest part
of our time, I expect, will be passed in our carriage,
the distances at Moscow are so enormous. The
French Ambassador lives seven versts from the
Kremlin, the Duke of Devonshire at the same distance
but on the other side, so that we must live fourteen

Allen & Co. Sc.

Lady Disbrowe.

versts apart; and as we intend visiting both very
frequently we shall be obliged to go post. Do
not you rather envy me going to Moscow? To
Moscow ! ! !

The Empress-Mother told Madame de Staël that
Moscow was compared to Rome, and asked her if
she thought it was so justly. '*Oui, mais Rome
Tartare,*' replied Madame la Baronne. We had the
Sardinian Embassy to dinner, Le Marquis de
Brignolle Sale, and Le Marquis de Sommarive,
with whom I pretended to claim acquaintance, and it
turned out I had never seen him in my life before.
They were Milanese, whom we knew of this name.
Mr. Disbrowe and I travel in the green chaise, Mr.
Jerningham and Parker in the yellow chariot. I
thought the *attaché* would not like this arrangement,
but he takes to it very well, preferring it to going in
an open carriage, or to buying one for himself. . . .
Tuesday. We are off in two hours; capital accom-
modation on the road : require to take nothing but
beds and eatables. Adieu, adieu."

From Mrs. Disbrowe.

MOSCOW ! ! ! ! ! ! !

(The last five added by Count La Ferronaye's desire.)

10 *August,* 1826.

"Who thought some thirty years ago that it would
ever be my lot to write from Moscow ? Well, but so
it is. Our journey commenced on Tuesday night,
the 1st of August, and terminated most prosperously
on Saturday morning, the fifth, only resting one

night on the road. I think I never travelled through such an extent of uninteresting country, and the only place to be admired is the town of Twer, which is prettily situated on the banks of the Volga.

At Torjok we slept and meant to buy shoes, sashes, and boots ; but the number of travellers who preceded us had so increased the prices and diminished the stock that we made very few purchases. On Sunday, the Emperor made his public entry into Moscow. He had previously resided at Petrowsky, an extraordinary Asiatic red brick palace, close to the town. There was nothing remarkable in the cortége, excepting the old-fashioned gilt carriages, in which the Empresses and ladies came. The Emperor was on horseback, dressed as usual. Next came the Empress-Mother, with a crown on the roof of her carriage. She looked wonderfully well, and bowed most graciously. The young Empress, accompanied by the Hereditary Grand Duke,* followed next. This was quite an affecting sight. The little Grand Duke is a lovely boy of eight years old. He was dressed in a hussar uniform, with his little star. The Empress was beautiful, as usual, the expression of her countenance even more than commonly interesting, but serious. Next came the Grand Duchess Hélène, a blaze of beauty and cheerfulness. The ladies of honour followed by four in old-fashioned gilt coaches made in the time of Peter, I should think. Adam, I believe, was never in Russia, or I should attribute them to his days. The rest of the procession was

* Alexander II.

composed of the *Maréchaux de la Noblesse,* anything but noble looking ; some squadrons of cavalry, the servants of the court ; that was all. We were fortunate in arriving in time for this sight, though I own I expected more show and more costumes. Our determination to come to this place had been so abrupt that very little time was given to find us a lodging, and poor dear John was nearly knocked up in trying to get everything ready for us. I do not know what we should have done without him. He found a house, carriage, servants, and linen ; and no easy achievement, I assure you. We pay enormously for a very tiny apartment—which just holds us, and is not over clean—2,000 roubles a month. As usual I was very nearly demolished the first night; the number of my enemies beats anything I ever saw in all my travels. They actually swarm on the walls.

The Duke of Devonshire is very kind to us. We have already dined twice with him, are invited to-morrow, and he gave me his opera-box last night. His house is really splendid, and he is doing his honours in great style. His *fête* for the Emperor will be magnificent. You cannot think what a treat the opera was to me, it was so long since I had seen one. The theatre is merely a long, large room, fitted up with two rows of boxes in a private house, and most oppressively warm. Madame de la Ferronaye has chosen Sunday for her *soirées.* The Duc de Raguse receives on Wednesday, and some Moscow houses are open the other nights. Mr. Disbrowe was presented this morning. The Emperor told him the

Coronation would take place in three weeks; so there
is plenty of time for my tail to come from Petersburg.
The Empress-Mother inquired after papa and John
with great kindness.   I hope now I shall manage to
be presented to the Grand Duchesse Hélène."

Friday $\frac{30}{11}$ *August.*

"We have been looking about us, but everything in
this place is so different from any I ever saw before,
that I do not know how I shall describe it to you.
The town is built irregularly, extends over a great
space, and the best houses on the scale of palaces in
other countries.

The Moska is a poor little river when compared to
the beautiful Neva, but still it adds much effect to the
scenery of the town.   The Kremlin seems a small
town walled round in the centre of the city, and
presents the most extraordinary diversity of buildings
of all ages it is possible to imagine : gilt and painted
cupolas dazzle the eye on every side, and their
glittering effect is really magnificent.   No two domes
are alike in form and colour, some are merely gilt,
others of a bright *lapis lazuli ;* others of a shining
green, some painted like mosaic ; in short, it is
impossible to describe the endless variety, and all
looking as bright and fresh as if only a few months
old, instead of having defied the elements during
centuries.   Yesterday, when I viewed the town from
the top of the Tvan Tower, I could not help envying
the unsmoked atmosphere, so different from that
which envelopes our own capital.

Ségur's story about the Golden Cross from this tower is a fond fancy.   It never was more than gilt, and the French did not carry it off, nor throw it in a lake, it still maintains its old post.   On Wednesday we dined at the Duke of Devonshire's, splendid repast to be sure, cuts out Marmont's completely, everything magnificent and costly, but no shining *Vermeil*, all in massive silver, elegance combined with simplicity, just as it ought to be at the Duke of Devonshire's, or a British Ambassador's.   .   .   .   .

We began gadding early this morning by going at eight o'clock to see ' *La Bénediction des Eaux.*'   A small temple or rather chapel was erected on the river, and the same ceremony performed as on the 6th January at St. Petersburg.   We were not very well placed, but had a tolerable view of the procession descending from the Kremlin, the priests all in silver robes, and the Empress and ladies of the Court in very smart morning dresses.   The chanting is always beautiful, and there is something very imposing in the ceremonies of this Church, though to my heretical eyes I see no difference in a picture gilt and ornamented with precious stones from an image, nor discover any more edification for the people in hearing the Mass performed in the Slavonian language than in Latin, as they do not understand either the one or the other.   Everything is typified in this Church, and every candle, every action is meant to commemorate some part of our Saviour's history.   The Sacrament is always attended by the symbols of the Passion and Crucifixion, such as the scourge, the sponge, the hyssop.   When a Metropolitan officiates, every prayer

is repeated three times over, every verse of the
Gospel, in short, the whole service is nearly tripled.
The costumes of the priests are very handsome, and
their flowing, bushy hair and long beards have a very
good effect. Some of them wear a sort of *Bretelle*
over their shoulders that has much to do with the
ceremony, and is frequently crossed and uncrossed.
To-day the Fast has begun, the long one at Easter is
the strictest, and then neither fish nor milk are
allowed, and they may only cut a sort of mushroom.

M. de Berg* was presented to me the other evening,
he begs to be particularly remembered to you
all.

The Duke's ball was extremely pleasant, and went
off with the greatest *éclat ;* he was in great despair,
for the first hour there were only four ladies arrived,
and the rooms already crowded with men, however
the *belles* appeared afterwards in great force in their
best looks and best attire. Prince Charles of Prussia
was the lion of the evening, and a very good-
humoured, lively one too. It is amusing to see how
thoroughly he hates all *etiquette*, and how cleverly he
jilts the grand old ladies for the pretty young ones ;
he did not choose to sit down to supper on account of
his rank pinning him down to two elderly dames, so
he walked about some time, and then took a plate on
his knees behind his would-have-been ' step-mother,'
Countess Catherine Tiesenhausen (you remember
her). She fully flattered herself some time ago that

* An old friend, had been an *attaché* at Berne, afterwards
Consul in London.

the King of Prussia meant to espouse her, all her preparations were made, and the mama already provided with due consequence for the occasion, when His Majesty sent her word he had found somebody he liked better. She now looks very sweet on the Duke of Devonshire, and even told him the other day, she did not go out for several evenings, '*Je me reserve pour vous.*' Quite a declaration was it not?"

From Mrs. Disbrowe.

Moscow, 22 August, 1826.
2 September,

"Hardly have I allowed myself to disrobe ere I attempt a description of the magnificent sight from which I have just returned. At half-past seven this morning the *Corps Diplomatique* assembled in the ancient Palace of the Tsars, in a low hall whose walls were covered with gilding and saints at full length. The procession began to enter the Cathedral of the Assumption about half-past eight, the Empress-Mother opened it, and took her seat upon a small throne entirely covered with turquoises, and under a canopy to the right of the Emperor's. It must have been a trying moment for her, as this is the third time she has performed at a coronation. The procession was composed of the several Imperial establishments, deputations from the provinces, and of the merchants, the general officers, etc., etc., and clergy. The Emperor was attended by his two brothers, the Grand Dukes Constantine and Michael, and the Emperor and Empress were seated on great

chairs yclept thrones, under a canopy, the great
officers of State arranged on either side of them, the
Grand Dukes close to the thrones, the *Corps
Diplomatique* stood on the left on raised benches
by the wall of the building, the ladies of the Court
were on the opposite side; the thrones, of course,
faced the High Altar, where stood the Priests
magnificently habited. The ceremony began by
music, which was quite divine, the Archimandrite or
Archbishop then approached the Emperor and read
him a long exhortation in very good Slavonic or
Russe, I know not which. H.I.M. then took another
book and also read aloud, these I conclude were his
promises to be good; his brothers and other
dignitaries then invested him with the Imperial
Mantle. Here began Constantine's fine part, placing
his younger brother in his own stead, voluntarily
resigning to him that Imperial sway to which he
himself had so just a right, performing the duties of
a subject in a manner that showed he was one of his
own free will, and apparently happy in so doing. It
was very fine indeed, and is I believe an unparalleled
trait in history. In appearance he is greatly inferior
to the Emperor, being short, thick, and *sans trancher
le mot*, remarkably ugly, with a most disagreeable
expression of countenance, quite a caricature of the
Emperor Alexander; but his want of beauty does
not militate against his noble conduct, for which we
must give him full credit.

When the mantle was arranged the priest presented
the crown to the Emperor, who took it and placed it
on his own head, he then bent over the Bible, and the

Archbishop prayed over him.   The Empress-Mother now approached and embraced her son ;   this was quite affecting, for Imperial dignity and grandeur seemed forgotten, and it looked like the happy union of a domestic circle, the Grand Dukes and the little Hereditary Prince followed, and the Emperor seemed quite overcome with emotion.   The young Empress now approached and knelt before the Emperor, who removed the crown from his own head and placed it upon hers for a few seconds, he then resumed it and put a smaller one on her head, which four Ladies of Honour advanced to fasten on — she was next invested with an Imperial Mantle—the Emperor then raised and embraced her, and she received the felicitations of the Empress-Mother and the Grand Dukes.   They both descended to the Altar and received the Sacrament, after which the Archbishop delivered an extemporary discourse, and prayers and psalms were sung.

The whole lasted about three hours and a half ; it had been curtailed on account of the Empress, otherwise it would have been much longer.   It was delightful to see the Emperor's solicitude about the Empress, he looked round to see how she was every five minutes, and insisted upon her sitting down almost the whole time.   She looked fatigued, but seemed to bear it very well altogether.   She wore nothing on her head but her pretty little crown, and her hair was arranged in a profusion of curls and long ringlets hanging to her shoulders.

It is impossible to describe the spectacle that presented itself on the exterior of the Cathedral, the

K

immense crowds of people that were assembled and arranged on raised benches to a great height. It was quite beautiful, even the sky seemed crowded with spectators, for some of the scaffolding was raised to the steeples. Only the two first classes were admitted into the Cathedral, the crowd on the exterior was chiefly composed of the nobility of the other classes.

I should much like to know what pretty things the Emperor said to the Grand Duke Constantine when he delivered him up his sword previous to receiving the Sacrament, he smiled so kindly.

Amongst the favours dispensed at the Coronation old Countess Lieven is made a Princess, and the title to descend to her children ; the Ambassador, her son, has the Order of St. André, the first of this country, but I do not know whether he becomes a Prince at once or waits for the death of his mother—Madame de Lieven would be greater than ever as a Princess. Prince Pierre Volkonsky is named *Ministre des Appanages and Ministre du Cabinet* with 50,000 *roubles per annum.* Princess Kourakine is made *Dame du Portrait,* and her spouse raised to the rank of Field Marshal. Princess Volkonsky received the Order and Star of St. Catherine in diamonds; Count La Ferronaye has the St. André ; Count Blome, St. Alexandre Newsky, General Schaëler ditto. Mademoiselle Salahoub is *Demoiselle d'Honneur.*

And now, my dear Sophy, having told you all I know, except that my dress yesterday was much admired, my silver gown, you know, and a silver embroidered train over lilac satin, English plumes on my head, I will e'en take leave."

From Mrs. Disbrowe.

MOSCOW, $\frac{1}{13}$ *September*, 1826.

"The ball at Court was a splendid assembly; it was held in the Banquet Hall, which looked very handsome, and well suited for the occasion. It was hung in crimson velvet, with the arms of the provinces emblazoned. We met at seven o'clock, in full court dress, habit Russe, which means the train and body separate from the gown. The Countess Zitta was the most splendid in diamonds. She wore two plain rows of great size round her neck, and her toque was covered, even the crown of it, with brilliants. The Empress Alexandrine polonaised with the great men in turn, the Emperor with the great women, your humble servant included, of course. He again spoke to me about our remaining and repeated, '*qu'il faut mettre tout sur son dos.*' There was no other dancing, and it was over in an hour, which was as much as the Empress could support. She was covered with diamonds, but did not look as pretty as usual, but always graceful. The Grand Duchess Hélène was in great good looks . . . . . . Sposo asked me who I danced with? Such a question! as if I should condescend to dance with anyone besides the Emperor and Prince Charles of Prussia!

There were many rich Russian merchants with long beards and their wives covered with diamonds last night. Amongst the company, the Khan of Tchergise and the Kahness, or '*Madame la Canne,*' as the French chose to call her, were in a box. She wore a rich caftan in some dark coloured stuff, a fur

cap pointed on the crown, and a large veil. She is
very young, fair, and as pretty as Calmuck features
can permit, little twinkling eyes set very far apart in
a flat broad face. It always appears to me as if those
faces were originally made without eyes, and then
slits cut for them to be sunk in. The Grand Duchess
Hélène asked her the other day how she liked her
husband having several wives. She said she did not
mind ; that he had only *one* besides herself whom he
liked very much, and that she was the one he liked
and esteemed most, but she believed he meant to take
a third. She speaks German, Russian, and I believe
some French. The wife of the Hetman of the
Kossacks was also there. She is very like an
ambulating feather bed, mounted on bed posts, wears
a dark cloth gown up to her chin, a coloured sash,
diamond buttons down the front of her dress, and a
blue silk handkerchief tied flat round her head. She
has followed her husband in all his campaigns, and it
seems to have agreed with her. She says she has
retained her national costume because the Emperor
Alexander approved of it.

I have just seen Count Matzusewich, who says
there were 5,300 at the *fête* last night. The theatre
looked extremely handsome. The centre lustre is
quite remarkable for its size ; it held 2,500 lights, in
circles that diminish towards the top. It was curious
to see the man lighting it ; he was suspended by a
rope from the ceiling, and hung in the centre of the
lustre ; it is not glass, but bronze. We assembled at
seven, supped at nine, and it was all over about half-
past eleven. Nothing but polonaises were danced.

The Ambassadors were at the Imperial table, the rest
of the diplomatic corps were at a separate table,
which was fixed round orange trees, and ornamented
with very handsome ancient gilt silver, embossed and
very curious.

Mama asks John in her letter of the 20th if people
exiled in Siberia are allowed to see their friends?
Not without a special permission from the Emperor.
Indeed, the immense distance almost renders it
impossible, except in similar instances with the
present, where the parties are rich ; but the present
example is without precedent, I believe, and neither
the crimes nor the punishments have been conducted
as formerly.   The great change of feeling and
civilization within the last fifty years in this country
prevents the example of former days being followed.
The condemned are dead in the eye of the law ; they
lose not only their property but their *names ;* but
these families are preserved from these sufferings by
the clemency of the Emperor, who has not punished
the children for their fathers' crimes.   He has also
given their wives and friends permission to follow
them.   The punishment even annuls their marriage,
and their wives may marry again if they chose to
take advantage of such divorce.   In this case, however, most of these unhappy women intend following
their wretched husbands, but any children born in
exile will be considered as *peasants ;* they do not
share the nobility or name of those born previously.
It is yet uncertain whether the poor people will be
allowed to see each other more than once a week ; only
fancy, the misery of such an existence.   Princess

Troubetsckoi must travel four thousand versts before
she can learn the ultimate destination of her husband,
and it is possible he may be sent to the frontiers of
China, seven or eight thousand versts further. She is
only twenty-five ; it is dreadful to think of such a fate !
The old Princess Volkonsky is determined to follow
her son, and give him her blessing. To my great
surprise her family do not discourage this idea, but
seem to think it feasible. I think, however, the
Imperial Family who are much attached to her, will
contrive to prevent it ; it seems to me impracticable,
and yet Princess Zeneide V. talks of it as nothing
extraordinary of having a tent pitched on the Steps
or Desert, a physician to attend her, that the climate
is better than at St. Petersburg, and that in the winter
the trainage will avoid the great fatigue of bad roads,
etc. The journey from St. Petersburg to Moscow
they consider as a mere step, not worthy of being
called a journey. Five hundred miles, is, however, no
joke in my eyes.

As there is no answer yet about our moving, I mean
to go to the ball at the theatre to-morrow, as a
Russian, a pretty little compliment we strangers pay
to the natives in adopting their costume : light blue
and gold for a serafin or gown, and *ponceau* embroidered in gold and pearls for a cap, not exactly
like my old blue one in shape, but very nearly. I am
still without a veil, and am now going to hunt
for one.

On the 20th, the Duc de Raguse gave his ball, and
a very handsome one it was too, upwards of 800
persons attended it. Madame de la Ferronaye

assisted the Marshal to do the honours and acquitted herself to admiration. Both the Emperor and Empress were dressed in white in compliment to France ; her gown was trimmed with marabouts, and diamonds studded down the front and over the whole of the body of her dress—she looked extremely well. A room had been built expressly for the supper. It was painted in flowers, and the lamps were all hung with wreaths ; a semi-circular table was placed at the top of the room for the Imperial Family, the Ambassadors, Madame de la Ferronaye, the *Dames d'Honneur* and *Dames du Portrait* (they wear the portrait of the Empress), the rest of the ladies were seated round small tables dispersed about the room ; it was very handsome and perfectly served. Each lady received a bouquet of natural flowers on arriving, but the hopes of a fan as well proved vain. Months ago we were told that the Marshal intended distributing some, also nosegays from Natier's, but it was a fib.

On the 22nd the Duke of Devonshire gave his *fête,* and here *I* did the honours, went to the door to receive the Imperial pair, handed the Emperor upstairs, polonaised with him, remained by the Empress the whole evening, supped with her, talked with them both, in short I was greater than great, and they were kindness itself to me, and I was very happy and only very little nervous. The Duke was in raptures, for the Empress danced a mazurka with him, and they both were delighted with the *fête.* The ball-room was the prettiest thing possible, the walls were white stucco or *faux marbre,* and it shines very much and is quite smooth. The only ornaments were pink roses without leaves, an immense circle of wax lights supported on a wreath of roses was suspended in the centre by very fine wires, so that it appeared to be held by magic. Our King's and the Imperial cyphers were traced in roses on the walls. The supper was laid out in the *Orangerie*, on two long tables, the Imperial table was placed across in a raised alcove at the end of the gallery, the hangings were in crimson and blue silk. Their Majesties were in red for England, and in great spirits. Papa's delight, the Grand Duchess Hélène, looked uncommonly pretty, and was so pleased that she danced more than she ever did in her life, and stayed until half-past three : she gave me such a sweet kiss when she went away.

15/27. Now for the Russian entertainment given by Prince Yowrousoff—it was quite an enchantment.

The company assembled in a pretty little theatre fitted up in blue and silver. A short opera was performed, which lasted one hour all but two minutes, for everything was timed. The Imperials then polonaised through the suite of rooms, and dancing commenced. In less than two hours supper was announced, and we were ushered into what had been the theatre, but now a floor was laid down, the roof was covered with a netting of silver cloth, two beautiful silver lustres suspended each holding 200 lights—tables laid in the first tier of boxes which faced the Imperial Family, who were seated at the extremity of the stage, and two parallel lines of tables extended to the boxes.   It was a fairy scene, and seemed to have been done by magic.   The floor was laid in twelve minutes, and five minutes allowed for hanging each lustre.   In one of the dancing-rooms the supper tables had been laid behind silk hangings, and no one suspected they were there.   The entrance to the house was like a garden, and the Russians are enchanted at the success of their countryman.   The Empress looked better than ever ; these amusements seem to do her good and make her forget all her anxiety and the dismal scenes of the last nine months.

Leave-taking has seriously commenced.   The Swedish Extraordinary Ambassador, Marshal Stedingk had his audience yesterday, and the others will probably kiss the Emperor's hands on Friday.   The Duke of Devonshire is quite sorry to go away.   I hope he has really liked his embassy to this country, nothing could have been done in better style than he has performed his part, and he has made a most favourable impression upon the society at large.

I believe I have given you all the gossip of the place, excepting that Prince Boris Yourousoff* is to marry Madlle. Narischkin, who has such a slender waist.   Marie Narischkin or the four thousand peasant girl, or the daughter of '*votre devouée à iamais servante*,' Anne de Narischkin, takes M. Bulgarine for a husband; the widow, Princess Zoubofft

* Youssoupoff (?).

† Princess Zouboff as Comtesse Schouvaloff was mother of the Ambassador, Prince Schouvaloff.

with 8,000 peasants, means to espouse Count Schouvaloff; she was Lord Clanwilliam's flame last year at Carlsbad; she is very young, notwithstanding her former husband was prime favourite and Minister of Catherine II."

Thursday, $\frac{16}{28}$.

"Just returned from the *fête populaire*, some say there were 140,000 people assembled, the Emperor says 200,000. The guests had full liberty to carry away whatever they could lay hold of. The table cloths were torn to pieces, the tables broken up, the provisions appropriated, the wine was swallowed in a twinkling, and no sooner were the contents disposed of than they began to demolish the very buildings. Prince Menschikoff* has been liberated."

The next letters by my mother are written from St. Petersburg. Reference is made to the departure of the Duke of Devonshire, the dignified and altogether delightful way in which he "fulfilled his trust," and how he gained the good-will of the people of the country of his sojourn, and showed himself generous to many distressed Russians. Madame de la Ferronaye and her daughter Pauline, are also mentioned as leaving. The latter is described as "looking beautiful, and a dear, little, spoilt, saucy, wayward, clever body that everybody indulges, and cannot help it." This delightful creature was known

---

* He had been seized by the Persians.

in later life as Mrs. Augustus Craven, author of " Le Récit d'une Soeur," " Fleurange," etc.

The next event of importance looked forward to with interest was the arrival of Lord Hertford with the Garter.

CHAPTER IX.

LORD HERTFORD AND THE GARTER.

From Mrs. Disbrowe.

St. Petersburg, $\frac{3}{15}$ *June,* 1827.

"I AM quite in despair about our return, no one seems thought of as ambassador here but Sir William A'Court, and in common reason it is easy to suppose that some time must elapse before this nomination could take place, and every delay is misery to us.

Our party on board the steamboat was a magnificent *fête,* and did the Ambassador and his factotum infinite credit. Indeed it was quite wonderful how everything was arranged, and a certain Duke would have been perhaps a little piqued to see how completely he was surpassed in his own water-party. I mean in respect to arrangement and order, for I think *his,* altogether, was the merriest affair of the two. We were upwards of eighty persons; the vessel ornamented with shrubs and flowers, the band of the *Chevalier Garde,* three or four bonnetted cooks, and plenty of attendants on board. Madame de Nesselrode, to her cost, was on board before eight o'clock, and so

was dear, little Madame de Guerrieros, who on
general occasions is always too late. The Ambassador
delayed his arrival purposely, for he said, 'Had I
told Pontcarré to be off at a certain time, nothing
would have prevented its being put into execution
and half of the company might have been left behind.'
The little man is punctuality itself. An *avant
déjeuner* of coffee and tea was first offered to us, and
in less than half an hour afterwards we were all
regularly seated at table to partake of a more solid
repast. This, with the help of ices and oranges,
sustained us until we reached the fleet, which was
drawn up in a line just below Kronstadt. The ships
appeared in great order, and we were quite satisfied
with their outsides ; but no means were offered us of
examining the interior. Instead of coming at twelve
as they promised, the Imperial Family never appeared until past four ; so to prevent time hanging
heavy, dancing and gaming were resorted to, the
young in the gambling line, and these were chiefly
ladies, took to '*la Mouche*,' the more experienced
gamblers had recourse to quinze and cress ; I joined
in neither. . . . .

A steamer towed the beautiful little Imperial yacht
in sight, and as soon as the standard was hoisted, the
firing was begun, and such an uproar as it was, the
thirteen ships besides every battery and fort and
gun-boat in the neighbourhood saluted with their
whole force and almost at the same moment. It
really was a very fine sight, so many ships of war on
one side, Kronstadt and its crowds on the other, and
several steamers moving about. The lovely Empress,

as usual, was distinguished from afar, and seemed to take great pleasure in the magnificent sight. We played 'God save the King' whenever we approached her yacht, and she saluted us repeatedly.

Some of the party landed at Oranienboom* and saw the old-fashioned palace and terrace; but at ten we were all on board, partaking of a substantial dinner, served in a manner that would have done credit to the Hôtel de l' Ambassade on shore. Dining at ten o'clock in the open air without the aid of candles or lamps is a circumstance worth noticing, and in no other latitude of the civilized world could nineteen hours of daylight and amusement be enjoyed. We reached our respective homes at three o'clock, the sun already risen, and the working world on foot. Only two or three ladies were sick, and excepting a few mistakes of seizing hold of a head or body, imagining it was the much wanted cloak of some shivering *beau*, we had no adventures. One poor lady who had monopolized several of these comforts, upon perceiving an attack about to be made, called out, ' *Ce n'est pas tout manteau, Monsieur*,' much to the poor man's astonishment, who had no idea anything living was near."

From Mrs. Disbrowe.

ST. PETERSBURG, 10 *July*, 1827.

" It must be your turn, darling dad, to have a letter from me, and I have a great deal of small talk to communicate, mostly about myself, so of course it

---

* Oranienbaum (?).

cannot fail of being extremely interesting to you ; besides I am quite certain that you will take a wee bit pride in hearing how very highly *I* have been distinguished by the Imperial Family, quite enough to turn a less thick head than my own ; perhaps, in truth, honours conferred on me were intended as a compliment to Lord Hertford and his embassy, and something perhaps to my better half; but as neither of them seems particularly elated, I may as well take the whole to myself.

Know then that, contrary to all established etiquette, the charming Empress-Mother invited me to dine at Paulofsky, with the Marquis and suite, Mr. Disbrowe and John. At first, when I expressed a wish to go to Tzarskoselo to see the ceremony of the Investiture of the Garter, I was told it was out of the question, and Sposo said it would not do for me to go as *badeau* when he was invited officially. Judge then my surprise at one o'clock on Saturday to receive an express invite from His Imperial Majesty. Such a scouring of mantua-makers and milliners, a *fête* day besides, so there were very few shops open. However, my amiable Madame Turin did wonders for me, and half-past seven on Sunday morning four new gowns were brought home, for as usual there was great uncertainty about trains or no trains, but both must be ready. The embassy was present at Czarkoselo in great state, but neither the Emperor nor Empress dined at Paulofsky. The latter is not allowed to encounter the least fatigue, and the former did not *choose* to come, so that there were only three of the Imperial family at dinner, the Empress-Mother, and

Grand Duke and Duchess Hélène. One hundred and twenty sat down, and there was a beautiful display of *demoiselles d'honneur*. The dinner was very plainly served and the table ornamented with a quantity of cornflowers, which looked extremely pretty.

Lord Hertford sat opposite the Empress, and Garter King-at-Arms next to him, nodding and grinning at a great rate, not comprehending a syllable of what was said; not even when the Grand Duchess spoke in English. We were dismissed early after dinner with an invite to meet Her Majesty at the *Pavilion des Roses*, and spend the evening with her, which we did. I played at her table at *Mouche*, and she gave lessons to Lord Hertford in the game with the greatest good humour and affability. The young people played *aux petits jeux* and amused themselves famously. They were very romping games, and the Empress was highly diverted with the peals of laughter that could not be repressed now and then. Little Francis Seymour and young Midshipman Murray amused her particularly. Our young men say they never saw ladies romp with such propriety. The Empress did not sit down to supper, but walked about talking to her guests and doing the honours like a private person. We returned about half-past eleven, all delighted with our day's amusement; but I fear poor Lord Hertford suffered from fatigue and gout very much.

Next day, as soon as I was up, I received the reigning Empress's command to go to see her privately. She received me on a balcony, and gave me strawberries and cream, and was kind and amiable as possible. The dear little Grand Duchess Alexandrine,* at whose christening you attended, came in and was very gracious to me, and made me cry. She was just what Albinia was when I left her. At one o'clock the Investiture of the Garter took place, so privately that the public saw nothing but the actors in it get out of the gilt carriages and walk across the colonnade. Even the Empresses were not admitted ; but a curtain was placed before a doorway, and they and the children peeped through. The Empress told me that to her dismay she found that towards the end of the ceremony the little Olga had contrived to thrust her head through a hole in the curtain. Mr. Disbrowe saw the pretty face come through, and was so enchanted and amused that he nearly forgot to bow in the right part of the ceremony. Lord Hertford was splendidly dressed, indeed all the costumes were much admired. The Marquis and Sir G. Naylor, Garter King-at-Arms, headed the procession ; next Lord Marcus Hill with the George on a cushion, Lord Seymour with the sword, Captain Meynell the hat for the Emperor, Captain Seymour the mantle, Windsor Herald and attendants with the seals and admonition, and then the two pages, Francis Seymour and young Murray, with Lord Hertford's hat and King Garter's crown. The day was lovely, and the crowd round the palace gaily dressed so that it was altogether a very pretty sight.

The Embassy and the Mission dined with the

* Afterwards Queen of Würtemberg.

L

Ministre de la Maison, Prince Pierre Volkonsky. I
was with the Modènes, and just as we were thinking
of getting into the carriage to return to St. Petersburg, the Empress sent to beg me to come to tea
with her at the *Sauvagerie*, which of course I did,
nothing loath, and she stuffed me with bread and
' *buther* ' as she called it, showed me the place, and
then sent me home charmed and as proud as needs
be.   After that we met the Marquis, and *ligned* it
round the grounds, then went and played and danced
at Countess Modène's, and finished at a soirée at
Princess Troubetskoï's, after which we returned to
St. Petersburg, and now I am making all haste
to write a great deal by the messenger to-morrow."

From Mrs. Disbrowe.

St. Petersburg, $\frac{6}{18}$ *July*, 1827.

"Only think, I have been invited to another
Imperial dinner, and on Sunday last I had the
honour of feasting with the Emperor at Czarskoselo.
His Majesty and the Empress-Mother were at table,
but the lovely Empress could not bear so much
fatigue and therefore only appeared after, looking
more beautiful and interesting than ever.   All the
Imperial children came in, and even the little one
made a pretty curtsey and seemed to understand all
about doing the honours, and observing that the
young *demoiselles d' honneur* stood with their hands
crossed, she did the same, and looked very saucy the
whole time.

Young Francis Seymour received a present of a

diamond ring from the Emperor. Now he is going
for a year to Weimar to learn German, and then he
becomes a Guardsman. Lord Hertford has left
10,000 roubles for one of the Empress Mother's
benevolent establishments. Is not that handsome?

$\frac{12}{24}$ *September*, 1827.

"We are all rejoicing here at the happy event
which took place last Friday, and you cannot think
how pleased everyone is at the arrival of the young
Prince—the Imperial Mother too is so well that there
is nothing to alloy the joy of the Emperor. The
Empress had spent the day at Ylegen, had an evening
party until eleven o'clock, went to bed at twelve, and
before three Constantine-Nicholaivitch was in the
world, and at six the event was announced to the
public by 301 cannon, which I in vain tried to
count, sleep having overtaken me half through the
task.

Whether we are sent to Munich, Stuttgart, or Rio
Janeiro, is still to be conjectured, for those three
posts are still unoccupied. It is more than probable
that Lord Erskine will accept the move to Munich
that is offered to him, and then I suppose Würtemberg is our destiny. Of only one thing am I certain
and that is the idea of leaving dear John is most
painful.

My next grievance in leaving this place is the idea
of parting from whom do you think?—The Emperor
and Empress! See how high I soar, but really they
have been so kind to me I have quite an affection for

them and cannot bear the idea of never perhaps
seeing them again. I have seen so many affecting
traits of them, and have witnessed, to them, so many
important events, that I must ever feel a warm
interest about them, and I always think of them as
individuals, not Sovereigns. I always think of the
Emperor as the best of husbands, and the Empress
as the most amiable and excellent of women, and so
lovely too : if you had but seen her at the Masquerade
the other evening! She never looked so beautiful
before, she seemed so happy and gay too."

Once more my mother referred in these letters to
her attachment to the Russian Imperial Family,
saying : "On Sunday they received our *adieux* so
kindly, so very kindly, that I forgot all *etiquette* and
felt just as if I were parting with dear relations, and
in short behaved very ill. . . . You cannot think
how kind everybody is to us." And now the definite
news of the appointment to Stuttgart had come, and
the joyful hour of being homeward bound to Walton,
"the pets," and many dear ones. My father also
wrote : " The Emperor and the Grand Duke Michael,
as well as the Prince of Prussia, did us the honour of
calling here after we had taken leave, as I was consequently no longer Minister, an honour which is the
greater from its extremely rare occurrence." This
brought the sojourn at St. Petersburg to a close. The
return journey was by Riga, Memel, Königsberg,
Berlin, and Frankfort, begun on February the 23rd,
1828, and Walton was reached apparently on the
20th of April. At Berlin, my parents dined at the

Duke of Cumberland's, to meet the King and Royal Family of Hanover, and the Grand Duke and Duchess of Weimar.   On this occasion the King was mentioned as " most gracious," and Prince Charles as very amiable and an old friend.   My mother said : " Little Prince George of Cumberland is an uncommonly fine boy, very clever and lively, and has exactly the manner that a child of his age should have."

Then followed the delightful announcement of the prospect of seeing children, parents, and sisters once more in less than three weeks, which anticipation was duly fulfilled.

PART II.

CHAPTER I.

FROM WALTON TO WÜRTEMBERG.

ON leaving Russia my father was offered and accepted the post of Envoy Extraordinary and Minister Plenipotentiary to the Court of Würtemberg. The post was called a "*Mission de Famille*," because the Queen Dowager was the eldest daughter of King George III. and Princess Royal of England. But she died on October 6th, 1828, the day after our arrival at Stuttgart. My father thus lost the advantage of being head of a family mission, and I believe also part of his salary.

Soon after their return from Russia my parents had come to Walton, and we all started together from thence for London, travelling in our own carriages with post horses. The journey occupied two days. Old-fashioned carriages accommodated a remarkable quantity of luggage. Our big green coach had two large imperials on the roof, two other trunks under the driving box and rumble, and a bonnet-box which hung behind the carriage, and must have rested on the knees of whoever was seated in the rumble or "dickey," as the seat behind was called. Behind that seat yet another trunk was suspended.

And this was not all. Beneath the floor, between the hind and front wheels, were so-called wells, whilst inside the carriage there were chaise seats, and under the seats, both back and front, were sword-cases. Room was found somehow also for sundry carpet bags. We had four horses to the coach, and, when abroad, three to the chariot, in which my father travelled. London was our first halting-place after leaving Walton. We put up at Marshall Thompson's Hotel, in Cavendish Square, in order to be within reach of the Regent's Park, to which locality the oldest charitable Foundation in England, St. Katharine's, had recently been removed from the spot now occupied by St. Katharine's Docks. My father's sister was married to the Grand Master, Sir Herbert Taylor. My grandfather, Colonel Disbrowe, had been the previous Master. His letter to my father (then at Copenhagen) announcing his appointment is dated April 27th, 1817. He says : "The Queen has been so good as to make me Master and Governor of the Free Chapel of St. Catherine, near the Tower. The emolument will be £500 or £600 a year. I am away with your sisters to take possession of my new appointment and write from Ludgate Hill."

Sir Herbert Taylor* was appointed on my grandfather's death in 1818. It was under Sir Herbert's auspices that, in 1825, the whole establishment was moved from the banks of the Thames to Regent's Park. The original Foundation of the Charity dated

* Sir Herbert Taylor was the confidential friend of King William IV.

from 1148, Queen Matilda being the Foundress.
There seems to have been a second Foundation by
Queen Eleanor in 1273, called "The Royal Hospital
and Collegiate Church of St. Katharine near the
Tower." Since those days there have been great
discussions as to whether Sir Herbert was wise or
had any right to move the charity from its ancient
locality. But the price paid by the Dock Company
made the move a profitable speculation, and enabled
him to erect all the present buildings. I may almost
say that the church was moved piecemeal. Pulpit,
windows, monuments, all travelled from near the
Tower to the Regent's Park. The building consisted of the church, the school, three sisters' and
three brothers' houses, and the house of the Master,
called St. Katharine's Lodge. This latter stood in
a large garden, in which I have spent many happy
hours of my childhood. All the brothers were
clergymen holding livings in the gift of the Foundation. It was obligatory for them to be in residence
and do duty at St. Katharine's for four consecutive
months in the year. The sisters were and are ladies
of limited incomes. In my time they were all
spinsters, but I believe widows have been given the
same advantages. There are also schools in connection with the Foundation, which includes, in
addition, bedesmen and bedeswomen, mostly old
servants in receipt of £10 a year. The sisters had
each a small house, £200 a year and sundry fines,
which later on were commuted, and the incomes
were raised to £250 per annum. The patronage
always belonged to the Queen Consort, whom failing,

the Queen Dowager or Queen Regnant; our beloved Queen Victoria taking it up on the death of Queen Adelaide. George IV. must have had the matter in his own hands from 1818 to 1830. Later on a certain number of outdoor sisters were named, each receiving £100 a year. Great was my joy when the first of these was my friend, the Honble. Jane Touchet, daughter of ths twenty-second Lord Audley, and goddaughter of the Duke of Kent. Her brother had done homage at the Queen's Coronation for the barons of England in lieu of the Lord de Ros of the day, the real premier baron, who was unable to be present. Miss Touchet thoroughly deserved and needed the help. A braver woman under the most overwhelming troubles I have never known. But I must leave the subject of St. Katharine's and return to the year 1828.

We had a very rough crossing from Dover to Calais, and remained on deck in our own close carriage, a most miserable proceeding I should think. It was, however, the custom in those days, and has since been forbidden, because somebody's carriage was washed overboard, whilst the inmates were drowned. Lord and Lady Stuart de Rothsay crossed with us, he being on his way to Paris as Ambassador to the Court of Charles X. We all remained at the famous Hôtel Dessein at Calais for the night, and we children were taken to see the Stuart de Rothsays and their daughters, who were so well known in after years for their great beauty and talents as Lady Canning and Lady Waterford. My recollection is of two girls both taller and older

than myself, dressed in red, and with close-cropped
hair. In those days this close-cropping was considered to be for the well-being both of children
and their hair. I never saw much of Lady Canning
in after years ; she married in 1835, before I was
grown up, but she used to call on my mother,
and came to say good-bye to her before going to
India. I had considerable correspondence in later
life with Lady Waterford, principally on the subject
of Miss Touchet, whose sad story she brought before
Queen Victoria, with the result of my friend's
appointment as a sister of St. Katharine. I also
spent some pleasant days at High Cliff with Lady
Waterford in 1878. She was still a very beautiful
woman, and had magnificent hair. She was always
occupied with some charitable object, to which she
devoted her artistic talents, and was, to the last,
always seen with a paint-brush in her hand. At
the time of my visit she was very full of the second
marriage of her first cousin, General Charles Stuart,
with Miss Louisa Murdoch. Sir Charles was also
my father's first cousin. My father's grandmother
and Lord Stuart de Rothsay's mother were sisters,
daughters of Lord Vere Bertie, one of the sons of
the Duke of Ancaster. A great friendship existed
between Lord Stuart and my father, whose diplomatic
career began under him at Lisbon in 1810. Lord
Stuart came to see us at the Hague on the way
to his last diplomatic post as Ambassador at St.
Petersburg in June, 1841. He was anxious to buy
a Chinese dressing-gown. The only one the Chinese
shop contained which was of sufficient length was

made of white silk, covered with pink roses. Lord Stuart was delighted with it, and as a joke put it on to start on his journey. He was a very big man, and we all thought he looked like a white bear when we saw him in his flowing robe, and were greatly amused. Alas! once *en route*, he found that he had forgotten his cloak, and had to travel all the way to St. Petersburg in the white dressing-gown!

My recollections of Paris are not distinct beyond that I was struck by the sight of yellow satin curtains and large mirrors, all of which were novelties to me; also that we were taken to St. Cloud, the Jardin des Plantes, and to the Tuileries garden, where our nurse was much impressed by the cleverness of the Paris children, who even when quite small *spoke French*, whilst her charges had only just begun to learn it. What most impressed me beyond that was seeing Charles X., the Duchesse D'Angoulême, and the Duc de Bordeaux together in a carriage. The latter aspired to be Henri Cinq, but was known in later years as the Comte de Chambord. In my early days I always liked to see great people connected with the history of olden times. Which way we posted to our destination I do not remember, excepting that we went through Mannheim, waiting in the carriage whilst my father went round to every gate of the town to learn if his sisters had passed by, for they were travelling from England by the Rhine. I cannot make out our route, although I have a vague idea that it was viâ Nancy, and that we passed through and some-

times slept in fortified towns, at which there was a
hurry-scurry to get in before the gates were closed.
I can recall my father urging the postilions at the
top of his voice to use their utmost speed, lest we
should get shut out, and have to spend the night
in the carriage. Of course I could not speak French
sufficiently to show my nurse that I was as learned
as the children in Paris, but I knew enough to be
surprised at hearing the post-boy say, "*Chameau
comme toi de te laisser tomber,*" when one of the
horses fell down. We were always preceded on that
journey by a courier on horseback in a sort of livery
or uniform, covered with small bells.

On arriving at Stuttgart, we went in the first
instance to the Hôtel du Roi d'Angleterre, a queer
old building with the upper floors overhanging the
lower ones. I believe many such houses still exist
in Germany. We looked out upon the Old Palace,
a gloomy-looking building with four square towers,
one of which contained an inclined plane, made
for a former Duke of Würtemberg, who liked to
ride up to his rooms on the upper stories.

The New Palace was built by the first King,
and I believe it was he who disliked the smell of
cooking so much that he instituted having dinner
prepared in the old Palace. One of our childish
amusements was to go and see the royal dinner
carried from one palace to the other at 3 p.m.
It was conveyed in boxes, warmed by hot water
vessels, and looking much like coffins on stretchers.

The first King of Würtemberg was one of
Bonaparte's creations. He was said to have been

the biggest king of the smallest kingdom in Europe. He was greatly pleased with his new honour, and placed crowns at every point where they could be seen. The one on the top of the Palace at Stuttgart was said to be large enough to seat eight people, and was highly gilt. The palace at Ludwigsburg was larger than those in the capital, and perhaps it contained a kitchen. It was there that Queen Charlotte Mathilda, second wife of the first king, lived and died. In our day it was used much as Hampton Court is used in England, and inhabited by the old ladies of the court. One of these was Countess Seckendorf, of whose daughter the tale was told that she had been three times divorced from and remarried to the same man. Both the above-mentioned king's wives were of English descent. The first was a niece of George III., being the daughter of his sister, Princess Augusta, and of the Duke of Brunswick-Wolfenbtütel, who fell at Jena. By her the King of Würtemberg had two sons, the future king and Prince Paul. The latter was father both of the handsome Princess Helena,* wife of Grand Duke Michael of Russia, and of Pauline, Duchess of Nassau, grandmother of the present Duchess of Albany, and daughter of Princess Catharine, wife of Prince Jerome Bonaparte, Napoleon's youngest brother. Jerome had been created king of Westphalia in 1806, but the kingdom came to an end after the battle of Leipsic, 1813. King Jerome had two sons and a daughter. The

* *See* Russian letters.

sons were another Jerome, who died young at the military academy at Ludwigsburg, and Napoleon, who always traded on his likeness to his uncle, and was known as "Plonplon." King Jerome's daughter, Mathilde, was well known in later years as the beautiful Princess Demidoff.

I wish someone could corroborate a story which always clings to my memory. I believe I have both read and been told it. My recollection is that when Napoleon I. raised the Duchy of Würtemberg to the dignity of a kingdom, he became anxious that the Crown Prince (the king of our time) should make a royal marriage, but there was a serious obstacle in the way. The Prince had a wife, *née* Mademoiselle Abeelen, but Bonaparte, nothing daunted, got rid of her. Whether she was carried off to Siberia, or what became of her, no one ever knew. It is a matter of history that Napoleon forced the Crown Prince into a marriage with Princess Caroline of Bavaria. She hated the idea as much as the Crown Prince hated it, so they agreed to separate after the ceremony at the church door. They never met again until after Waterloo, and then only to arrange the terms of their divorce. The Prince is said to have then become aware of the treasure he had lost. His next wife was a Russian Princess, sister of the Emperors Alexander and Nicholas, and widow of the Duke of Oldenburg. She was a clever and intriguing woman, and accompanied the Allied Sovereigns to London in 1814. It was she who was credited with having in great measure caused the breaking off of the Princess Charlotte of Wales' engagement with the Prince of Orange. She did not live many years after her marriage with the King of Würtemberg, and left two daughters, of whom the younger, Princess Sophie, married the Hereditary Prince of Orange, afterwards William III. of the Netherlands. But I am anticipating.

In those Stuttgart days the princesses were young, and being educated by two Demoiselles de la Harpe, nieces of the famous La Harpe, who had such great influence over Alexander I. of Russia in his early days. King William's last wife, Queen Pauline, was his cousin, daughter of Duke Louis of Würtemberg, and Duchess Henrietta, who was still alive at the time of which I write. Queen Pauline had three children. Her son Charles became the third King of Würtemberg, and his sister, Princess Catharine, married his cousin and eventful successor, Prince Frederic. The Queen's other daughter, Princess Augusta, married Prince Hermann of Saxe-Weimar, whom we met in after years at his brother's, Prince Edward's. We were often asked to the palace to play with the princesses and their beautiful toys, especially with a doll's house, large enough to admit us all. This latter made a great impression on me.

CHAPTER II.

MORE ABOUT STUTTGART.

On first going to Stuttgart my father was extremely
occupied with the affairs of the Queen Dowager of
Würtemberg. I do not know whether he was her
executor, but he had charge of all the remembrances
she had left to her brothers and sister in England, as
well as those sent to the Landgravine of Hesse-
Homburg, Princess Elizabeth of England, whose
letters acknowledging them, make great complaint
of not having been warned of her sister's increased
illness. She said she would willingly have gone to
Stuttgart, and had begged the ladies of her sister's
court to write to her, and give her all details. Her
letters breathe a true sisterly affection and great
sorrow for her loss, she always adds that the blow fell
specially heavily on Princess Augusta, as being
nearest in age to the Queen of Würtemberg.
Besides those letters on the subject to my father, I
have others from the Dukes of Cumberland and
Cambridge, thanking him for sending the various
articles, and a letter written by Sir John Conroy, in
the Duchess of Kent's name, on the same subject.

My father's two sisters joined us not long after our arrival at Stuttgart, and we all moved to an apartment in the Kronen Strasse, in the house of General Brenning. Among our visitors was Miss Cornelia Knight, who had been governess to Princess Charlotte of Wales. She was old and blind, or nearly so, and when she was announced, everything had to be moved out of her way, lest she should fall over it. I think she must have been either a guest of Queen Mathilde or attached to her Court. Another visitor was a Mr. Joseph Banks (who was celebrated in some way), and a Chanoinesse (or Comtesse) Talbot, who used to astonish the world of that day much more than she would surprise the present. I think she was a Talbot de Malahide, but I have failed to find her in the Peerage. She was masculine in her attire, and generally wore her riding-habit and a fur cap, but on state occasions, donned a very showy plaid toque or turban. My father was asked by his friend to escort her in that guise to the theatre. Of course he did so, but my mother would not be of the party. The countess or Chanoinesse (for she was called sometimes by one title, sometimes by the other, both having been granted to her by the King of Bavaria) travelled all over the Continent *en voiturier*, which means that the carriage was changed as well as the horses at every post. She had no escort of her own, but joined any chance traveller going the same way. She was fond of telling how once when her passport was being examined, the official put his head into the carriage and asked : "*Lequel de vous quatre Messieurs est la dame Anglaise de distinction ?*" She had

M

travelled in equally independent fashion in an open boat round the Greek Archipelago.

In the spring of 1829 we moved into a new house on the Friederich's Platz, from the windows of which we could see three pointed hills. On the top of the central hill stood a Greek chapel, dedicated to the memory of Queen Catherine, the King's Russian wife.

Two of Stuttgart's most celebrated men were still alive in our day. I would first mention John Henry Dannecker, born at Stuttgart in 1758, whose statue of Ariadne at Frankfort was sufficient to place him in the forefront of modern sculptors. His female figures have rarely been surpassed, nor his busts of Schiller, Lavater, and Gluck, as well as of many members of the Royal family at Würtemberg. He had studied both in Paris and Rome, but the greater part of his life was spent at Stuttgart, where he died in 1841. I was once taken to see him, and recollect him as an old man in a dressing-gown and skull-cap, but his mind was already failing. He is said to have cut off all the long locks from one of his busts.

The other great man was Baron Cotta, an eminent bookseller and proprietor of a political daily journal, the "*Allgemeine Zeitung*," as well as of several other papers, devoted to literature and the fine arts. I was often at his door with my father, who was in constant correspondence with him.

The poet Schiller was also a native of Würtemberg, though not of Stuttgart. He was born in 1759 at Marbach, a town within reach of Ludwigsburg, where we spent our summers.   I remember quite well being shown the house.   It was situated on a Platz, most likely where the market was held, and had over-hanging stories.   Schiller* died in 1806.

And now from celebrities I will return to our commonplace selves.   Our five summers in Würtem-berg were all spent at Ludwigsburg.   Our house, the Mathildenhof, belonged to the Queen Dowager.   It was situated close to the palace gardens, and had a large garden at the back, which was a great pleasure to us children after Stuttgart, where we had only public gardens and streets to walk in.   I believe it was in the Mathildenhof, that the Queen did most of her painting, and at the end of the garden, there was an oven for baking china.   One of my cousins has a whole tea and coffee set painted on china by her.†   A curious sale of her effects took place whilst we were at Ludwigsburg.   My father bought a complete suit of cloth of gold, now in the possession of my sister.   The Queen was said to have always kept a widow's cap in her pocket from the time the King died, and when anyone called she exchanged it for whatever she had on her head at the time.   With her *trousseau* she had received two sets of children's clothes, supposed to last for the three first years—one for a boy, one for a girl.   They were never needed, and were sold at her death.

* A statue to Schiller was erected on the Schiller Platz at Stuttgart, in 1839.   It was by Thorwaldsen and all Germany subscribed to it.—M.M.C.

† An account and photograph of this china, illustrating the Triumph of Love, appeared in the *Connoisseur*, November, 1901.—M.M.C.

Stuttgart was not considered healthy in summer as it lay in a sort of basin surrounded by vine-clad hills with the river Nesenbach flowing through it, and sanitary precautions were not then in vogue. Ludwigsburg, situated about nine or ten miles from the capital, was on much higher ground, and, I conclude, on different soil. In the stones used for mending the roads we used to find many sea-shells firmly embedded, which were no doubt relics of a pre-historic period.

There were several small *châteaux* belonging to the King, and we made excursions to many of them. *La Solitude* was, I think, the furthest off. It stood on a high hill, from which the Vosges Mountains could be seen. Then there was *La Favorite* within a walk ; we had leave to walk in the parks and woods. The old woman who had the care of this *château* was a great friend of ours, and invariably treated us to large slices of plum-tart. One day, when we were making our way to this favourite haunt, we saw our friend, the caretaker, standing on the high steps outside the house and making all sorts of signs to us not to advance. Our governess, who was much affronted at being waved off, persisted in walking on with us, but in a very few minutes we saw the reason of the warning. A mad bull came rushing down the road towards us, dragging four men with him, who were endeavouring to hold on to his horns, tail, and hind legs. We had only just time to hide ourselves in some brushwood when he passed. When we were safe, I hope our governess repented of her ire.

An excursion to a fortress called the Hohen-

Asperg made a great impression on me, for at the foot of the hill was a village being entirely destroyed by fire. It had been burning many hours when we came in sight of it. We could see all that was going on. There were some poor women approaching as closely as they dared, hoping to rescue some of their property.

I cannot exactly remember at what time of year we moved to and from Ludwigsburg. We cannot have gone there in the spring, because we were invited annually to a summer-house in a garden not far from Stuttgart, to a children's party given by Countess Beroldingen, for the young princesses. It was to eat new potatoes, *des pommes de terre à l'anglaise*, a great treat to the Royalties, and we were given butter to eat with them.

We were generally back at Stuttgart at the time of the vintage. Our doctor always asked us into his vineyard to play with his children and eat grapes. We were then taken to see the very primitive wine presses; men and women jumped with all their might on the grapes placed in large tubs. I must not forget to record our own never-to-be-forgotten picnic in a vineyard near Ober Türckheim on the Neckar. My father, following the custom of the country, hired a vineyard for the day, and invited a large party to meet there. The bargain was that all were to eat as many grapes as they liked, but no fruit was to be carried away. Everything seemed prosperous, and we all, great and small, started in high spirits, little thinking what was to happen. Food and fireworks were taken with us. Unfortunately, a lady let off a rocket and then took fright and dropped it whilst still burning on to the stack of fireworks. These instantly exploded, and set fire to the whole vineyard. There was nothing for it but for everyone to fly from the flames. How well I remember Comtesse Beroldingen seizing my youngest sister (now Mrs. Wise), then called "Baby," in her arms and rushing up the hill as hard as she could run. Our governess took us two elder children, one by each hand, and fled up the hill, and I do not believe anyone took breath until we were safe behind a stone wall. Soon my parents arrived breathless, but most thankful to find their three little girls safe. It really was an awful scene, the flames seeming to chase us, and the explosions sounding very alarming. We all returned home very disconcerted, but I trust with truly thankful hearts, for we had escaped a great danger.

I now come to the memorable year 1830. King George IV. died on the 26th June, and on hearing the news my father's two sisters thought it advisable to return to England to make sure of their apartment in Kensington Palace, which the King had granted to them on his accession, in exchange for a house given by George III. to their father, the Vice-Chamberlain, for life and to his unmarried daughters.

I do not suppose many people now give much thought to the events of 1830, so much has happened since ; but it was a memorable year. "*Les trois glorieuses journées*,"* as they were called—the 28th,

* A letter written in French to Sir Edward Disbrowe by a colleague from Baden-Baden on August 3rd, 1830, mentions

29th, and 30th of July, drove the last King of France
into exile, and he and all the Royal family fled to
England. On the 7th of August Louis Philippe
ascended the throne as King of the French. On
August 25th an insurrection broke out in Brussels,
and in September the separation from Holland was
resolved on. In February 1831, Prince Leopold of
Saxe-Coburg was chosen King of the Belgians, and
in November the Great Powers concluded a treaty
with Belgium, defining the limits of the new
kingdom. It was many a day before all matters were
settled, and as Belgium was not at once recognised
by all as a separate kingdom, my father, when at the
Hague, had to sign all passports for the new kingdom,
for the use of British subjects, and these were sent in

the serious riots on July 27th, owing to journals representing
the Liberal Press having been seized in various quarters of
Paris. The letter goes on to speak of the voluntary
mobilizing of the National Guard, of fighting all day on the
28th, of the Swiss being almost all massacred, of two line
regiments refusing to fire and the seizure by the Liberal Party
of the Invalides, Arsenal and post-office. The telegraph wires
had been cut in all directions, a provisional government had
been instituted, composed of eight members of the Chamber
of Deputies, including Casimir Perrier, Laffitte, Schoenau,
and Lobeau. Lafayette was commanding the National
Guard. The "tricolor" was hoisted on the Louvre, and the
revolution accomplished. The paving-stones of the Rue
Richelieu had been torn up to be hurled at the Royalist
troops, and the *fleur-de-lis* had disappeared from all buildings.
The King, " so brave in words, so prudent in deeds," was said
to be " at Lille, and the Dauphin with 10,000 men at St. Cloud
doing nothing;" 12,000 Zouaves had lost their lives. '93 was
reported not to have been more terrible.—M.M.C.

batches to the English Legation at Brussels. This
went on, I suppose, until 1839, when the treaty was
concluded between Holland and Belgium, and it was
certainly only then that all the property left behind
by the Prince and Princess of Orange, in the beautiful
palace at Brussels, was restored to them and sent to
the Hague.

In these troublous years the Greeks were also in a
state of insurrection, seeking to free themselves from
the Turkish Dominion, and Prince Leopold having
declined the throne of Greece, the establishment of
Prince Otto of Bavaria as King was settled and
signed in London on May 30th, 1832.

King Otto was a minor when he was chosen, and
Count Armensberg went out with him as Regent and
Governor. I remember that most particularly,
because a Miss Murray, whom we knew, and who
had been English governess to the elder Princesses
of Würtemberg, went as lady-attendant to Comtesse
Armensberg. All seemed settled and we had
bidden her good-bye, when, one evening about ten
days later, my father came into our schoolroom and
turned us children out, saying he must see our
governess alone. This greatly excited our curiosity,
especially as on the staircase we saw Miss Murray
closely veiled. She was handed over to our
governess's care for several days until plans could
be settled, and afterwards, at the request of the
Margravine of Baden, she was received by my
grandparents at Carlsruhe. They (my mother's
parents), Mr. and Mrs. Kennedy and four daughters,
had come out to Germany in 1830, and after a

summer spent with us at Ludwigsburg had settled
in Carlsruhe, where they remained until my grandfather's death in 1843. The house they were in was
an old palace belonging to the Margrave William of
Baden, and was said to be haunted by the presence
of a white lady "*die Ahnfrau.*"

In 1831 my father went to England to be received
by William IV., who knighted him and made him
Grand Cross of the Order of the Guelphs, so that
from that time he was known as Sir Edward
Cromwell Disbrowe. The name of Cromwell was
given him in consideration of his direct descent from
Jane Cromwell, the Protector's sister, who married
Major-General John Disbrowe, a famous General of
the Commonwealth. The latter was supposed to
have had much influence with his celebrated brother-
in-law, and to have been in great measure the cause
of Oliver Cromwell refusing the crown. General
Disbrowe certainly did not sign Charles I.'s death
warrant, of which I have a copy. Major-General
John Disbrowe, who spelt his name as we do, was
great-grandfather to my father's grandfather, George
Disbrowe, who married Margaret Vaughan, of
Trederwyn, in Montgomeryshire, whose son Edward,
my grandfather, born 1754, inherited the property at
Walton-on-Trent in 1773.

How I am rambling backwards and forwards, but
thoughts come and go as they will to-night, as I
dream by my own fireside.

My recollections of Stuttgart are nearly at an end.
We remained there until the autumn of 1833. Our
move was caused by my father being appointed to

Stockholm, to carry on the Mission there, until diplomatic relations should be resumed with the Netherlands, he having had the promise of that appointment, when things should be ready for a minister. We left Stuttgart early in November, at least we children and my mother, my father remaining behind to wind up affairs, while we went to Carlsruhe to my grandparents.

How well I remember my sorrow at learning that Hannah More had just died. She was one of my heroines, and I had so much hoped to have a sight of her when we got to England.

We had not been many days at Carlsruhe, when my sister Albinia sickened with scarlet fever and died after three days' illness. She was just over nine years old. It was a great grief to us all, and my mother was terribly distressed at not being allowed to nurse her, though she of course knew how carefully she was tended by my grandmother and our old nurse. My little sister was laid to rest at Carlsruhe, and as soon as it was thought safe for us all to travel, we started for England, posting in two carriages, mostly by the banks of the Rhine.

We reached England about Christmas, and stayed in Chapel Street, Belgrave Square, for a short time, in a house lent to us by our dear old friend, the Dowager Lady Kilmaine. After that we moved to Brighton to a house on the East Cliff, to be near Sir Herbert and Lady Taylor, who were living within the precincts of the Pavilion. Sir Herbert was private Secretary to William IV., and very hard worked, but he always made a point of his daily walk, and took his little girls and myself with him. Lady Winchelsea often joined us at the pier, which I think was then quite new.

One of our great amusements was to see the King taking his daily drive along what I believe was called the Marine Parade.   He drove almost every day from Kemp Town to Shoreham—accompanied by one or other of the FitzClarences—in a chariot with four horses and postilions.   There was no driving-box, therefore His Majesty was in full view of his loyal subjects, who generally had the satisfaction of seeing him fast asleep.

Who these FitzClarences could be puzzled me. Lady Augusta FitzClarence, who had married my mother's first cousin, the Honble. John Kennedy Erskine, son of the first Marquis of Ailsa, used often to spend the evening with us, and was always talking of "papa."   How the King could be her papa was a question I always asked myself, but, child-like, never broached to anyone else.   A great event to me was a children's party at the Pavilion, given by the King, and presided over by Lady Mary Fox.   We had famous games of hide-and-seek, hen-and-chickens, and I know not what else.   Lady Mary joined in all of them; she was the eldest of the King's FitzClarence daughters.

I wish I could remember who the other children were, but I was a stranger and knew none of them. The only girls I remember were the daughters of the Marquis of Anglesea, Lady Eleanor and Lady Constance Paget, the latter afterwards Lady Winchelsea.   When tea was over the King came in,

and patted us all on the head and gave us each a
present. Mine was a pair of china candlesticks, doll's
size, which are carefully kept and in good preservation to this day.

Though I remember her kindness to the Fitz-
Clarence's, I do not remember seeing Queen
Adelaide on that occasion, but she was often ill,
and I do not think she was present at the feast.
My sister saw her constantly in later years when
spending evenings at Marlborough House with the
Princesses Anna and Amelia of Saxe-Weimar, and
she still treasures a little basket made by winding
silks of diverse colours which the Queen taught her to
make.

We all left Brighton early in the spring and went
into Staffordshire to stay with my uncle and aunt,
Mr. and Mrs. John Levett, at Holly Bank, and then
my father took leave of us and started for Sweden,
travelling over land.

In April or May the rest of our party went to
London, and on the 5th of June, 1834, my brother
Edward was born. It was in Sweden that my father
learnt of the birth of his first son. I cannot find
many letters from him to my mother, but one I
remember well in which he described some days at
Count Wetterstedt's, the Minister of Foreign Affairs,
at his country seat Finspong, and a banquet at which
all the household were present, as well as many
retainers ; the latter *dining below the salt.* My
father said it was a very impressive sight.

He returned to England in July, and then my
brother was christened in St. Marylebone Church.

The Queen Dowager stood godmother ; the Marquis of Bute and the Earl of Ripon were the godfathers. My brother was named Edward Amelius, the second name being intended to represent Amelia, one of Queen Adelaide's names.   Had he not had a royal godmother, he would have been given Cromwell as a second name.   My father wished it very much.

As soon after the christening as possible, preparations were made for our move to Sweden.   The London house was given up, and we all went to Eastcombe, in Kent, the residence of the Dowager Lady Buckinghamshire, second wife of the fourth lord, and known as " Pitt's only love."   She was the Hon. Eleanor Eden, eldest daughter of the first Lord Auckland.   I do not think that when she gave a hospitable invitation to such a large party, she expected us to stay long under her roof.

An Admiralty steam yacht had been told off to take us from Woolwich to Stockholm, but this vessel, the " Lightning," had in the meanwhile been sent to Hamburg to fetch the Crown Prince of Hanover to England, the blind King George as he was afterwards.   For some reason he did not start at once, and when the vessel arrived, certain repairs were needed ; so we were three weeks at Eastcombe.

CHAPTER III.

AN ADVENTUROUS VOYAGE.

AT last, on the 13th of September, we were able to go on board the " Lightning," an Admiralty steam-yacht, a party of thirteen and on a Friday. Our old nurse took my father to task for embarking under such circumstances, and she was the only one who did not return, for she died in Sweden.

Our vessel was a small one even for those days, only I believe a hundred horse-power. We did not get to sea until the Saturday afternoon, and had a rough passage across the North Sea. I do not feel sure whether it was on Monday evening or Tuesday morning that those on deck saw the extreme point of Jutland, and the dangerous rock of Skagen with several wrecks upon it, but it was not until nearly dark or by the light of the moon that we sighted the coast of Sweden. I quite remember that my father called us on deck to see it, and then we children were sent to bed.

Very shortly after that we heard a great commotion on deck, and the captain calling, " Port, port hard aport, for God's sake, hard aport"—then came a most awful crash, and the vessel stopped dead.

My mother exclaimed, " We are on a sand-bank," but my father came down to tell us we were on the Kulen rocks, though he hoped we should soon be towed off by anchors and boats.   It seems that the captain and the North Sea pilot had been quarrelling as to whether the light on the shore was the real or the false Kulen.   In one case we ought to have hugged the shore, in the other to have put out further to sea. I conclude the captain was right, as the pilot was under arrest for the remainder of the voyage.   It was considered a shameful business, those rocks being in every chart.   As it was a beautiful calm night with the moon very bright we were told there was no possible excuse for the accident, which I believe happened about eight p.m.   For some time we were listening to shouting, rattling of chains, pulling of hawsers, orders issued in loud tones, and we lived in hopes that our father would come down to the cabin to tell us we had got off the rock.   Alas, the next time he came was to say all efforts had been in vain, the anchors would not hold on the rocks.   No hauling by the boats, not only by our own, but from those that came to our help from the Swedish shore was of any avail, and we must leave the ship.   No time was to be lost as the weather was fine and the sea calm.   Every morning since we had left Woolwich, a stiff breeze had sprung up at sunrise, and it might have happened again.   On being told of the necessity to leave the ship, my mother exclaimed in a voice of agony, " Oh, must it be ?   The poor children ! "

We were only two miles from the Swedish shore,

but had we landed there should have been sub-
jected to a rigorous quarantine, which in those days
meant forty days in huts on the shore. It was an
absurd regulation, for cholera was raging in Sweden
at that time, and there was none in England from
whence we had come. It was therefore settled that
we should make for Elsinore, in Denmark, which was
much further off, and from there send a tug-boat to
the help of the " Lightning." The two additional
reasons for our leaving the ship and making for
Denmark were that when the captain found we
could not get off the rock he told my father he
must send the largest of the boats for help to
Elsinore, in which case he would have nothing in
which to land our party should a storm come on ; the
other reason was that our clean bill of health was for
Denmark.

It was about eleven p.m. when we got into the
boat, seventeen people including steersman and
rowers. We were all placed most carefully according
to weight, by the captain's directions, so as to
balance the boat. My mother held her three months'
old baby in her arms. My sister, as next smallest of
the children, was seated in front of the steersman, who
could see over her head. The first mate was at the
helm, and one of our rowers was a Swede belonging
to a boat which had come to our rescue. This man
was to act as pilot, but on no account to make his
nationality known and not to say one word within
hearing of those on land. At sea he and my father
conversed, the Swede in his own language, my father
in Danish, for whoever can speak one of these two

languages can generally understand the other. Our
butler was placed at the prow to keep a look-out for
whatever might be ahead of us, and we were all told
to sit still, and that in two hours and a half we should
reach Elsinore. Unfortunately, a fog came on, and
then there was a ground swell, and once we were
found to be too near a dangerous rocky part of
the Danish coast, which, as the fog lifted for a few
minutes, my father recognised as " Hammer Müller,"
where he had been for shooting nearly twenty years
before. Of course we had to go further out to sea
again. The four rowers were sadly exhausted, and no
refreshment had been provided for them. My mother
had told our nurse to bring something, meaning food,
for the children with her, but when the bag was
opened it was discovered to be full of sashes and
ribbons. The poor woman had quite lost her head.
It was then found that the boat was leaking, and my
father gave orders to bale. The mate's answer was,
" I have brought nothing to bale with." " Then I will
take my hat," said my father. " No, Sir Edward, it
is too late, no one must move," was the reply.

As daylight appeared we saw the Castle of Kronberg and sang the morning hymn together, which
cheered the poor exhausted rowers, and towards eight
we got into the harbour of Elsinore and made for
the Quay. We were accosted by an official who
called out, " Where come you from ? " My father's
answer was, " From London," but he had the bills of
health, his passport, and his credentials to show, and
at last his request to be allowed to land for the sake
of the poor women and children was attended to,

N

and we left the boat which could not have held out
another half-hour.

When we started to walk to the little inn pointed
out to us by the harbour-master, we all found it
quite painful to do so on the rough pavement of
Elsinore. Our feet were so very tender from having
been so many hours in the water that filled the
bottom of the boat. When we got to the inn we
found it under repair, smelling strongly of paint, and
there was no food, no attendance or any comfort to be
had, nothing but the shelter of the roof. My mother
found an old box to sit on to attend to her baby,
and the rest of us stood about until my father came
back with the Consul, Mr. Chapman, who most kindly
took the whole party to his own house, where he gave
us a very good breakfast and many much-needed
comforts. We could never forget his kindness.

After a rest my father took my aunt, Margaret
Kennedy (my mother's sister), and myself to see the
Castle of Kronberg, where Caroline Matilda, daughter
of George II. and wife of Christian VII., the mad
King of Denmark, had been imprisoned. It was a
grim-looking old place, and it was sad to see the
many hands of the prisoners for debt stretched
through the iron bars to beg of the passers-by. We
had barely walked round when, on returning towards
the harbour, we saw a steamer approaching, and to
our great joy recognised our own "Lightning." I do
not know how it had been released from the Kulen
rocks, but there it was within sight, and the carriages
had not been thrown overboard, which the captain
had threatened to do. The vessel came on in festal

array, the sailors in their best clothes, the ship all
be-flagged ; an awning covered the deck where dinner
was laid, and Captain Allen was ready to receive us
quite *en fête.*

We embarked with as little delay as could be,
steaming along the Sound towards Copenhagen. On
our left the coast of Sweden and the island where the
famous Tycho Brahe, the astronomer, had worked—
on our right the island of Zealand, with its beautiful
beech-trees coming down almost to the water's edge.
I believe that nowhere but in that part of Denmark
do forest trees grow so near to the sea. The Baltic
having no tides is the cause of their flourishing there.
I trust it was with very grateful hearts that we
reached Copenhagen, when we disembarked and took
up our abode at the Hôtel du Nord.

Captain Allen informed my father that the
"Lightning" had been very seriously damaged by
contact with the sharp Kulen rocks, and had lost six
feet of keel, therefore must be repaired before proceeding to Stockholm. It was consequently settled
that we should remain at Copenhagen long enough
for the repairs to be done, besides which we were met
by such bad accounts of the cholera at Stockholm,
that it was not thought wise to go there until
absolutely necessary. It had always been arranged
that we should stay some days in the Danish capital,
that my father might see his old friends and make
my mother acquainted with them ; but in consequence
of continued accounts of the cholera at Stockholm
and the needed repairs to our vessel, we prolonged
our visit to quite a fortnight.

My recollections of Copenhagen are of wide streets and large squares or *Plätze*. On one of these, four buildings joined together by archways thrown across the streets formed a palace. We went there to see some pictures. We children spent most of our time with my father's cousin, Lady Harriet Hagerman, *née* Hobart, wife of General de Hagerman. We were also taken to Sir Henry Wynn's country-seat some way from the town. He was the British Minister to the Court of Denmark, and had been my father's *chef* in Switzerland. At Sir Henry's we met the Duke and Duchess of Montebello. The Duke was the son of Marshal Lannes, the Duchess had been a Miss Jenkinson. They soon followed us to Stockholm, as he was transferred from the Danish to the Swedish Court.

Thorwaldsen's *atelier* and its contents made a great impression on me, especially a most beautiful font which he had executed for his native town of Skaholt, in Iceland. The bas-reliefs were most beautiful; on one side our Saviour was represented blessing the little children; on another was His Baptism in Jordan. The font was in the form of a plinth. Curiously enough, years afterwards, when calling on Lady Bayley at Lord Caledon's house in Carlton Gardens, I saw either the same font or a replica. Sir Joseph Bayley had taken the house for the season. I think it was in the year 1867.

It was at Copenhagen that I saw a man-of-war for the first and only time in my life. We were conducted over the dockyard by a young officer, who was most kind and attentive in explaining and in

showing us everything. He talked of the bombard-
ment of Copenhagen by the English fleet in 1807, of
which some traces were still visible, and then stopped
the whole party on a bridge of rafts, and turning to
my father said, " Do you remember how twenty years
ago this bridge gave way under the pressure of the
crowd and many lives were lost? And do you remember saving the life of a little child, and handing
it over to a woman who was crying on the quay?"
My father answered that he recollected something of
the kind happening.   Then the young officer continued, "I was that child. The woman was my
mother. I have always longed to see you again, and
when I heard that you had arrived, I requested that
I might be your guide to thank you on the very
spot." To me this is a touching tale, and according
to what the young officer said, it must have happened
in the year that my father was appointed Secretary of
Legation at Copenhagen.

One more recollection of Copenhagen before
pursuing our way to Stockholm. We were taken to
the theatre, and above the stage was written, " Ei blot
till lust," which means, " Not only for pleasure," and
my father pointed out an old lady in the royal box,
telling me she was the last of the direct royal line of
Denmark. I have since been told that she was
Princess Julienne, grand-daughter of the unfortunate
Queen Caroline Mathilde.

We resumed our voyage on the 1st of October with
our new pilot, the former one being under arrest for
striking us on the rock. We had not been many
hours on our way when a most fearful storm arose

Our poor little steamer creaked and strained terribly. Captain Allen was much alarmed and owned to my father that he was so because he had not had the repairs done at Copenhagen as he had led him to believe. We took refuge in the harbour of Carl-scrona, the principal dockyard of the Swedish navy, and remained there until the weather improved. On leaving again we made our way through the Straits of Calmar. It was an anxious experiment, as our steamer was the first that had ever attempted the passage. We positively crept along, sounding the whole way, and preceded by boats sounding also. We remained on deck the whole time, and dinner was put off until we got into deep water. The shores on either side seemed quite close, the mainland on our left, the island of Oland on our right hand. We saw the castle and town quite distinctly during our slow progress through the Straits. Calmar is famous for the treaty signed in 1397 known as the Union of Calmar, by which Sweden, Norway, and Denmark were united into one kingdom under Queen Margaret. The Union was finally dissolved by Gustavus Vasa in 1523. I cannot help thinking, as I note this down, how poor Denmark has suffered by treaties, con-cluded, marred, and disregarded. I cannot say how grieved I was for her when she fell under the hand of Prussia in 1864. The Schleswig-Holstein question is a very old one. I have a letter of the time of the Empress Catharine II. of Russia, showing that even then it was under discussion. The Russian Minister of that time was Bernstorff. In after years we find that name in Prussia.

After leaving the Straits of Calmar we never lost sight of land again, and on Sunday, October 5th, found ourselves in the lovely Archipelago of Stockholm. I recollect it as being exquisitely beautiful, with countless islands of every possible shape and form. These latter seemed so close together that one could hardly fancy there could be any passage between them, and yet the largest ships of those days found their way through. Some islands were mere arid rocks, others were covered with fir-trees, and a few showed green fields. Sir John Ross, the explorer, gives an account in his book of an old woman of a hundred and eighteen, who lived all alone on one of these islands. Once a month she allowed a man to bring her provisions. The picture in this work (written a year before we left Sweden) represents her as stout and dressed in a loose striped dress with a girdle round her waist. She is wearing a close-fitting cap and has bare arms and feet.

On our way we saw many remains of wrecks, and were told they were caused by vessels being caught in the ice. The Fort of Væholm treated us to the usual salute due to a Foreign Minister, and we returned it, much to my terror.

After that all of us were very busy, trunks were got out of the hold, and we were made smart in honour of our arrival at Stockholm. As I have said, the first view made a great impression on me, and young as I then was I feel as if I could draw it from memory. Certainly it is a far more striking sight than Copenhagen. The south part of the town rises like an amphitheatre. At the entrance of the port it

is surmounted by St. Catharine's Church. The
palace at the extreme end of the port is a very handsome pile of stone buildings and close to the Norrbro,
or North Bridge, which unites the island on which
the royal residence is built and the mainland. Under
the bridge Lake Mälar flows into the sea.

As soon as we arrived many friends and acquaintances of my father came on board to greet us. The
first to appear was the Consul, then the Secretary of
Legation, then Baron Hochschield, the Swedish
Minister at Copenhagen, who was anxious to secure a
passage in our ship to return to his post, and who
would, I believe, have been better pleased had we not
tarried so long on our way.

It was good to be safe ashore at last. Whenever I
think of that eventful voyage, my dear mother's image
rises to my mind with her baby boy in her arms ; how
she held him all through that long night in the open
boat and during the storm which we encountered on
leaving Copenhagen. The young life of that dear
brother, of whom we were all so proud, was cut short
by his dying a soldier's death on the field of Inkermann, on the 5th of November, 1854. On that day
victory was turned into mourning, owing to the fearful
losses of the Coldstream Guards, in which my brother
was lieutenant and captain. My poor mother, then a
widow, never got over his death, and did not long
survive him.

Allen & Co. Sc.

Lieutenant and Captain E. A. Disbrowe.

Coldstream Guards.

Inkermann.

CHAPTER IV.

IN SWEDEN.

WE landed at Stockholm on Monday, the 6th of October, and drove to the Drottning Gatan (Queen's Street), where our house, or rather apartments, were situated. In these days they would be called flats. They had been used as the English Legation by several preceding Ministers.

On arriving we happened to have on tartan shawls, and some of the maids of honour told my aunt, on becoming better acquainted, that they had thought these shawls were a kind of livery for the maids, and wondered when the ladies were coming.

Our street was one of the finest in Stockholm, but it was narrow and ill-paved, and as far as I recollect, no two houses were alike, either in height, size, or colour. There was no foot pavement of any kind, nothing but an inclined plane on which one could stand to let a carriage pass, with one's heels against the house and one's toes in the gutter. The respective owners always paved before their own houses ; all did so according to their special fancy, the prevailing style being sugar-loaf stones with deep holes on each side. Our friends at Copenhagen were quite right in saying when we grumbled at their pavement, "Wait until you have been to Stockholm to judge of that."

The house we lived in was a very large one, and had need to be so, for it held many people. I will begin with our side. On the ground floor, next to our *porte-cochère*, was Madame Friedrich, the Court milliner. On the next floor, extending over the *porte-cochère*, was the flat of his Excellency Count Rosenblatt, Minister of Justice, who had served I know not how many Sovereigns and dynasties in Sweden. We occupied the two upper floors and the attics. The other end of the house was inhabited by two painters. Above them was the Ministre des Douanes, Count Posse, with wife and family ; and the apartment corresponding to ours belonged to the Dutch Minister, M. de Kronburg, and his wife. Our rooms were all heated by large earthenware stoves of the height of a man, and built in three divisions, with sundry valves to open and shut according to the state of the fire. These stoves threw out a great deal of heat, and consumed but little fuel. Wood was burnt in them. All our rooms had double windows, but each window had a *Was-ist-das*, a solitary pane made to open. It seems to me that a very small portion of air was allowed for the rooms, considering that they were without fireplaces, but it may be that in those northern climates the keener air penetrates through loop-holes which would puzzle an English atmosphere.

The stone staircases at either end of the building were open to all comers, and nearly as public as the street. Each apartment was separated from its respective staircase by an ante-room, called a *tambour*, where footmen, cloaks, and over-shoes were left. No one thought of calling without having an extra cloak and goloshes to be left in the *tambour*.

The first object that greeted our eyes on reaching our drawing-room was a most beautiful pink porphyry vase or *jardinière*, presented to my mother by King Charles XIV. John (Bernadotte) on her arrival at Stockholm. There was only one other in existence at that time, namely, the king's famous vase at Rosendaal, in the Djurgard, and the porphyry was so hard that only one inch a day could be cut, so the vase was, and is, most valuable. I have it still at Walton. The circumstances under which the present was made were rather peculiar. In olden days, when a treaty was concluded between England and another Court, the Minister or Ambassador who negotiated it was presented by the foreign Sovereign with a snuff-box. My father had concluded a treaty on the Sound dues with Sweden, and the King was much affronted to find the decree had gone forth from the Foreign Office forbidding all English representatives to receive any presents. He then said no one could prevent him from offering a present to a lady, and the porphyry vase was the result.

The view from our front windows was over a yard across the street where market carts were put up, and on a higher level still was the market-place. We were promised a great deal of amusement from that view, and a sight of Laplanders and reindeer,

should the winter prove a severe one, but although
the lake was frozen over, no Laplanders or reindeer
were seen.   At the back of the house we could see
beyond the courtyard a branch of the Mälar lake,
and a steep, rocky island on which stood a large
windmill.   It took fire one evening after dark, and
was the most beautiful exhibition of fireworks I have
ever seen.   The whole scene was reflected in the
lake below.   The fire-engine could not be taken up
the almost perpendicular rock.

One of the first events I remember was my father
going to Court.   The Master of the Ceremonies
came to fetch him in a huge glass coach, which
was followed by his own carriage conveying the
gentlemen of the Legation—Mr., afterwards Lord
Bloomfield, Secretary, and Mr. G. Gordon, *attaché*.

Next, my mother and aunt went to be presented
in black dresses with a peculiar shaped slashed
sleeve, the required Court costume.   There were a
few occasions on which the ladies were dressed in
white, and when they attended Court they wore grey,
but the particular sleeve was never dispensed with.
The dinner hour was five ; after it visits were paid.
I have personal recollections of the following
courtiers : Comte de la Gardie, Marshal of the Diet,
a fine old man with snow-white hair, always in
uniform, covered with Orders, and never without his
bâton, the sign of his office, in his hand.   Count
Magnus Brahe, one of the highest in the land.   I
forget his office, but he was in constant attendance
on the King, and had suffered much in health from
his Majesty's habit of always transacting business

at night, when he either kept up his Ministers the whole night long or sent for them between three and four in the morning. Count Wetterstedt was Minister for Foreign Affairs. He had not long lost his wife, and it was said he was sorely puzzled whether to attend her funeral as chief mourner, or to cede that post to her first husband, Count Gyldenstolpe, from whom she had been divorced to marry him. The two men were great friends, notwithstanding their peculiar positions. Count Gyldenstolpe constantly went to play whist at Count Wetterstedt's house, the Countess playing with one or other of her husbands, and the fourth hand being taken by her daughter, Comtesse Jacquetta Gyldenstolpe, also a divorced woman.

Of other visitors I remember Comtesse Brahe and her daughters, Ebba and Ulla, sisters of Count Magnus Brahe. Another Comtesse Gyldenstolpe was "grande Maitresse" to the Queen and her daughter. The Löwenskydds and Wedel Yarlbergs were old Norwegian families, too ancient, too proud, and too grand to have any title, their names were enough. Then there were Hamiltons, Bruces, and Wrights, all become Swedes in the lapse of centuries, and who may have been descendants of the Scotch adherents of Gustavus Vasa.

Amongst the worthies of Stockholm I must make honourable mention of Mr. Owen, to whom we owed our English Service. He was the head of large ironworks, in which he employed numerous English workmen. Being most anxious they should not be deprived of the services of their own Church, he tried, but in vain, to get a clergyman of the Church of England to come to Stockholm. When he found that none would come at his request, he applied to the Wesleyans, who at once sent a missionary, Mr. Scott, to whom, as well as to his wife, Mr. Owen gave a home.

Every Sunday we had a very nice English Service in an *Orangerie* on the Carl XIII. Torg. Mr. Scott always used our liturgy, the only difference being the introduction of an extemporary prayer before the sermon. We all grew very fond of Mr. and Mrs. Scott, and saw much of them, and they stayed with us in the summer. I think both Mr. Owen and the Wesleyan community emulated the good Samaritan, I hardly know which most deserved the name, when the English dwellers in a foreign land had been "passed by on the other side."

The cholera was not quite over when we arrived. We were shown the cholera pit, into which the victim bodies were thrown, some distance from the town. For some time we all wore camphor bags round our necks, and large plates of pitch were placed in every corner of the room. The visitation had been most severe, and the panic very great. The Swedish doctors, or many of them, refused to go when called to attend patients at night; but Mr. Smith, an English medical man, whose presence there was also due to Mr. Owen, was most zealous and kind, never refusing to go where he was wanted, and was of very great use. Consequently the Swedish doctors were most jealous of him, and the chemists were forced by the doctors to refuse to make up his prescriptions. An appeal was made to my father, and after a great deal of trouble he settled the matter by naming Mr. Smith doctor to the Legation, and I believe all his prescriptions were dated from our house.

The environs of Stockholm were very picturesque, consisting of rocks, pine woods, and lakes. We had some very pretty drives on first arriving, and later on sledging across the frozen lakes. Drottningholm, on the Mälar lake, was a summer palace of the King, with gardens imitated from Versailles. It was reached by one of the long bridges of rafts so common in Sweden, and which open in the centre to let the boats go through. The Park of Haga with its small palace was very pretty, and in the spring the wild flowers were our great delight. The lake of the same name was soon frozen over, and we often drove across it in sledges. One day, on arriving on the bank, we found the ice near the edge covered with water. My father wished to turn back, but was assured by the Swedish servant that it was quite safe to drive through the water as long as it remained on the surface. It showed that the ice had not become porous. So we splashed through the water for some distance, and found the ice quite firm. We returned home, however, by another way. The Djurgard was also most picturesque. It was situated on a small peninsula in the Gulf of Stockholm, and commanded a beautiful view of the town. It was a long way off by road, but there was a ferry which helped to considerably shorten the distance, and it was amusing to cross in those queer-looking boats, rowed by Dalecarlian women, wearing grey cloth dresses, yellow cloth caps and aprons. When there was ice, the ferry-boats were replaced by a bridge of rafts. My father and aunt and Mr. Bloomfield and I went one fine frosty afternoon across this bridge to scramble over rocks and through the pine woods of the Djurgard. We found it most enjoyable until Mr. Bloomfield, who had been much longer in Sweden than the rest of the party, recognised the footprints of a wolf in the snow. I was terrified, and my seniors were quite ready to exercise the "better part of valour"— *i.e.* prudence—so we left the interior of the park for the outside road, on the edge of which were several habitations, and so took our way home.

Amongst the visitors I had forgotten to name General Suchtelen, the Russian Minister, who had been in Sweden from time immemorial, and was supposed to have come out of the ark. He was made very much of at that Court, indeed was allowed privileges not granted to other diplomatists, and my father had some difficulty in consequence of obtaining the proper position due to him as the accredited Minister of the Court of St. James. General Suchtelen had two brothers attached to his Legation as secretaries, of the name of Bodisko. They were known as *Beau* Disko and *Laid* Disko, for obvious reasons.

M. Cartoni, the Neapolitan Minister, was a great curiosity. He gave a grand ball that winter, throwing open all his rooms to his guests, who were much amused at the bed hangings being

supported by cupids, who for the occasion were
dressed in pink satin unmentionables ! The invitation ran thus : " *On prendra du Thé le soir chez
Cartoni. On dansera, et puis nous mangerons le
Macaroni !*"

On Sunday all the *bourgeoisie* paraded up and
down our street. It was amusing to watch them.
All the women wore dark cloth pelisses, and large
silk handkerchiefs on their heads, supported by very
high combs. Such was also the dress of our maid-
servants. Some handkerchiefs were black, others
figured, and very gaudy and expensive. I believe
they were all made in Sweden, but besides this and
scissors and paper-knives, like the Damascus work,
and a few porphyry ornaments, I cannot remember
anything worthy of being purchased in Stockholm.
Shops were scarce, dear, and bad, the ladies sending
for all their finery to Copenhagen or Hamburg, and
most likely the Court dress being black prevented
much enterprise. Of course the great trade of the
place was iron, and in the south part of the town
there were always extensive depôts of iron bars
ready to be shipped to England. I do not remember
seeing any large quantities of wood ready for exporta-
tion ; probably that was shipped from further
south, and mostly from Norway, but it was from
Stockholm that the produce of the mines of
Danemora was exported.

The Palace, the historical Museum, the Riddar-
holme Kerke, and the Chamber of the Diet were
all on the same island. The church was partially
burnt down whilst we were in Sweden.

O

We were present at the closing of the Diet, then composed of four orders—nobles, clergy, burghers, and peasants. Bernadotte did not attend. He was ill and angry. The Queen and Prince and Princess Royal were there, and the Prince read the Speech from the Throne. He generally did so, as Charles XIV. John spoke but little Swedish. Queen Désirèe had never learnt the language at all. She was by no means queenly in her looks, and had no wish to forget her origin. She said one day, in talking of the power of standing possessed by royalty, " *C'est fort bien pour ceux qui sont neés pour le metier, mais cela ne me va pas.*" Her spouse also talked of " *Quant j'etais petit lieutenant.*" The Princess Royal was a tall, distinguished-looking woman. She was a Beauharnais, daughter of the Viceroy Eugènie. Prince Oscar was also a fine-looking man. They had four sons and a daughter, Princess Eugènie. The Queen, like the King, turned night into day. She always drove after dark in winter, and dined after the play. The King remained in bed many weeks that winter, not that he was ill, but he was afraid of being poisoned, and part of the time he lived entirely on raw apples, often eating eleven at a time.

My father had the stage box, or " *Oeil de Bœuf* " (as it was called), at the theatre, on leaving which Gustavus III. was murdered. We were taken there to see a piece called *Birgir Yarl*, from the name of the founder of Stockholm, in 1252 or 1260. The piece was supposed to represent his dream, which led to his founding the town. The scenery introduced the Gustaf Adolf's Torg and the Norrbro, the most picturesque parts of the town.

Whilst in Sweden we heard from home of the burning of the old Houses of Parliament, also of sundry ministerial changes, and of the Duke of Wellington for a time holding all portfolios. It was then that Mr. Hudson (afterwards Sir James) made his rapid journey to Rome in search of Sir Robert Peel, which gained him the name of " Hurried Hudson." It was also then that Sir Charles Lyell made the discovery that it was the shores of Sweden that were rising, not the level of the Baltic falling. I can remember hearing my father tell Mr. Bloomfield the fact, which I did not at all understand, till I read about it years afterwards in a book called " Gales and Shores of the Baltic."

Letters from England were very precious, coming once a week by steamer to Gothenburg, from whence a messenger brought the Minister's bag to Stockholm. He always had a cariole to himself, so that he could bring parcels and books, and many were the nice things my dear aunt, Lady Taylor, used to send "for the children."

How happy I was when the days lengthened. The elders voted the long, bright evenings, when it was too cold to play at summer, very dull, but to me anything seemed better than those endless hours of candle-light. On the 1st of May it was the custom for the Court and society to drive in open carriages round and round the Djurgard, the ladies being all as smart as the weather would permit. The court then dined at the Rosendaal, the summer palace in the park, and the rest of the world made up parties at some of the small wooden refreshment houses that were dotted about the park.

On the 1st of May, 1835, we played at summer in that way, though there were no leaves on the trees. Summer and winter in those northern climes are divided by a brief spring. The vegetation makes the most of a short time, and hardly has the snow disappeared when all is green. Soon after that drive we went to the camp on the Larger Holm to hear the soldiers sing their evening hymn, and beautiful it sounded, the Swedes being very musical.

It was in consequence of the death of the young Prince of Holstein-Augustenburg, that Bernadotte had been chosen as Crown Prince of Sweden, and successor to Charles XIII., the childless King, who in 1809 had deposed and succeeded his nephew, Gustavus IV., so well known afterwards as Colonel Gustavuson.

The Prince of Holstein-Augustenburg died of sunstroke at a review in Pomerania, and when his body was brought back to be buried at Stockholm, a report was spread that Count Fersen, who had accompanied him to Pomerania, had poisoned him. Consequently, as the funeral crossed the Norrbro, the populace fell on the poor man and literally tore him to pieces. Umbrellas, sticks, and legs of chairs were hurled at him, and all this in sight of the Guards, who never moved to help him. They even wanted to wreak their vengeance on his sister, Countess Piper, who had to fly for her life; and whilst crossing the lake in a boat she heard from the rowers that they were in pursuit of her. She had been bedridden for many years, but the fright restored the use of her limbs, and she lay concealed at Steninge, where her brother's tenantry were faithful to her. I believe she owned the property after her brother's death, and that it was from her that my father took the house at Steninge for the summer.

We went there on the 18th June, in a steamer that plied between Upsala and Stockholm, and which we hired on one of its free days. Steninge was in a small bay and somewhat out of the beaten track, and had a pier of its own. It is situated on the Mälar Lake, which was about sixty miles in length, but nowhere more than six miles wide, and at one place called Staket the shores approach so closely that there was only just room for the steamer to pass. Steninge had been built by Queen Christina for one of her favourites. It was in the Italian style. Up the first flight of steps were two pavilions : one was for a kitchen and offices, the other the Queen kept for herself. This last was devoted to visitors. The main building was a flight higher up. It had a very fine staircase, large rooms, and a marble gallery. The gardens were stiff, in the French style, and if I remember rightly, there were not many flowers. If Stockholm was dreary, Steninge was all brightness. We spent a delightful time there. Everything was charming, including the scrambles over the rocks and through the pine woods. I remember an old oak-tree with a balcony and a staircase leading up to it, and a small fortification made by Charles XII. when a little boy.

The ant-hills were immense, and whenever we saw one deserted, we were told it was a proof that bears had been on the spot in the winter.

Wild flowers and strawberries existed in great profusion. The only drawbacks were the mosquitoes. They drove us nearly wild. Our greatest delight was our little yacht, the "Shamrock," in which we used to sail on most fine days. It had three masts, lateen sails, and a tiny cabin. Sometimes we met the steamer on the way to Upsala, and brought back any friends who happened to be on board to stay with us. My father was told it was a most dangerous proceeding, that no one had ever heard of a sailing vessel boarding a steamer to take off passengers, but the feat was performed many times in safety.

Rosenberg, where the Royal Family spent the summer, was in the next bay to ours. My father, mother, and aunt went several times to dine and sleep there, and during one of their visits the King and Queen announced their intention of coming to dine at Steninge with my parents, and of bringing a party of more than thirty people with them. They gave most inconveniently short notice. Stockholm had the nearest market, and we were nearly thirty miles from thence, and besides we had nothing with us in the country in the shape of plate, linen, or china, fit to set before a king.

My mother obtained leave to shorten her visit, and having the loan of a royal carriage, returned as quickly as possible to see what arrangements could be made. She dispatched the English butler and French man-cook to Stockholm, whether by boat or by road I do not know, but they came back in the steamer next day with all that was needed, and that included bread and meat and a best gown for my mother. A carpenter was found by Count Flintberg, not only to concoct a dinner-table, but to erect sheds for carriages and horses. Lessons were dispensed with for two days previous to the feast, as the schoolroom was used as the dining-room, and all hands capable of holding a needle were needed to mend rents in the yellow satin coverings of sofas and chairs. This work was very much like Penelope's web, for as fast as we stitched on one side another rent gaped opposite to it.

Fortunately all went off well. The day was fine, their Majesties were gracious. We children came in to dessert and saw the King crumbling bread and rubbing his hands with it. We heard him say it was a habit he had acquired, "*Quand j'etais petit lieutenant*," and could not afford anything else to keep his hands white. This did not sound to me like a valiant soldier.

On one occasion my parents accompanied the Royal Family on a visit to Skoekloster, a castle belonging to Count Brahe, also on the Mälar Lake. They crossed in the King's small private steamer, and when they got on board, the Queen, who was short and stout, stuck between the paddle-wheel and the top of the cabin, and all the rest of the party were stopped. The King kept shouting,

"*Mais Désirèe avancez donc,*" and she kept on replying, "*Mais non, mom ami, je ne puis pas. Cela m'est impossible.*" At last my mother suggested that two chairs should be brought, and the Queen hoisted on to them, so as to raise her above the obstacle, and so the difficulty was overcome. But when the question came of the return journey, her Majesty got a fit of terror and vowed she would not start again until daylight. So the King and Count Brahe read "Racine and Corneille" aloud to the assembled company until the sun rose. I daresay that happened between two and three in the morning, for in the far north there is of course hardly any darkness in the summer. Quite early in August my father took my aunt, Lady Harriet Hagerman, and myself for a little northern tour. We started in our light *calèche* with three horses abreast, and with our servant Peter as coachman. I do not recollect what Peter's special post was in the household, but he was most useful as interpreter also on board the yacht, having been a sailor. Soon after leaving home we had a very steep hill to descend, down which he drove Swedish fashion, as hard as he could go. My father, who was on the box beside him, remonstrated, and asked whether accidents did not frequently happen from such driving. Said Peter, "I have heard of people being killed, but of nothing worse happening."

Our first halt was at Upsala, where we visited the famous library and the Museum, and were shown the chests containing papers left by Gustavus III. not to be opened until 1841, fifty years after his death. I have never heard what became of them. Upsala is the seat of the Bishop of the Swedish Protestant Church,* and it also has a university. We slept in the modern town, and the next day drove to Gamla Upsala, to see the church, once a heathen temple, in which there was an old idol, supposed to be the god Thor, and with tumuli outside sacred to the gods Thor and Odin. From thence we went to see the famous iron mines of Danemora, driving through pine woods and changing horses in the midst of them. The horses had been bespoken, and we found them fastened to a post. Peter harnessed them to the carriage, and fastened the three tired ones to the post, and off we went again. Who took charge of the horses and who received the money for them I do not know. There was no one in sight when the exchange took place. We spent some hours on the edge of the mine, sitting or lying down on a sort of overhanging stage, made for landing the ore. No visitors were allowed to stand upright on them. The mines were very open at the top, and one could see a long way down and watch the men at work. To me it was a very awful sight, and when a rock was blasted the noise was terrific. We saw the workmen let down in buckets, and they went down quite fearlessly, sometimes standing on the outer edge holding on by

* Here I have ventured to delete the words "like our own," because the Swedish Orders are not recognised by the Anglican Church, and their validity is still a matter of controversy. The latest book on the subject was written by the late Dr. Nicholson, of Leamington.—M.M.C.

ropes. The buckets in which they descended came up full of ore, the machine being worked by a blind horse.

From Danemora we proceeded to Löfsta, Count de Geers' seat. I believe he was the owner of the mines. On the way we were shown the most northern oaks in Europe, three stunted little miseries. We spent several pleasant days with Comtesse de Geers and her family. She was very anxious to live in the English style, but customs and hours were not like our own. Dinner was at three o'clock, with soup, etc. Before dinner the assembled company went into another room to whet their appetites with brandy or some other spirit, and either anchovies or oysters. This preparatory meal was called a *schaal*. After dinner, before our hostess left her seat, all her descendants went to her and kissed her hand, and said, " *Tak for mat.*" It meant thanks for food. Even her little grandchildren were carried down by their nurses, who repeated the same phrase, if the children were too young to speak. In the evening supper was brought into the drawing-room and placed on sundry little tables, but I was sent to bed before that. What struck me most was seeing all the common garden shrubs and plants treated with the greatest care, kept under glass, and only occasionally put out in the sun. One thing existed of which we cannot boast in England—namely, transparent apples which looked like wax. When such trees are transplanted to England the fruit becomes like ordinary apples in appearance after the second year, though both in

Russia and Sweden it would retain its original peculiarity.*

On leaving Löfsta we went to a house belonging to Count Platen, at one time Swedish Minister in London. It is one of the finest properties in Sweden, and contained endless statues, pictures, and works of art, collected by the Count from all parts of Europe. It was also celebrated for having been the place of confinement of King Eric IX. of Sweden. He had been for I know not how many years a close prisoner in the cellar, and the walls were covered with his writings, which had been most carefully preserved by successive owners, till alas! during the absence of Count Platen in Italy, and not long before our visit, an officious agent or servant had the whole place painted and whitewashed, obliterating all these precious relics, much to the disgust of his master.

In the evening we went to Salsta, a fine, old, gloomy-looking castle belonging to Countess Brahe, not half as pleasant an abode as Löfsta. I think we only dined and slept there, and then returned to Steninge.

On the 23rd of August my younger brother was born, and about six weeks later we returned once more to Stockholm in the steamer " Upsala."

---

* Bozen, in Southern Tyrol, has a large export trade of similar transparent apples, produced in the environs.— M.M.C.

CHAPTER V.

HOMEWARD BOUND.

IN October my father had orders to return to England, preparatory to proceeding to his next post, the Hague. It was already late in the year for travelling in these countries, and therefore no time was to be lost.

Lady Harriet Hagerman and her daughter, who had been spending the summer with us, left for Copenhagen soon after our return from Steninge. Our great trouble was the sad state of our good old Nurse Halliday. She had been with us almost ever since my birth, and now was so ill that it was impossible to move her, and very sad it was to leave her to die in that foreign land. My parents made all possible arrangements for her comfort. They kept on the apartment and sent for her daughter from St. Petersburg, where she was in service. An excellent woman, Peter's sister, who had attended her for months, remained to nurse her; Mr. Smith, the doctor, was to establish himself in the house as soon as we left, and good Mr. Scott was to pay her constant visits. Her sufferings were terrible, but we had the assurance of both gentlemen that the ten days she survived our departure were days of peace. On the 9th of November, the day on which we left the Swedish shore, she was released.

On the evening before our departure we were all arrayed in travelling garb, most of the furniture was packed, nothing remaining but a few very old blue satin chairs, that had passed from one Minister to the other, for I know not how long, and the kitchen table had been brought into the drawing-room to hold the bottles in which candles were stuck.

Suddenly we heard the King was coming to pay us a farewell visit. It was most kind, gratifying, and inconvenient. The news produced a fine hurry-scurry. Mr. Smith said he possessed a table cover, and brought it to hide the kitchen table. Mr. Bloomfield ran for something else, my father went to Count Rosenblatt, to beg for the loan of lamps and candle-sticks, which the latter promptly sent up, so that by the time Charles XIV. John had arrived, every-thing was as it should be. The King was most gracious, and complimented my parents, who were very much pleased and flattered by the visit. Just as he was leaving, he said he must go and see his old friend Rosenblatt, who, as it happened, was sitting in the dark until his lamps could be returned. What was to be done? The only resource was to light the King ceremoniously downstairs, my father taking one lamp, and Mr. Bloomfield the other, whilst Mr. Smith seized the candles. Was there ever such a reception for royalty?

And now for our journey. There had been some talk of our travelling by the Gotha Canal, but by the

time we were ready to start the boats had ceased
running on account of the ice, and were laid up for
the winter.   Thus there was no alternative but to
post to Gothenburg, where the frigate " Cleopatra,"
which had conveyed Lord Durham to St. Petersburg,
was to call for us.

The queer old travelling carriages were again in
requisition.   Besides the two original ones we had a
light *calèche*, a *fourgon* for the luggage, and one or two
peasants' carts.   In the *fourgon* besides clothes were
several iron beds and bedding, as there were not often
enough beds found in the inns.   That reminds me
that I have still several of the identical iron bedsteads.
In those good old days the nursery-maid used to put
them up without any help, but now, if I want them
moved or made ready for use, the blacksmith, and I
know not who else, has to be called in to get them
ready.   So much for the march of intellect !

The peasants' carts belonged to the owners of the
post-horses.   The postmasters were bound to furnish
travellers with horses, but neither with drivers nor
harness ; nor were they bound to keep horses.   They
collected them from their neighbours, and if one had
not ordered them twelve hours in advance, one had
no right to complain unless kept more than two hours
and a half at each stage.

We had twenty-one horses, and always travelled in
the same order.   First came the green chariot in
which my mother travelled with the baby and nurse.
She was driven by Peter with four horses abreast.
Then came the green coach with six horses, four
abreast and two leaders.   This Zittesberg the coach-

man drove, and a boy rode one of the leaders. Inside
were governess and children, and my mother's maid.
Behind the chariot sat the French cook with a lamp
before him on which he cooked broth. My father,
my aunt and I were in the *calèche*, with three
horses abreast, driven by Orlande. Then came the
fourgon and peasants' carts.

We started at seven every morning, and never
stopped until we got to our night's lodgings. We
spent the first night at Baron A. O'Keigelm's at Stäket,
who was indeed hospitable to take in so large a party.
We then crossed the Mälar Lake on which we had
spent the summer, and went on to Westeras, sleeping
at a bookseller's.

The length of our day's journey depended not only
on where we could find lodgings, but also on where
the markets were, as fresh meat and leavened bread
were only to be procured in the large towns. We
travelled from Westeras by way of Arboga, Orebro
(not far from the head of Lake Wetter), Maria Stadt
and Lidköping, on the shores of the Wenner Lake
which looked like a sea. No opposite shore was
visible. I think it was at Lidköping that we slept in
the town hall, a very large room with a gallery above.
The country was very thinly populated, we often were a
great part of the day without seeing a soul on the road,
and the villages consisted of a very few wooden huts.
The land was barren, excepting near the lakes, where
there were pine-trees.

Our last halting-place before Gothenburg was
Trolhätten, where we stayed to see the falls. Very
beautiful and picturesque they appeared, though when

we saw them they were not at their best, at least not as full as they were at times, but the volume of water must always be very considerable, as they are the chief outlet from the great Lake Wenner, which empties itself into the River Gotha, and from thence into the sea. We also saw the great lock by which vessels are put to sea. In those days they were looked upon as a wonderful triumph of engineering. We found Lord Hillsborough, afterwards Marquis of Downshire, and Mr. Lloyd, the great bear-hunter at Trolhätten. On the day we left we saw three wolves taking their morning walk, close to the high road, and were told that they were the scouts of a pack, and had our party been less numerous we should have been in danger of being attacked by them. As it happened they eyed us carefully and trotted back into the wood. We gave notice of this in every village we passed through, so that the children should be kept indoors.

That day we descended the steepest and longest hill which I remember in all that journey, and as there was a good deal of ice and snow my father was very uneasy about our heavy carriages, particularly on account of the Swedish fashion of driving down full tilt. Mercifully nothing happened and we got down in safety. We waited two days at Gothenburg for the "Cleopatra," but learning that she had passed through the Sound without communicating with the shore and gone straight to England, my father determined to push on to Copenhagen, so we travelled on to Helsingborg, sleeping one night at Falkenborg. Had it not been for the promised passage on board the frigate, our journey might have been considerably shortened by going direct to Helsingborg, taking the road on the Baltic side of Sweden and the eastern shore of Lake Wetter. We crossed from Helsingborg to Elsinore in open sailing boats, and then had a wet, dark drive to Copenhagen, where we learnt that the "Cleopatra" having arrived in England without us, the "Lightning" had been sent to Hamburg to take us home. We remained two days at Copenhagen and then went on board the last steamer that was to ply for that year. It was called the "Frederic VI.," and was most crowded and uncomfortable, but took us safely to Kiel. We had snow and wind to contend with, so were much longer than we had expected. Instead of the usual six hours the passage lasted from nine in the morning until eleven at night. As soon as we landed Captain Allen came to beg my father to re-embark at once, or at least on Sunday morning, on board the "Lightning," as the season was so far advanced, but my father (who never willingly travelled on Sunday) refused, as he wished us all to attend church together. He however consented to our sleeping on board on Sunday night, that there might be no delay in starting on Monday morning. Such a bitterly cold night it was, and in the morning when we ought to have started we were caught in the ice.

A first night's ice is not very thick, yet our small pair of 100 horse-power engines could not push through, but by twelve o'clock the sun had sufficient power to allow of the regular packet, the "William Joliffe," a much larger vessel than our own, breaking

P

through the ice, and we followed in her wake and got some way down the river. Then a fog came on, and we anchored opposite Glückstadt. On the Tuesday we got to Cuxhaven, and put into that port on account of the stormy weather. The harbour was already very crowded, yet there was no need to stick us on a sand-bank at the entrance, as the pilot contrived to do. As the tide fell, our position became most unpleasant. We gradually heeled over, and at low tide found ourselves with the cabin floor, if not perpendicular at least very far from horizontal, and until the tide rose and the vessel righted we could get no dinner, for the coal would not stay in the grate, nor the food in the saucepans.

At high tide we got off and moved further up into the harbour. The next day it was still too stormy to put to sea. Some of us went on shore and saw the lighthouse, also a large cannon standing close to it, and a small bathing establishment. Cuxhaven was the name of the harbour. These were the only things of note in the small town of Reichenbüttel. We returned to the ship in the afternoon in the hope of starting next morning for England.

The storm continued to increase as the day wore on, yet no one as far as I knew anticipated any danger for the vessels in the harbour. We retired to bed, but at about ten o'clock the noise of the wind and waves became terrific. I was sleeping in the stern cabin with my governess and the maids, the rest of the family being in the saloon. The first warning I received of any danger was when the nurse rushed in and said, "You must all get up and dress,

for we are all going to the bottom." I scrambled
into my clothes as best I could and joined my mother
in the saloon. She was sitting in her berth with her
two baby boys in her arms, one seventeen months
old, the other only three months. She was nursing
them both as calmly and tranquilly as if in her own
house. My sister, a very little girl, was lying half-
asleep in the next berth, my aunt with her. I lay
down on the floor at my mother's feet, our governess
and the nurse sat by the table. My mother's maid
was helping everybody. She was wonderfully
courageous when there was any danger, but full of
needless alarm when there was no cause for it. She
was engaged to our butler, and in the middle of the
night he rushed into the saloon in small attire, threw
his arms round her neck, and said, "Harriet, my dear,
good-bye for ever." Her touching retort was, "You
old fool, go to bed, and leave me to take care of the
children," which speech had the desired effect, for he
returned to his own berth. We passed many a weary
hour in hoping and fearing. My father looked in
upon us every now and then, but did not dare to
leave the deck for long at a time.

The sailors were in open mutiny, and he alone was
able to keep some order. They had proclaimed him
captain, and he told them his first order was for them
to obey Captain Allen. Part of the time was spent
by him and the French cook and English footman
with their backs to the spirit-room door, each with a
pistol in his hand, because the crew had threatened
to break in and die drunk. They were all so indignant at the want of care and precaution taken by the

captain, and well they might be, for we were moored to another vessel instead of to the shore. The pilot was on shore without leave. No preparation had been made for getting up steam, if necessary. The boats were all left swinging instead of being hauled on deck, and consequently two out of the three were utterly smashed.

All the vessels in the harbour had broken loose and also a huge engine for driving piles, which did terrible damage. Seven vessels in the harbour and many lives were actually lost, and fourteen other ships were wrecked near the mouth of the river. We could hear the screams of the drowning and the noise of vessels colliding whenever there was the slightest lull in the noise of the wind and waves. Long and dreary the time seemed, though I believe we were not more than six hours in this trying position. Three of our hawsers broke, but the fourth held out till the tide fell at about four in the morning, and we grounded on the sand-bank on which we had been stranded on first approaching the harbour.

During the storm the captain had been seen close to the last remaining hawser, apparently in the act of cutting it, having quite lost his head. Whether the lurch of the vessel was the cause of his falling over-board, or whether he was pushed over will never be known, anyway, overboard he went, and was rescued by two of our gallant tars without being recognised. It was not until they had got him down to the cabin that they found out who he was, and then some regrets were expressed that it was not known sooner whom they were saving ! As soon as possible after the tide fell we were all taken on shore in a large barge, which Mr. Dutton, the Consul, had sent for us. We did not know until afterwards, that my dear father had landed previously in the captain's gig to fetch help. It was a most perilous undertaking in that awful storm, and when on land he had the greatest difficulty in finding his way.

Our walk between four and five o'clock in the dark was most trying. The landing steps had been washed away and we had to scramble over the stones which were all slippery and slimy from the waves. It poured with rain, and the wind was still so high we could hardly face it. My mother always said, that walk was far the most trying part of all we had gone through. When we were in so much danger on board she was resigned and felt we should all go down together, but during that walk her dread was lest some of those who were carrying the children should fall and her little ones be lamed for life.

We first made for the little bathing-house, which we had seen the previous day, but found it not only deserted, but with every door and window blown in, therefore we could not shelter there.

The lighthouse had been much injured and the cannon upset. We walked on to the Consul's and found him and Mrs. Dutton ready to receive us. The latter had already prepared breakfast and beds for us. Nothing could exceed their kindness and hospitality. My dear mother as we crossed their threshold fell on her knees and returned thanks for our most merciful preservation, and for the first time was unable to restrain her feelings. I believe that if my aunt and I had not caught hold of her in time, she would have fallen on her face on the floor.

Thinking of it now, I must say it was wonderful that of all our large party only one should have lost his presence of mind—the love-sick butler. I am proud to say *his*, for all the women were calm and collected.

Years afterwards when my father was crossing from Rotterdam to London in a severe storm, he was accosted by a stranger who said to him, " You and I, Sir Edward, have seen worse weather than this." My father asked for an explanation, and the stranger said, " I was on board the 'William Joliffe' in Cuxhaven Harbour on the 18th November, 1835, when all the vessels broke loose." " What hopes had you of being saved ? " asked my father. " Some hopes," answered the stranger, " for *our large vessel—but none for your small one !* "

All Thursday we remained with the kind Duttons, and during the day heard most dreadful accounts of the number of wrecks and terrible loss of life occasioned by the storm. My father and Mr. Dutton went to look at the poor little "Lightning." She was found to be greatly shattered and battered, and the crew was in a mutinous state, having been badly commanded, so that it was determined in spite of Captain Allen's entreaties that we should not return to England on her, but only to Hamburg. We re-embarked on the Friday and arrived once more at Hamburg, just the day week after our first arrival, having wasted a week on the Elbe.

We saw many of the results of the gale ; amongst

others, a ship stranded high and dry in the middle of
a green field. As soon as we had once more cast
anchor, my father went ashore to secure rooms at the
hotel. On the way he met an acquaintance, who
seeing how ill and worn he looked did not dare to
ask him about any of us, being persuaded that we
were all drowned. The disaster at Cuxhaven had
been heard of, but the details were not known, only
that many lives had been lost.

We remained all Sunday at Hamburg, and had the
comfort of returning thanks in the English church
for the great mercy shown us in having been brought
safely through such danger. We then made acquaintance with Mr. and Mrs. Canning; he was the English
Consul, and a near relation of the statesman George
Canning. They told us that a few years before, they
had found a young Scotch lad fainting on the door-
step. He proved to be Lord Alexander Kennedy,
who had been sent away ill from some school in
Germany. They took him in and nursed him for
some weeks until his grandfather, the first Marquis
of Ailsa, sent his agent to fetch him home, alas to
die.

Once more we started from Hamburg, this time in
a river steamer for Harbruck, and on landing posted to
Zell, where we went to look at the palace in which
poor Queen Caroline Mathilde died. The following
day we reached Hanover, and were detained two
days, as some of the party were knocked up, and all
the carriages needed repairs after the wear and tear
of the hard roads of Sweden, and being knocked
about in the storm.

My father went to pay his respects to the Duke of Cambridge, then Viceroy of Hanover, and we took a long drive to look at Herrenhausen, but saw nothing to admire in the flat sandy country.

From Hanover, we journeyed *viâ* Bietfeld and Lippstadt to Cologne, where, the wheels just needed sufficient attention to enable us to see the cathedral. Aix-la-Chapelle and Brussels were our next halting-places. At the latter place the carriages were again kind enough to need some repairs, so we visited the palace the nation had presented to the Prince of Orange after the battle of Waterloo. It was just in the state in which he had left it before the Revolution of 1830, indeed the custodian tried to prove that he had fled from thence, and a pocket-handkerchief and pair of gloves were displayed on the Princess's writing-table. This was a romance, for all the Royal Family were at the Hague when the Revolution broke out, and although the Prince of Orange and his brother, Prince Frederic, were with the army, I do not believe they were ever in Brussels again. The beautiful malachite candelabras, the pictures, the pietra-dura table, etc., we afterwards saw at the Hague. They were removed there after affairs were arranged, but I doubt whether they looked as well in their new summer days as in the bijou palace at Brussels.

Mont-Cassel and Calais were our next halts, but our progress was much impeded by the little Vienna calèche breaking down at each stage, and finally it struck work altogether and was left at Calais. We seemed very near dear old England then, and expected no further trouble. Something however happened to one of the paddle-wheels of the packet-boat, and we were between six and seven hours crossing to Dover. At last, on the 8th of December, we reached London, having left Stockholm on the 31st of October, and never having voluntarily relaxed our efforts to get home. Those were the good old days before the pleasure of travelling had been spoilt by railroads !

We took up our abode at St. Katharine's Lodge, in the Regent's Park, the residence of our uncle, Sir Herbert Taylor, and were very glad to find ourselves there. But, alas ! the house caught fire. The damage was not so great as the alarm, yet it gave our friends the opportunity of saying we were born to be hanged, as we had escaped perils both by fire and water.

My aunt, Lady Taylor, and her daughter, came from Brighton to spend a few days with us, and carried me back with them. We travelled down four in a chariot, and as my cousin and I were big girls it was rather a tight fit.

I was given as many lessons as possible during the short time I was at Brighton, to make up for the idle time on the journey, but in spite of that I was very happy, and my cousin and I were often taken on the Chain Pier by Miss Bagot, afterwards Lady Winchelsea, and at that time maid of honour to Queen Adelaide. My aunt, Margaret Kennedy, who had shared all our perils, left us to join another sister, Mrs. Levett, in Staffordshire; and about the middle of January, 1836, the rest of us set off for the Hague, crossing from Dover to Calais. This time nothing impeded our progress until we got to Ghent, where we were delayed two days by the illness of the baby. There Sir Alexander Malet, the Secretary of Legation, and Lady Malet joined us, it having been decreed that we were to cross the frontier together.

Peace had not been declared, and the Dutch and Belgian armies were still facing each other, the former at Grodzundel, the latter at West Wessel. The Dutch headquarters were at Tilburg.

We slept at Antwerp on leaving Ghent, and just managed to glance at Rubens' famous "Descent from the Cross." Then came the important event of crossing the frontier in face of the hostile armies. I was a little disappointed that the whole thing passed off so quietly. We drove very slowly, and our carriages, four in number, were constantly stopped by some official or other, each of whom in my childish mind I settled must be the Commander-in-Chief. On these occasions my father invariably got out of the carriage and displayed his passports and special pass, and as we left the Belgian territory, three soldiers were drawn up on the side of the road with muskets pointed at us. No other sign of the army did I see, nothing but this outpost. We only got as far as Breda that night, owing to having taken some time crossing the border, and being inspected and stopped, but we had no custom-house to encounter. The next day we crossed the Moerdyk in a steamer, besides crossing two very wide ferries, for which we engaged two or three sailing boats. The last ferry was over the Meuse to Rotterdam, where we were received by Sir Alexander Ferrier, the kind-hearted and well-known Consul. He held the appointment for forty-seven years.

A fourteen miles' drive brought us to the Hague. There we took up our abode at the Hotel on the 26th January, 1836.

CHAPTER VI.

THE NETHERLANDS.

So many recollections and thoughts crowd into my mind about those Hague days that I scarcely know where to begin.

Diplomatic relations had been suspended between the Kingdom of the Netherlands and England and France ever since the Revolution of 1830, and my father and Baron Mortier were the first Envoys and Ministers accredited to the Hague from those countries. England was by no means in favour with the Dutch, who considered that we had deserted their old friends, and particularly resented Antwerp having been given over to Belgium. A Minister must have no politics, but I believe that in his heart my father agreed with the Dutch, and thought Belgium too much favoured. He certainly would not have held to some ideas of Baron Stockmar. French influence however came in, the Queen of the Belgians being a daughter of Louis Philippe. Those were that king's halcyon days, and I always thought Lord Palmerston leaned to his side.

Mr. George Jerningham, afterwards Minister at Stockholm, had been *Chargé des Archives*, which was

not quite the same as *Chargé d'Affaires.* It showed
that no actual intercourse had been going on between
the governments. He must have had a very dull
time, as hardly a soul in society would speak to
him.

A great many of the Legations had remained at
the Hague through all the troublous times. Amongst
these were the Danish, Russian, and Prussian, but I
believe that was in consequence of their not having
recognised the independence of Belgium. It was a
long time before affairs were finally settled, and the
famous twenty-four articles discussed. If I remember
rightly, the Plenipotentiaries did not meet in London
until the following year. I am uncertain as to dates,
nor do I suppose that in those days anyone took the
trouble to enlighten me on public business. Still I
remember the almost invariable greeting to my father,
when we met anyone in the street, was, " *Quelles
nouvelles de Londres, et des vingt-quatre articles ?* "

These were the days of the first King and last
Stadtholder of the House of Orange. The old Queen
was still alive when we arrived, but in very infirm
health, and she died not many months later. She
was sister to the Duchess of York, George III.'s
daughter-in-law, and to the King of Prussia of
Napoleon's days.⁵ Baron Verstolk von Zoelen was
Minister of Foreign Affairs. M. Van Maanen
(against whom it was said Belgium had originally
revolted) was Minister of Justice, and his daughter,
who had saved his life at the risk of her own and who
deserved the Victoria Cross, had such a thing existed
then, was still suffering from the effects of her

exertions. Baron de Selby, the Danish Minister, and his wife were *Doyen* and *Doyenne* of the Diplomatic Corps, so presented all new-comers. The Baron had been accredited to Jerome, King of Westphalia, and when that kingdom broke up had to leave Cassel under the escort of Cossacks. One of his daughters, afterwards Comtesse Bille Brahe, was christened Jeroma—King Jerome being her godfather. Count Lottum was the Prussian, and M. Poteinkin the Russian Minister. Monsieur de Baze was the Spanish representative for Queen Isabella, and a second Spaniard tried to be acknowledged as sent by Don Carlos. Of course the latter never came near the English Legation, but he was received by some of the others and so to some extent in general society. When we first arrived neither of them had been received at Court. Mr. Davezac was Minister from the United States, and Baron Mortier from France.

As I was kept up to make tea, and all visits of ceremony were made in the evening, I had the amusement of hearing all the long and wonderful names announced. "Baron et Baronne de Tuyll de Serooskerken et Mesdemoiselles leur filles" called very soon, and invariably called my father "Sir Charles," which they thought was the proper name for the English Minister. They talked a great deal of when Louis Bonaparte was King; praised him and said he meant well, but his brother would not allow him to do his duty to the country. They had no good word for Queen Hortense.

There were also the Snouckarts van Schanbourg.

Mademoiselle S. S. had been a great beauty at the Court of King Louis at Utrecht. She was still a handsome woman in spite of the starvation which it was said she and her sisters underwent at home, thanks to the stinginess of their mother. Report said that the old Comtesse, who always went about with a black bag, used to fill it at her friends' houses with fruit, cakes, and sugar-plums, or anything else that she could "requisition." I can answer for the existence of the old lady and her bag, but never saw its contents.

Madame d'Hoguère, a Russian by birth, also deserves mention. She had been Maid of Honour to the Empress Catharine II., and had accompanied her on her famous journey, when she went to take possession of the Crimea in 1773.

Madame d'Hoguère had an old Swiss reader who lived with her, who was bound to find books as well as read them to her. Neither mistress nor companion were really literary characters, and the latter found it less trouble to read a book over again than to get a new one ; and up to the sixth time nothing was said, but at the seventh reading, the old lady would say : "*Il me semble que l'auteur se répéte un peu.*"

My great delight was when Madame d'Estorff came to tea, as was often the case. She was "*Dame du Palais*" to the old Queen, and had been with the Royal Family through all their years of exile at Hampton Court. She had many English friends and always had a great love for England, was full of anecdotes of olden days, and used to tell many of the old Electress of Hanover, the mother of George I.

As she looked very old I had a sort of floating idea
she had known her. Madame d'Estorff lived for
many years after we left the Hague, and throughout
our stay was always the same kind friend. She was
supposed to have been considerably over a hundred
years old when she died, but as no one knew any of
her family the fact could not be ascertained. I can
see her now attending regularly at our English
Service, in her close-fitting black bonnet, large white
Queen Bess frill, and long black silk cloak, and with
her black silk bag containing her books. She never
would sit on a stuffed chair or sofa. When she was
announced we always had to find a straw chair for
her, and in her own house we always found her
perched on a high wooden stool. I never saw her on
horseback, but I was told she rode a great deal when
at the Loo, even when long past threescore years
and ten.

Comtesse Henriette d'Oultremont, who afterwards
married the King, was one of the Maids of Honour.
She was said to be very clever, but I have little
recollection of her beyond that she was a tall
masculine woman.

Baron Westreenen de Tiellandt, "*premier
bibliothécaire du Roi,*" was amongst our constant
visitors. He was one of the most learned of men,
and as eccentric as he was learned. His memory
was marvellous, but as he did not wish to be thought
old, he always added after relating anything that
had happened more than ten or fifteen years
previously, " *Vous comprenez que mes parents me
l'ont raconté.*" He had a wonderfully good library,

but no one was permitted to approach it but himself and his *chasseur*, dressed in white from head to foot, for the purpose of dusting the books. He left his library to King William II., and I am sure that if his ghost ever had any hairs they must all have stood on end when in after years his treasures were shown to the public by Mr. Campbell, his successor, and handled by unlearned folk. His manuscripts were most beautiful.

Duke Bernard of Saxe-Weimar held a high military command in the Dutch army, and it was always said that had he led the troops in 1830 and 1831 instead of Prince Frederic, all might have turned out very differently. He was Governor of Ghent at that time, and the Duchess and her children were pelted with stones by the mob as they drove out of the town. The Duchess was sister to Queen Adelaide and used constantly to come to see us. The Duke was not able to carry off all his important papers before leaving, but they were saved by the cleverness of the housemaid, who collected all she could find, putting some into a waste paper basket, and others amongst the logs of wood ready for burning. When the mob, after ransacking the drawers in vain, asked her for them, she said : "Do you think the Duke would have left any papers behind but what were ready to be burned? Of course not, but he left the cellar door open and I can show you the way." This she did, and whilst the mob were getting drunk, made off with the papers. I saw her several times in later years.

Another tale of those days was told by Baron van

Q

Doorn, a great friend of ours. He held some high civil appointment at Ghent at the same time as the Duke, and received a letter from a man who was greatly alarmed by the disturbances. He wrote to say he was in terror of his life, as someone had threatened to *suicide* him. The Baron wrote back : "You need have no fears, no one but an ass would *suicide* you," after which the poor fellow felt quite safe.

When first we went to the Hague, Mr. Holworthy, the Chaplain to the Embassy, was still there, but was withdrawn soon after our arrival, although he had been there the whole time of the suspension of diplomatic intercourse.

The Foreign Office granted Chaplains to Ambassadors and Consuls, not to Ministers. This seemed wrong, but it was said to be thanks to a mistake in the Act of Parliament.

Then and for some time afterwards a clergyman came over either from Rotterdam or elsewhere to conduct the Services in a small church in the Noordeinde, which had been built for the mother of William II. Princess Mary, daughter of Charles I., and Queen Mary had also worshipped there, also Anne, daughter of George III., who married another Prince of Orange, and was Regent for her son. Her marriage was the last which took place between our Royal Family and the House of Orange. A few years after we arrived the little church was pulled down. My father tried to claim it, as having been built for our English Princes, but the claim was not allowed.

Mr. Holworthy, the aforementioned Chaplain, had a good many pensioners whom he handed over to my father's care. Most of them founded their right to be helped by the English Legation from having been left behind by the Scotch regiment. The most notable among them, was old Nancy Pant, who at one time was pew-opener in the little church. The good old woman with all her poverty had found some-one still more to be pitied than herself, a poor lad named Jacob Robinson. He was also said to have been left behind by the Scotch regiment and had been entirely dependent on the charity of the poor, sleeping first on one floor then on another, and living on scraps and often on potato peelings, until Nancy took him in. She let him sleep on her hearth, and divided her scant food with him. She also taught him all she knew, namely, to read the Bible and knit stockings, and between them they earned some honest pennies, and as he grew older he gained a trifle here and there by cleaning or helping to clean, and load and unload the canal boats. Poor Jacob was a sad object. He had a club foot, a misshappen arm, one blind eye, and not many brains, but he was honest and kept out of scrapes. He came to the Legation to weed the garden, and was even promoted to clean boots and shoes, and thus became ambitious and bethought himself of a grand speculation, nothing less than holding a booth at the fair. It answered well, because we and our young friends bought toys for it, and then bought them back again. The next thing we heard about him was that he was going to marry an heiress, and on inquiry found she had £3 10s. and *one silver spoon!* From that time all went well with him, as the heiress proved to be a good charwoman.

In olden days the English Ambassador had had a residence allotted to him, but the house had been confiscated by the French when they took possession of Holland, and instead of being restored to the English Embassy it was taken possession of by the House of Orange and used by them as the Royal Library. Lord Auckland had resided there, but I do not know who was the last fortunate Ambassador who was so sumptuously lodged. Meanwhile we poor folk could find no house at all. Month after month passed in fruitless search, and found us still at the Hotel Stanislas, a great expense and inconvenience to my parents ; but we had a very cheerful look-out on the plain with its fine lime-trees and what was called Princess Marianne's Palace. Two of the public offices, "*les ministeres des justices et des colonies*" were also on the same square ; and we were not far from the Museum where Paul Potter's famous bull, Rembrandt's wonderful and horrible picture representing the College of Surgeons attending the dissection of a dead body, as well as countless other treasures of the Dutch, Flemish and other schools were to be seen. On the lower floor of the same building was what was in those days a unique collection of Japanese curiosities. There were also sundry historical relics in the Museum, including the clothes which the favourite Dutch hero, William the Silent, wore at the time of his assassination, and a model of a house made for Peter the Great, and left behind because not paid for.

There were no very fine buildings in the town. Neither churches nor palaces were remarkable, but altogether it was a very pretty place. The houses with gable ends and *perrons* or *stoops* as they called the double flights of steps up to the house doors, the irregularity in which houses of different sizes and heights were dotted down side by side, not always in line, the beautiful avenues of lime-trees, all combined to produce a very picturesque affect.

The flower-market on the Prinse Graacht was also well worth seeing. Not only were the quays covered with flowers, but so was the canal, for there were so many flower-laden barges close together that the whole looked like a vast *parterre.*

In May the good folk at the Hague were enlivened by the annual fair. The whole town was dotted over with booths. We had a circus and Martin's wild beast show in front of our windows, and the roaring of animals at night was tremendous. The Tournooiveld was covered with what were called "Pofferje Wafel Kram," booths where peculiar kinds of cakes were made. In front of each of these erections sat a woman either in Friesland or North Holland costume, perched on a very high stool, continuing without ceasing to pour a mess of milk, flour, and melted butter upon a hot plate, indented with either round or square holes according to whether a "Wafel" or "Poffertje" cake was to be made. A "Wafel" was a kind of wafer, the "Poffertje" was pronounced by our Belgian servant Joseph, who considered it his duty to enlighten us as to the customs of the country, "*pas un manger pour son Excellence.*" One custom of the

fair I must name, that of the *bourgeoises* of the town
and the peasant girls from the neighbouring villages
hiring *beaux* to escort them to the fair. I do not
know what the exact tariff was, but a man with an
umbrella, a watch-chain and seals might command
almost any price. A soldier was also highly valued.
Occasionally two fair ladies not much blessed with
this world's goods would hire one between them, and
put up with an arm apiece.

Sometime that summer, the Prince of Orange
visited England with his two eldest sons, William,
afterwards William III. of the Netherlands, and
Prince Alexander, who died young in 1845. They
went in hopes that Princess Victoria would smile
upon them, but their hopes proved vain. It was
then also that the Marquis and Marchioness of
Londonderry came to the Hague, and Baron Mortier
and Mr. Newton Scott, the English *attaché*, both
came with their newly-wedded wives. That summer
also my father gave me a pony and took me for
many excursions in the neighbourhood. We saw
Delft with its fine old churches and the tombs of the
House of Orange. On the spot where William the
Silent was murdered, a bullet-hole is still shown
in the wall. Delft is a pretty little town, five miles
from the Hague on the road to Rotterdam, and
boasts of a military academy. Leyden, the seat of
learning, contained much that was worth seeing—the
beautiful Museum of Natural History and the
Egyptian Museum. The Japanese collection had
not yet arrived. It was collected by Doctor Siebbold,
and wonderful was the enterprise, courage and

perseverance he had to exercise. He knew it was high treason to collect or copy any Japanese curiosities, and therefore got duplicates of everything and let himself and his collection be seized, while his servant escaped to Europe with the counterpart. He was seven years in imprisonment, and suffered severely from the confinement and from having been bastinadoed. Indeed he never recovered from the effects of that torture.

We also visited the great flood-gates at Katwyk, as well as the salt-works, the salt being extracted from the sea-water by evaporation. The old Rhine flows into the North Sea at Katwyk, and in olden times that part of the country was continually under water. In the seventeenth century the channel was deepened and the great sluices were made. They were self-acting, closing and opening with the rising and falling tide. The whole time we were at the Hague the subject of making similar flood-gates at Scheveningen was being mooted. It was merely for the purpose of having an outlet for the canals ; and one large one had been completed for that purpose to within three-quarters of a mile of the sea. There it stopped, for no engineer was found daring enough to cut through the sand-hills and thus interfere with the natural sea-wall. Every now and then there is a rumour that the canal is to be completed, and Scheveningen included, but as far as I know the twentieth century finds the plan no nearer completion.

All this time we were living at the hotel, and could hear of no suitable house. However, in October someone told my mother that General and Madame Constant (she was "*Grande Maitresse*" to Princess Frederic) were about to leave their house, which had in former days been inhabited by Lord and Lady Clancarty. Our old Dr. Wachter undertook to make inquiries about it. Madame Constant was very wroth and sent word they did not mean to leave it as long as they lived. Within a very few days she was taken ill and died at the end of the week. General Constant could not bear to remain on in the house, and gave it up to us. Of course the next few weeks were very busy ones, and there was much to be done to it, and furniture to be procured. My parents took me with them to Amsterdam on a furnishing expedition, and we were in time for a great sale, where they bought some very handsome blue satin chairs and a sofa and hangings in Louis XIV. style. We visited several of the public and private galleries during our stay.

In the Museum the picture that struck me most was Vander Helst's famous "Garde de Nuit"—the figures seemed almost to walk out of the canvas. The companion picture was Rembrandt's "Meeting of the Town Council."

On our way home we stayed at Haarlem to hear the far-famed organ; often as I heard it in later years, I do not think I ever was so much struck by it as on that dark autumn afternoon. I could not believe that the *vox humana* stop was part of the instrument, and not the song of a concealed choir. The quaint little old organist looked as old as the organ, if not as the cathedral itself, and it seemed

wonderful how such an apparently feeble old man
could play with such execution. He certainly did ·
justice to his instrument, and his successor was by no
means his equal. The organ itself was said to have
come from Spain, and its twin was believed to have
been on board the Spanish Armada and destined to
be erected in England as soon as the conquest was
completed. No one knew if the tale was true. If it
were so, then there was something to be regretted on
board the Spanish Armada.

One custom which we saw at Haarlem caused us
much amusement. It was that of sticking up a piece
of lace made up in the shape of a cushion on a
house-door to note that there was an addition to the
population. The custom dated from the time of the
Spanish Dominion. In those days every house thus
adorned was exempted from any soldiers being
quartered there ; but the custom had since been
continued as an announcement of a birth. The lace
was lined with white or pink according as a son or
daughter was born to the house. At the Hague such
an event was announced by being written on the door
with a bulletin, and on the ninth or tenth day afterwards a statement appeared that the bulletin would
be stopped, and that on such and such a day
" Madame " would receive her friends. Mother, baby
and nurse were then dressed in their best, and only
married ladies were expected to attend. The nurse
made a good thing of it, as each visitor presented
her with a florin (1s. 8d. English money).

I wonder whether anywhere else the system of
perquisites is carried on to such an extent as in

Holland—one cannot dine out without giving the servant a florin.* It is even done when near relations dine with each other. The Dutch ladies when they engage servants tell them the number of dinner-parties they are in the habit of giving each year at which the servants receive gifts of money, which are deducted from their wages. The lady of the house keeps a cash-box in which all the perquisites are deposited and distributes them once a year. The *Corps Diplomatique* all agreed not to give anything in each others' houses, which I believe gave some offence.

In November of the year of which I have been speaking there occurred one of the most frightful gales I have ever witnessed, reminding me of the night at Cuxhaven. The trees in front of our windows were torn up by the roots. I saw six fall down one on the top of the other, like Prussian soldiers, as we used to say in our childhood. We had ordered the carriage to drive to Scheveningen to see the sea, but the master of the hotel came to beg we would not attempt to drive out as it would be very dangerous. Many buildings were injured, and amongst them our new house, which retarded our moving into it. That same storm nearly cost the life of Prince Alexander, the then Prince of Orange's second son. He and his eldest brother were returning from Leyden, where they went most days to pursue their studies. The road through the wood

---

* This is also the custom in some parts of Germany.—
M.M.C.

was so entirely blocked by fallen trees, that they were obliged to abandon their carriage and proceed on foot. As they reached the part of the wood nearest to the Hague, the trees were falling on all sides. The Prince's tutor, Baron Forstner, was just explaining to them that if they saw a tree falling the safest plan was to run towards the roots, when one fell from a direction from which they did not expect it. The Baron seized hold of the Hereditary Prince who was walking next to him and pulled him out of danger, but Prince Alexander was caught by the branches and thrown down. It was some time before help was obtainable to extricate him, for it had to be done by digging away the ground. At first he was not supposed to be much hurt, but after some hours fever and delirium set in and he was very seriously ill. His mother, the Princess of Orange, had spent the day in great anxiety about her sailor son, Prince Henry, who had not long entered his profession, little thinking of the danger so much nearer home.

CHAPTER VII.

MORE ABOUT THE HAGUE.

IN December we moved into our house on the Voerhout, facing the former Embassy, afterwards the Royal Library. It was well suited for a Legation, as it had five rooms *en suite* on the ground floor, one of them fifty feet long, which was used either as a ballroom or dining-room. We had a nice little garden at the back of the house, and some flags that we dignified by the name of "the terrace," which in summer were covered with pots of flowers from the market.

As soon as we were settled sundry teachers were engaged for myself and my sister. Our musicmistress was a Jewess, a fact we did not discover at first. I believe the Jews were very privileged people in Holland, more so than in other countries. They were possessed of great wealth, which however they never displayed, and a house built either by or for Jews was known by having the best rooms at the back, often behind a small court-yard. The rooms toward the street were small and shabby. I do not remember whether at that time Jews were admitted to the Chamber, but later on this was allowed.

On New Year's Eve it was the custom of the
country for all families to assemble and have an
oyster and champagne supper, and to begin the New
Year together. The *Corps Diplomatique* considered
themselves one large family, and assembled at the
Doyen's, Baron de Selby. He was the Danish
Minister and had a large house called the " Hotel
d'Espagne," from having been formerly the residence
of the Spanish Governor. Amongst others, the
cruel Duke of Alba had lived there. Behind the
house was the Jesuit Church.

One of the first parties that I remember my
parents giving that winter was a large card party ;
such was the fashion of the day. The master of the
house was expected to place the players at the
different tables. My father did so to the best of his
ability, but he saw that two old gentlemen whom he
had invited to play together looked very uncomfortable
though they made no objection and played on to the
end of the rubber. He asked his friend, Mr. Dedel,
if he knew what was the matter, and was told that
one of the partners at whist had ran away with the
other one's wife the previous year.

Nothing of note occurred that winter. The Con-
ference of London continued to sit on the Dutch and
Belgian question. The new Belgian kingdom was
not yet recognised by Russia, Austria, or Prussia, and
in consequence passports to be used by the Legation
at Brussels were signed at the Hague, as well as passports to cross the frontier, which was called Grodt
Zundel, from the name of the last village on the
Dutch border.

Many relations of both my father and my mother
came to see us in the following summer, and the
possibility of visits from relatives proved to us what a
pleasant change of residence we had made from
Stockholm. Meanwhile, we had become familiar
with many wonderful names, Botzelar Van Dobble-
dam, Nievekerk dit de Nievenheim, Schimmelpennick
Van der Oye, Van der Poll et Nymagen, and many
more. Like the Scotch the Dutch call themselves
after the names of their estates, so father, sons, and
brothers have different second names.

There were not many counts in Holland, and
generally speaking the barons claimed to be of older
and better families than the counts. The Dutch are
very proud of good old names, and intermarry a
great deal. There is a strong feeling of clanship
amongst them, and hardly any invitations are allowed
to interfere with family gatherings. They wear very
deep mourning, and the seclusion the ladies practise
lasts much longer than in England. The men do
much as they like. You can tell when you pass a
house for how near a relation the family is mourning.
The shutters are shut one, two, or three folds
according to the degree of kinship.

There was always a great deal of jealousy between
the good folks of Amsterdam and the Hague; the
first being the capital, the second the seat of government and residence of the Court. The residents of
Amsterdam sneered at the people at the Hague as
"courtiers" given to foreign ways. The dwellers at
the Hague retorted by dubbing the good folk of
Amsterdam "merchants." All the same, many

patrician families who had reason to be proud of their names and ancestry continued to reside in the capital. There is a great deal of wealth in Holland, and as the people are very frugal and with rare exceptions live within their incomes, they can generally provide liberally for their families. There is no law of primogeniture, therefore everything is equally divided, and when a man has married an heiress and survives her, he takes two children's portions. For instance, if there are four children, the fortune is divided into six, and he gets two shares. I do not know what happens if there are no children.

The death of King William IV. having released my uncle, Sir Herbert Taylor, from his long and arduous duties, he determined to go abroad for my aunt's health. Therefore my parents went over to England to take leave of them, and had a most fearful passage of fifty-two hours in lieu of the usual twenty-four. Those of us who remained behind were too near the sea not to be quite aware of the weather they were encountering, and the recollection of the storm at Cuxhaven was still too fresh in our minds for us not to be anxious. Long indeed seemed the day between their departure and the arrival of the next mail, which brought the welcome letters. What a comfort a telegram would have been!

Our parents were absent for about a fortnight, and on their return the whole society of the Hague came to condole on the death of the King and congratulate on the accession of Queen Victoria, every one saying as they came in, " *Vous avez une bien jeune Reine.*" No one then knew what a great and glorious Queen she was to be, a blessing to the whole world. " We ne'er shall look upon her like again."

That same summer we made a tour in a canal-boat. We were a large family party. My grandfather and grandmother Kennedy, and my mother's four unmarried sisters,* with my father and mother, us two girls and our governess, and Count Thun, the Austrian Secretary. We were indeed a boatful. When it rained, which it did during a great part of the time, we had only just room to sit round the cabin table. We drove to Leyden and embarked there, first making our way to Utrecht by the old Rhine, which was as calm and sluggish as any canal. Our vessel was called a *Binnenyacht* (an inland yacht), and belonged to the King. It was drawn by two horses, and was altogether very superior to the common *Trakschüyt*. We were allowed to pass other boats at a trot, and any *Trakschüyt* that we met was bound to drop her rope, and when that was not done we had a right to cut it, and very angry the good folks were when we did it. We had our French cook on board, and fared sumptuously. The chief cabin just held our party of fourteen if we sat close, and we were very merry and happy. We passed many pretty gardens and saw snug parties sitting at tea in the little *gloriettes* built out into the river. Our first halt was at Utrecht, where we slept and ascended the lofty

* Jane and Margaret died unmarried; Frances married 1845 to Baron von Weiler, Chamberlain to H.R.H. the Grand Duke of Baden; and Isabella Matilda married 1844 to Hugh Montgomery-Campbell, Royal Scots Greys.

church tower, from which the most extensive view in
the United Provinces was obtained. The Zuiderzee,
the Lake of Haarlem, and many of the seven Provinces were visible. The tower was originally
attached to the church, but in the time of King Louis
the church was partially burnt. When we saw it
there was considerable space between it and the
remainder of the church, and there was no talk at
that time of rebuilding it. A very curious feature of
this town was that a row of warehouses was built
along the side of the canal ; whilst over them were
the street and houses. The canal was of the same
level as the rest of the country, but the town was on
higher ground, and could boast of ups and downs not
to be found in other parts of Holland.

I have no recollection of being shown any palace
or building in which King Louis lived, beloved and
respected though he was by the subjects he had been
forced upon. I heard many old people say he would
most willingly have done justice to his adopted
country, and would have done much more for it
but for his brother Napoleon, and that at last he resigned his crown rather than act against his conscience.
Queen Hortense very seldom troubled Holland with
her presence. As far as I could make out no one
regretted that, and I never heard her mentioned with
any respect though in modern memoirs she is made
out a martyr.

From Utrecht we made our way to Amsterdam,
where we spent two days. We landed literally in
the Hôtel du Vieux Doelen, one wall of which is
built into the Canal. Amsterdam is called the Venice

R

of the North, and certainly is most picturesque. Our
next move was to Saardam, where Peter the Great
worked as a ship's carpenter. His shed is most carefully preserved and is now covered by a much larger
shed built by the Queen-Mother, Anna Paulowna, a
daughter of the murdered Emperor Paul of Russia,
and wife of King William II. The curious village of
Brock was not far from Saardam, and said to be
the cleanest place in the world. No animal was
allowed in the street, and as my grandfather was
too lame to walk he was put into a very small boat*
that just held him, and was propelled by a boat-hook
from the edge of the canal.

One was bound to take off one's shoes on entering
a house, and the families always lived in their cow-
houses during the winter. The principal door of the
house was never open excepting for a marriage or a
funeral, and the inhabitants all intermarried. I
suppose they thought they would have lost caste by
alliances with their neighbours.

We returned home by the end of the week well
pleased with our expedition, and our family party
dispersed in the course of the summer. Soon after
our return the Dukes of Cumberland and Cambridge
came to the Hague. The former was going to take
possession of the kingdom of Hanover, the latter was
returning to England, after giving up his post as
Hanoverian Viceroy. Both changes were consequent

---

* Another member of this delightful party told me that
Mr. Kennedy was conveyed through some of the streets of
Saardam in a wheel-barrow.—M.M.C.

on the death of William IV., the Salic Law prevailing
in Hanover. The Duke of Cambridge stayed for
several days, generally dining at our house. My
father gave one state dinner in his honour. Prince
and Princess Frederic were present. H.R.H.
refused to take the Princess in to dinner, telling my
father it was *his* duty to do so as the Queen's representative, and my mother was to go in with the
Prince. He then inquired who was the lady of
highest rank, and was told it was the wife of the
Minister of Justice, the senior Minister of the country,
but he pronounced her too old and ugly for him. My
father, sorely perplexed, said, " Then, your Royal
Highness must take your own choice," so he chose a
Comtesse d'Aubremè who had no particular rank,
but was certainly younger and much smarter than the
wife of the Minister of Justice. In the course of the
evening he repented of his breach of etiquette and
called Comtesse d' Aubremè " Madame Van Maanen,"
and so contrived to affront both ladies, the right one
because she was passed by, the other because she did
not like to be mistaken for her senior. H.R.H.
remained until two a.m. playing at whist, and then
reappeared most unexpectedly at eight o'clock for
breakfast. My father and mother, never early risers,
were still in bed, so he sent for us children, the girls
from the schoolroom, the boys from the nursery,
and we had a famous game of romps. Great was
my mother's consternation when she came down to
find what was going on, and that we, who had appeared in proper mourning at dessert, were in our
schoolroom attire of coloured cotton frocks. I
wonder if H.R.H. noticed the garments!

The old Queen Frederica died in October 1837, having long been very feeble, and in consequence there had been no receptions at the King's Court, all the *fêtes* having been given by the Princes and Princesses. The Queen was buried at Delft on the 17th of November, on a bitterly cold day, and if I remember rightly, there was no intermission of frost from that time until well on into March. It was a dreadful winter. There was not much snow, but the rivers and canals, and even the sea were frozen. We could walk on the broad band of ice on the German Ocean, and see large banks of ice floating on the waves. Our large rooms could not be kept warm, and at last we had to give up depending on English fireplaces and have stoves everywhere. They were not like those stoves in Germany and Sweden, but open, showing the fire in front, and with valves each side for hot air. They stood out some way into the rooms and the pipes went into the fireplace. I have never seen any other stoves like them. They certainly answered their purpose, throwing out a great deal of heat, and without making the rooms close. The theatre was closed during the greatest part of the winter as neither actors nor spectators could stand the cold ; but acting is not much appreciated by the Dutch. Young and old, rich and poor, men and women, all go perfectly wild about skating, and to keep either men or women servants at home during the skating season is an impossibility. One afternoon we were told we must go to the Vyvyer to see a most wonderful skater, so we all went, the whole family and Legation together, and found that this wonderful

skater was our own stable-helper. It was such a
sight on a Sunday afternoon to see all the peasants
in their best dresses skating on the meadows outside
the Rotterdam Gate. As far as the eye could see
nothing but fields of ice were visible, with booths and
gaily decorated boats like at a fair, and strings of
thirty and forty skaters sailing along as quickly as
the wind. The peasants almost always skate in
single file, holding hands behind their backs. They
begin to skate almost as soon as they can walk, and
have ample opportunity of doing so. Most winters
the frost lasts for several weeks. I was told that an
old woman of seventy had skated all the way from
Friesland to present a petition to the King. The distance was more than seventy miles. She slept one
night on the road, stayed two days at the Hague, and
then skated back again, carrying with her a stock of
skates for her grandchildren. I saw a gentleman on
the lake who had skated forty-eight miles from
Utrecht before two o'clock in the afternoon. He was
followed by his servant, also on skates, carrying a
carpet-bag slung on his shoulders. Two ladies whom
we knew skated from Amsterdam to the Hague,
thirteen miles in three hours and a half with only half
an hour to rest by the way. The Dutch wear their
skates very loosely. Good Friesland skaters only use
two pieces of tape, one is fastened across the toes, the
other across the insteps, and yet with these loose
skates they will take tremendous leaps with long
poles over every obstacle in their way.

  I think it must have been in 1838 that we heard of
Colonel and Madame de Stuers' most wonderful

escape both from shipwreck and starvation. They were sailing from Java to Amboyna, the Colonel having been appointed Governor of the latter island. They had with them their family, suite, and a number of soldiers—altogether with the crew numbering over two hundred and fifty souls; and were wrecked on the Lucifara reef, where they had no shelter at first but that afforded by one or two boats, which sufficed for the women and children. Afterwards a few huts were made from the wreck. Thus they lived for nearly five weeks, and were very short of food, though suffering even more from want of water. One boat sent to Amboyna for help was never heard of again, but the other reached Java in safety, and as the mail-boat was leaving for Holland it brought a verbal account of the disaster but no letters.

It was a fearful time of anxiety for all their relations and friends, and the greatest sympathy was felt for poor old General de Kock, Madame de Stuers' father, at that time Minister of War, a man greatly beloved and respected. For three months he was kept in uncertainty about the fate of his only daughter, her husband, and four young children. The report brought by the mail-boat was that there was little if any hope of their food holding out until they could be rescued. In addition, there was the possibility of their being attacked by Malays, who I believe were cannibals; and lastly, it was well known that but two spots on the reef remained dry at high tide, and these were of so inappreciable an extent that it was feared that a severe storm might at any time cause some or all of the party to find a watery grave. It was an

awful time of suspense, till in the month of May the
Java mail arrived.   General de Kock was with the
King when His Majesty's letters were brought in.
The kind old King sent at once for the General's
letters, but the poor man was so utterly wretched
and bewildered that he could not open them till his
royal master succeeded in rousing him to read.   It
was from Colonel Stuers announcing not only their
safe arrival at Amboyna, but that within a week of
their reaching the shore Madame de Stuers had been
safely confined of a daughter, who had been christened
Lucifara.   In after years we knew the whole family,
and that child was a martyr to asthma, whilst
Madame de Stuers was much shattered in health.
Poor General de Kock looked twenty years older
after three months of terrible suspense, and even when
he knew of the safety of his loved ones could not
bear any allusion to the subject.

Madame de Stuers' journal was most interesting ;
her brother presented a copy of it to my mother,
which I value greatly.   She, like most ladies of the
country, wrote in French, but they had many French
relations.   Paul de Kock, the novelist, was a brother
of the General.   As a rule the Dutch ladies
correspond in French and the men in Dutch.   Many
of my young friends told me they did not know how
to write their own language, but they always spoke
Dutch in the family circle.   The written and the
spoken language are quite different.   It was always
said of Queen Anna Paulowna that she spoke the
written language and that her way of speaking was
so pure and correct that she never could be taken for

a native. Queen Sophie learnt to speak more like her subjects.

Although these were my schoolroom days, as I was kept up to make tea for evening visitors, I used to hear many interesting things discussed. One evening the French Minister, Baron Mortier, and M. de Falck, the former Ambassador from the Netherlands to England, had a great discussion about the safety of the quays at the Hague. Baron Mortier contended that the canals ought to have some sort of parapet, as in such a country of fogs and ice the danger of driving into them was very great, and M. de Falck maintained that in all his long life he had never heard of an accident of the kind happening, and as M. de Falck was very positive and Baron Mortier very hot-tempered, the discussion became very warm indeed, more so than my father liked. Within a week of the discussion Baron and Baronne de Mortier were upset in the middle of the Korte Noordeinde, the broadest street in the town, and Madame de Mortier was so seriously hurt that for many days her life was in danger. Strange to say M. and Madame de Falck were also upset, not in but on the canal, for the ice bore their old-fashioned coach, coachman, and footman and horses—no light weight! They were all unhurt. The accident happened close to their own house, and Madame de Falck gave us a most amusing account of how their servants all rushed out, not exactly to their rescue, for they made up their minds that both their master and mistress were dead, but she heard them quarrelling as to which of themselves was most to be pitied for losing such kind friends.

Her maid was furious with the butler for saying that
M. de Falck would be a greater loss to him than her
mistress would be to her. At last she made herself
heard and begged they would cease quarrelling and
pull her out. I shall never understand how that feat
was performed. They were indeed clever folk who
got M. and Madame de Falck through such a small
window.

CHAPTER VIII.

EVENTS IN ROYAL CIRCLES.

THE old Queen of the Netherlands' death put everyone into mourning. At the "*cour de deuil*" held by
the Royal Family to receive condolences, all the
ladies wore black crape caps tied under their chins
and over them black crape veils, the length of their
black cloth dresses on each side reached to their
waists both before and behind. In later days this
mourning was modified. At the first "*cour de deuil*"
which I attended we were allowed to lift up our veils,
and the next time, some of the young Princesses
having come out, rebelled against caps, consequently
young ladies appeared without them and wore veils
only.

The old King kept on all his Queen's ladies, and
they had regular waitings just as when she was alive.
Baroness d'Estorff and Comtesse Goltz were "*Dames
du Palais*"; Medemoiselles Constant, Stamford, and
Heckeren-Kell, and last, though not least, Comtesse Henriette d'Oultremont, were all "*Demoiselles
d'Honneur*" in turn, three at a time. They dined
with the King at 4.30, then left to pay visits, coming
back to tea with his Majesty at eight o'clock. The

King's daughter, Princess Marianne, wife of Prince
Albert of Prussia, and her children came to stay with
him, and he was supposed to be bearing his grief as
well as possible.   He could not, however, make up his
mind to retire to the Loo, where the Queen had spent
the last days of tolerable health, therefore he spent
the summer of 1838-39 at the House-in-the-Wood,*
where is the famous *Salle d'Orange.*   This was
painted by Rubens and Jordaens and their pupils,
and was designed as a mausoleum for Prince Moritz
of Nassau,† son of William the Silent.   It represented all his feats of arms and the most remarkable events of his life.

One night there was an alarm of fire whilst the
King and Court were there.   His Majesty aroused his
daughter and her children, and it was said was seen
rushing across the court with them to the coach-house,
followed by Madame d'Estorff with his dressing-gown,
and Comtesse d'Oultremont and Comtesse Goltz with
sundry other garments, and the King was so pleased
with these attentions that after being dressed by fair
hands he suggested that they should all breakfast
together in the coach-house, which they did at his
usual hour of between four and five o'clock.   The
King always rose at four, and invariably lighted his
own fire.

By degrees we heard of the ladies being tired of
this life.   Mademoiselle de Heckeren was the first to

---

* Huis ten Bosch built in 1647 by Pieter Post for Princess
Frederick Henry of Orange, *née* Princess of Solms.—M.M.C.

† Should this not refer to Prince Frederick Henry, Prince
Maurice's brother ?—M.M.C.

leave. Her parents wanted her in Guelderland.
Mademoiselle Constant used to excuse herself from
attendance at tea, and honoured society more with
her company. Mademoiselle Stamford's health was
not good. Good old Madame d'Estorff could not
find any fault with Court life and needed no change
but that of visiting friends between dinner and tea.
Comtesse d'Oultremont needed even less change, and
soon it was whispered that the King found her very
clever and agreeable. There were also other whispers
in regard to the management of public money. It
had something to do with a commercial speculation.
I have no clear idea of the business, but later on,
when his probable marriage with Comtesse d'Oultremont was talked about and great horror expressed
at the idea of his marrying a Belgian and a Roman
Catholic, a caricature was found stuck on one of the
walls of the palace, showing Comtesse d'Oultremont
dragging him by main force to the confessional, and
he saying, "*Mais ces cinq millions. Je ne les
confesserais jamais.*"   However, attention was taken
away from the old King's doings by another royal
marriage in the family. The Hereditary Prince of
Orange, afterwards William III., was considered of
age to marry, consequently German Princesses were
ordered sea-bathing, and came to Scheveningen. It
was soon known that Princess Sophie of Würtemberg
was the chosen one. She was the second daughter of
the King of Würtemberg by his second wife, widow
of the Duke of Oldenburg, a Russian by birth, and
sister to Anna Paulowna, the Prince's mother. The
latter objected greatly to the match. She had the

greatest horror of first cousins marrying, as that was then positively forbidden by the Greek Church. It was said that the marriage was made up regardless of Princess Sophie's wishes, for that she was bent on becoming Duchess of Orleans. Her father would not give his consent to that, as he would not sanction a Roman Catholic marriage, also he looked upon the Orleanists as usurpers. The marriage took place at Stuttgart in 1839. My mother and grandmother, my aunts and I went from Carlsruhe to Stuttgart for the *fêtes* which lasted a week. The heat was terrific and made such gaiety very hard work. I must own, that although I was included in all the Court invitations I was not out of the schoolroom, and was only allowed to go to an afternoon dance at the Rosenstein about a mile from the town, and to dine once at our Minister's, Sir George Shee's, that I might see our old house ; and to witness the marriage from a gallery overlooking the chapel of the palace, in which the ceremony took place according to the Lutheran rites.* The ladies all wore trains. The Queen's train was of scarlet velvet, and thanks to the hot weather, her Majesty's face was of the same colour. The bride looked very fair and pretty. The illuminations that night were quite beautiful, and we drove round the town for some hours to see them. The palace was one blaze of light, and the crown with which it was

* Although the *Almanach* de Gotha designates the Würtemberg Court as " Lutheran," " Evangelisch " appears to be a more correct definition. Würtemberg received the Reformation in 1534, after Duke Ulrich's return, Johannes Brenz being the leading reformer.—M.M.C.

surmounted never was seen to greater advantage. The afternoon dance at the Rosenstein was a very pretty sight, the world being in duty bound to wear fresh new gowns in such broad daylight. The "*polonaise*" danced on state occasions gave a capital view of it all.

What pleased me most at the Rosenstein was seeing our favourite old servant Jean again. Though he had risen to be *Silber Diener* at Court, and was really much too grand to hand trays, he served lemonade himself, that he might see "My lady and *la petite demoiselle*," whom he had so often carried to her dancing lesson at M. St. Leon's. M. St. Leon was to the best of my belief father of the celebrated ballet-dancer of that name.

In the midst of these festivities one face looked sad and suffering. It was that of the bride's eldest sister, Princess Marie. Some said it was on account of the separation from her sister, which she felt deeply. Others declared she was already in love with Count Neipperg, whom she afterwards married. He was stepson of Marie Louise, Napoleon's second wife. It was stated that the Princesses Marie and Sophie had fixed upon him as a suitable husband for their cousin, Comtesse Marie, who since her father Duke Stephan's death, had always lived with them, and been their constant companion. Her mother not being of royal blood was not styled princess. The royal cousins commissioned a lady of the Court to see how the marriage could be brought about. In course of time she reported to them that nothing could be done, as his affections were already engaged. For a long time she would not tell them who the lady was, but at last yielding to their importunity said, " He loves you, Princess Marie." The King was very long in acceding to his daughter's wishes to marry Count Neipperg, but she became ill and miserable, and at last obtained her father's consent, and was married to the Count on the 9th of March, 1840. At first she called herself Comtesse Neipperg, left cards as such, and attended to her household like a true German *hausfrau.* Later she added "*née* Princesse de Würtemberg." The next change was to put " Princesse Marie" only on her cards, and when we saw her at Baden-Baden in 1843 she had given up visiting and gave audiences instead.

My father did not accompany us to the *fêtes* at Stuttgart, but came with us as far as Coblentz by the Rhine steamer. My uncle, Sir Herbert Taylor, had died at Rome in March 1839. His widow, with her daughter and sister, and Sir Brook Taylor, started as soon as they could on their sad homeward journey, and we agreed to meet them at Coblentz. In the days before railroads and telegraphic communication it was not easy to manage a meeting on a given day between one party from Rome and another from the Hague, therefore it was settled that whoever arrived first was to wait twenty-four hours for the other, after that each party was to go its own way, we to Carlsruhe, the Taylors to England. So well however were our movements timed that as we landed from the steamer we saw our relatives' carriage crossing the bridge of boats. Never was a *rendez-vous* better timed. We spent one day together, we juniors being taken

to see the Ehrenbreitstein fortress, and I believe we
were allowed much more liberty in wandering over it
than we should have been given under Prussian rule.
The following day we all dispersed, my aunt and her
party to travel by slow stages viâ Belgium and Calais
to England ; my father to return to the Hague, and
then to proceed to England by Rotterdam, to be in
time to receive his sister when she reached home. My
mother and we four children steamed up the Rhine
to Mannheim. Our big green coach was landed
there, and we posted on to Carlsruhe. We had with
us a Dutch footman who had never seen any rising
ground in his life, and was quite horrified at one or
two very small hills we had to pass over. When
later on we went to Stuttgart his horror at having to
get off the rumble to put on or take off the drag
knew no bounds, particularly as on one occasion he
burnt his fingers, and I believe he then and there
registered a vow that he would never leave his
beloved Holland again, where all was nice and flat
and drags were unknown. Perhaps the men of these
days, used to a brake, would be equally indignant if
they burnt their fingers with an iron shoe placed
under the wheel.

I believe it must have been in 1838 or 1839 that
an invading army passed through Holland into
Germany with no declaration of war, but only a passport given most unwittingly by my father. He was
only asked for a passport for two officers of the
English army and their suite. He was somewhat
puzzled at the number of valets they seemed to have,
and had no idea of the object in view. They were

bound for Kniphausen, which dominion had had
Sovereign Counts as rulers, for I know not how long.
The sovereignty was so small that the Congress of
Vienna forgot to mediatize it at the same time as the
other small states, therefore the reigning Count was
left in possession, and was no doubt forgotten by
most of the world. The right of the Count could
only be established by his proving the possession of
sixteen quarterings. But a day came when the
Sovereign Count forgot himself and married his cook.
He was left in peace all his life, but on his death, his
son's rights were called in question, no quarterings
being found on his mother's side. The son was
popular and perhaps few of his subjects were aware
of the flaw in his pedigree. For a time he reigned
without interference, but at last his good cousins
determined to assert their rights and to come to the
Hague and demand special passports as English
subjects. They kept everything about their plans
and so called suite very close, and my father had not
the least idea that said suite consisted of ten valiant
Irishmen, armed with pitchforks and shillelahs, all
eager to attack the Castle of Kniphausen.

The army travelled by coach, contrived to enter
the town unseen before the dawn of day, possessed
themselves of a German *leiterwagen*, a cart with sides
of upright rails, which they turned into scaling
ladders, and confident of victory they marched to
the castle and demanded admittance, knocking down
the solitary inmate, the housemaid who opened the
door. For three-quarters of an hour they kept
possession of the Castle of Kniphausen, but the

S

housemaid escaped, roused the subjects, who rose *en masse* and drove the army and valiant leaders out of the town and across the frontier. The force of arms having failed, the lawful owner had recourse to the arm of the law, and to leave no stone unturned to strengthen their right two of the brothers scoured Germany in search of wives with eight quarterings, and succeeded in their quest. The noble wife of the elder one did not do her duty in presenting her husband with an heir, but the younger lady was more fortunate and had several sons. The magnanimous eldest brother then assembled every one of his name that he could collect, and in their presence abdicated the sovereignty he never possessed, and the family went to law with the cook's son. Over and over again have I heard from the eldest brother's lips " our *procès* " (he always called it so) " is going on well. The Duke of Oldenburg protects us." Some people believed that the Duke of Oldenburg was playing a double game, and that the revenues found their way into his pocket. I have never heard of the result of the lawsuit, but perhaps Bismarck swept away the state and revenues and both sides of the question.

We returned to the Hague in the following September. My parents paid a round of country visits in Guelderland and North Holland, and I was left to complete the last year of schoolroom life. The Hague world continued much occupied with the probability of the King marrying Comtesse d'Oultremont, and the report gained ground. The latter went for a tour in Belgium and Germany, and

his Majesty travelled to Berlin.   It is said, and I
believe with truth, that he had written from there to
his sons to announce his intended marriage.   It is
certain that Prince Frederic made a hurried journey
to Berlin, and the world said that he had extracted a
promise from his father to give up all idea of
marrying his dear Henriette.   In the meanwhile,
Comtesse Hagendorf, one of the Princess of Orange's
ladies who had been visiting some friends in Belgium,
was returning by the steamer from Antwerp to
Rotterdam, and it was rumoured on board that she
was Comtesse d'Oultremont, upon which a set of low
people vowed they would throw her into the water or
tear her to pieces ; in short, do anything that would
deprive the King of the possibility of marrying a
Roman Catholic, or what was still worse in their
eyes, a Belgian.   The captain of the vessel had the
greatest difficulty in preventing them from rushing
down into the cabin to carry their threat into
execution, and was forced to make a declaration on
oath as to whom she was.

On the 10th February, 1840, the marriage of our
own gracious Queen and Prince Albert took place,
and my parents gave a grand ball in honour of the
event.   We had an illumination over the front door
(which we did not see), a room built out into the
garden, favours for all the company, and wedding
cake.   All the world, with wife, sons, and daughters,
was present, beginning with the Royal Family.   I
was presented on the occasion.   There was a sit-
down supper for everybody.   Small tables to hold
eight people each were concealed behind curtains

and at a given signal moved into the various rooms. The scene was pronounced to be like fairy-land. The ball lasted from half-past eight until past four in the morning.

I was not considered quite emancipated, but as I was presented to the Queen and Royalties, I was invited to all the Court balls and taken to them, but not to other parties until the next summer, after we had been home and I had been presented at our own Court. On returning to England on this occasion, we arrived at St. Katharine's Docks on the 6th of May. We landed in boats as was then usual, and the first boat that came off to the steamer brought the news that Lord William Russell had been found murdered in bed that morning. For many weeks no one knew who was the murderer; then his valet, Courvoisier, was suspected. This was followed by news of his confession.

How well I remember dining at Lord De la Ware's one very hot evening. The windows were wide open, and men were bawling in the street, " Confession of Curveseer (*sic!*) for the murder of Lord William Russell." I was seated opposite to Lady William Russell, his nephew's wife, who was in mourning for him. How often in later years have I thought of that scene.

I was taken to Almack's several times, but am afraid I did not appreciate that privilege properly, as I never cared much for dancing. Now that Almack's exists no longer I am glad to have taken part in what was really considered an institution in those long past days.

The first *fête* I was at was a breakfast given by Queen Adelaide in the gardens of Marlborough House. It was meant for children, but as her Majesty knew I had recently come out, she most graciously included me in the invitation to the rest of the family. Queen Victoria and Prince Albert came in and walked round the tables at which the children were seated. I can see the Queen now in a white gown, a scarlet China crape shawl, and an immense leghorn bonnet. It was in the days when those fine leghorn hats were so much thought of, and were made up into bonnets without being cut.

Two days after the *fête* in question we went to the Drawing Room then held at St. James' Palace. My mother was presented by Lady Palmerston, and she in turn presented me. I was quite enchanted with the sight, and above all with the honour of kissing the Queen's hand. We were invited to two or three Court balls, and had other invitations besides, and I had my full share of gaieties. We were dining at the Duchess of Gloucester's on the 10th of June, the day that Oxford shot at the Queen. The ladies had just gone into the drawing-room when the present Duke of Cambridge, then Prince George of Cambridge, came in with the news, which he first imparted to the Duchess in private and then to the assembled company, and nothing else was thought of or talked about for the rest of the evening. The Duchess wanted to go to the Queen at once, but Prince George had brought word from Prince Albert that he wished Her Majesty to be kept quite quiet. Next morning we learnt more from the

Duchess of Saxe-Weimar, who came to see us after
accompanying Queen Adelaide from Bushy to Buckingham Palace. Oxford was at once set down as
a madman, and no conspiracy was feared. At first
every one was anxious as to the effect it might have
on the Queen, as it was said that she had completely
broken down when she reached the Duchess of
Kent's house in Belgrave Square. She had driven
there at once, her first idea being that her mother
should see her safe and sound, ere the news of the
attempt reached her.

In August of that same summer Louis Bonaparte,
afterwards Napoleon III., made his famous expedition to Boulogne with his tame eagle and small
following. He was laughed at throughout Europe
for his wild-goose-chase. I doubt whether any one
at that time foresaw his future career or gave him
credit for any cleverness or common-sense. That
year we very nearly went to war with France on the
subject of Mehemet Ali. "*La Question Orientale*,"
as it was called, was for long a vexed question.
Those who were so distressed at the poor reception
given to the Viceroy of Egypt when the Sultan was
in London in 1867, had better read up the annals of
that year and see how a difficult matter had to be
settled, and how the treaty of 1841 would have been
violated had the Viceroy been put in any way on a
par with his Sovereign, the Sultan. A ruler the
Viceroy certainly, but the name told its own tale
although the dignity had been made hereditary.

When we returned to the Hague late in August,
things were still in a very unsettled state in the East,

though I believe the fear of war with France was at
an end. On the 24th of September the Prince
of Orange was born, or rather, the son of the
Hereditary Prince. It was a subject of great
rejoicing in the country, besides being a very rare
event in the Orange-Nassau family to see four
generations. They are said to be a short-lived race,
very few either of the Orange branch or that of the
Dukes of Nassau attaining to the age of sixty.
Thanks to the new little Prince and Mehemet Ali,
the Comtesse d'Oultremont was in some degree
forgotten, and most people believed that the King
had yielded to his son's entreaties and given up
the idea of marrying her ; he having returned after
his travels to his usual mode of life. But in October
he astonished the world by going to the Loo for the
first time since the Queen's death, taking with him
almost all his suite, ladies and gentlemen. The day
after his arrival he sent for his Ministers, his two
sons, and his eldest grandson, assembled the whole
party in the dining-room, and then and there,
without giving notice to a single soul, announced his
intention of abdicating in favour of the Prince of
Orange. The deed was drawn up and the whole
business completed the same day, October 7th, 1840 ;
and on the following day everybody excepting the
ex-King and his Court returned to the Hague. He
reserved to himself the title of King and Count of
Nassau, and kept for his own use the Royal Palace
at the Hague and the House-in-the-Wood and the
Loo. The reason for his abdication was declared to
be to enable him to avoid inconvenient questions on

the subject of national finance. I give this for what it is worth. The first time the ex-King appeared in public after his abdication was at the christening of his great-grandson in the Kloster Kerk, and as far as I remember it was the last time he took part in any Court ceremony. All family gatherings were held by him in the Palace. Every Sunday at half-past four we used to see various Court carriages taking guests to the Noordeinde Palace for dinner.

The christening of the little Prince was a pretty sight, and our curiosity was soon relieved as to which of the two Kings would take precedence. The old one had no idea of anyone passing him, but rushed first into the church, and then in double quick time up the steps to the platform where the Royal Family were to sit. The King and Queen followed hand in hand, and then the rest of the Royal Family. The little hero of the day, smothered in lace and satin, was carried by the *Grande Maitresse* to the Princess of Orange. I do not remember any particular *fêtes* in his honour, but his mother was far from strong, and in addition, the Coronation and attendant festivities were approaching.

The Coronation took place on the 1st of December. The whole of the *Corps Diplomatique*, the Dutch Ministers, and officials of all degree, in short, the greater part of society went from the Hague to Amsterdam for the occasion. I do not remember that any special Ambassadors were present, but all the Foreign Ministers of the time were specially accredited for the occasion. The first sight was the entry into the town of the King and Queen and Princesses. The King and Prince were on horseback, surrounded by the *État Major* and various other dignitaries. William II. was well advised to ride, he always looked so well on horseback. But his riding on this occasion was found fault with by many, who said it looked as if he were commanding the escort of the Queen's carriage. I believe that Princess Sophie, the Queen's only daughter, accompanied her, and that the other Princesses of Orange preceded the Queen and received her there.

The town was most tastefully decorated with flags and evergreens, and the reception given by the citizens of Amsterdam was most royal and loyal, and nothing could be more gracious than the way in which both the King and Queen acknowledged the hearty welcome they received.

That evening the Royalties remained quietly at home, and we were invited to a regular Amsterdam party, the dullest entertainment I ever was at in my life. The room was crowded with whist tables, and the only non-players were a girl I did not know and myself. We had a very small space to stand on with our backs to the wall. I thought the evening interminable, and I have no doubt that my companion was of the same opinion, although perhaps that style of amusement was not so new to her as it was to me.

CHAPTER IX.

COURT FESTIVITIES.

THE ceremony of the Coronation was here called the "Inauguration," as no crown was used. The King only took the oath to govern according to the Fundamental Law, which it took Baron van Doorn, the President of the Council, one hour and a half to read aloud.

In consideration of the very cold weather and great size of the church (which there was no means of heating) the Queen had given leave to all the ladies to wear high dresses and long sleeves, in spite of their trains, which of course could not be dispensed with. Her Majesty also announced her own intention of being covered up, so there was to be no "*luxe d'epaules*," as we called it. Of course the combination became a great puzzle. I know it was so to my mother, both on her own account and on mine, for our dresses were all ready when the order came out, and it was not easy to match her silver tissue nor my pink silk. Then came the puzzle about heads, for the prejudice existed then and for some time afterwards that heads ought to be protected both against cold and heat, and the valuable

discovery had not yet been made that a rose and
a yard of ribbon about an inch wide were sufficient
protection for women's heads under a burning sun,
or in a bitter wind with the thermometer down
at zero. So the puzzle was great as to what to
do with the young unmarried ladies. Our elders
had turbans, toques, and all sorts of shaped dress
hats wherewith to cover their heads and display their
diamonds, but we girls were decidedly left out in
the cold on such occasions.

My mother and the Court hairdresser between
them contrived a most wonderful erection for me
of silver and pink satin ribbon. It covered my head,
hung over my ears, and between ribbon and silver,
flowers and loads of hair, I have no recollection of
any cold. The gentlemen wore wigs. We left our
various hotels between eleven and twelve, each
Legation in two carriages, and with all the state they
could muster, but I believe England alone boasted
of powdered coachmen and footmen. I do not
think that custom existed elsewhere. The *Corps
Diplomatique* occupied tribunes at the left of the
throne opposite the Queen and Princesses. Of
course we were there before their arrival, and in time
to admire the stately Queen Anna Paulowna as she
entered with her train borne by two pages. I do
not think I ever saw anyone walk as well as herself.
She was tall, had a good figure, and at that time
also beautiful fair hair. She had more diamonds
than any Princess in Europe, with the exception of
the Empress of Russia. All her jewels were said
to have been lost by the burning of the palace at

Brussels, therefore the Emperor of Russia, the King of the Netherlands, and her husband combined to replace them, and afterwards most of the lost stones were picked up amongst the ruins. The following year again all her jewels were stolen, and once more replaced as before, and within eighteen months the stolen gems were found in New York, and recognised at a sale by Madame Huygens, the wife of the Dutch Minister. Though the Queen wore a great number of diamonds at the Inauguration they had not as much effect there as at the ball, her dress being of cloth of silver and her train of cloth of gold, both deeply trimmed with ermine. The Princesses of Orange, Sophie, Frédéric and her daughter, Princess Louise (afterwards Queen of Sweden), who followed Queen Anna Paulowna, were also resplendent with diamonds and gold and silver. On the entrance of the royal party, the cheers were most enthusiastic, though nothing to those that greeted the King himself. He came on foot from his palace under a canopy borne by six generals. He wore his mantle of state over his uniform and the cap of maintenance, as it was called, on his head. This latter was a headgear he either invented or introduced, and which he always wore to the end of his life—a high, blue cloth cap, with a broad gold band. He looked so well, so dignified, and so chivalrous that everyone was moved when he took the oath to the Constitution, after the reading of the Fundamental Law.

This was followed by the taking of oaths of allegiance by his sons and brother, as well as by

the Ministers and officials of all kinds. Afterwards
came a sermon in Dutch from the Court preacher,
and a prayer, and then the King left the church,
returning as he had come, under his canopy. His
departure was the signal also for the Queen,
Princesses, and everyone else to leave the sacred
building.

There were two state representations at the
theatre on the occasion of the Inauguration, one in
French, the other in Dutch. In the evening the
whole town was beautifully illuminated. The
inhabitants of each street and quay agreed to
illuminate on the same plan, and as all lights were
reflected in the canals, the effect was splendid. We
walked round the town, my mother with Sir William
de Tuyll, my father and I following, avoiding the
streets through which the royal procession passed,
and so seeing everything without inconvenience.
Other people, more venturesome, were not so
fortunate, and several were crushed to death. A
few days before the Inauguration a stranger called
at a hatter's and ordered twelve cloth caps. They
were to be all exactly like, and he came for them
himself when ready. Being pleased with the design,
the tailor made himself a thirteenth cap of similar
design and wore it on going out to see the
illuminations. To his surprise, on returning home,
he found his pockets filled with purses and watches.
He took these all to the police, and learnt from them
that the ordered caps were intended to enable a
gang of thieves to recognise each other.

The ball with which the festivities wound up was

the finest of the kind I ever saw. It was given
in the magnificent *Salle de Justice*, which was a
hundred feet high and a hundred feet long, and
lighted entirely with wax candles. The *Salle de
Justice* was the building used generally as the Town
Hall. When we entered the ball-room and walked
up behind the Court, through rows of well-dressed
ladies and glittering uniforms, I thought the sight
most magnificent. But those already in the *Salle*
said the entrance of the Court was finer still. The
Diplomacy and Ministers of the country had already
been received in another room, and the King had
amused himself as he generally did by making
remarks on the ladies' dresses. His Majesty told
my mother, who was in white and gold, that she
appeared as Queen of Golconda.

After ten days of festivities we returned to the
Hague, where there was a Royal entry as at
Amsterdam. The next day we all attended a Court,
which was held that afternoon. We assembled in
an outer room, until it was announced that the King
and Queen had taken their places in the Throne
Room. We were then all marshalled in, in order of
seniority according to the rules of the Congress of
Vienna. First came the Diplomacy, headed by the
Doyen and Doyenne, Baron and Baronne de Selby.
The Russian Minister, Count Lottum, came next,
but as his wife was not there, my mother was next
to the Doyenne ; so it came to pass that I was
separated from her. All stood in their appointed
places, the Diplomacy on the right of their Majesties,
the Dutch Ministers on the left hand. I was to

stand with Mademoiselle de Selby, daughter of the
Danish Minister, whom I always looked upon as a
protectress during those early days, when I used to
be so alarmed by the foreign custom of girls not
remaining under their mother's wing. Ella de Selby
was a great stickler for etiquette, and had that day
warned me that we daughters of Ministers were to
pass before the wives of the Secretaries of Legation.
These ladies, I believe, had no intention of taking
the lower place.   I do not know exactly what
happened, but in the doorway I was seized by my
friend Ella, that I might pass on with her in front
of a Madame Pelaprat, who meant to go before us.
Both were much bigger women than I was, and
each pulled as hard as they could, and what with
my train to look after and my fright, I went the
wrong way, and when able to look up found myself
at the head of the column of ladies of the country,
which was quite incorrect.   I was consequently the
first person whom the King addressed when he
started on the round of the room, and he said,
"Young lady, I should like to know how you got
here ? "   I answered, " Sire, Madame Pelaprat pulled
so hard."   He was so much amused, that for a long
time after he used to say, " Charlotte, tell me, what
has Madame Pelaprat done to you lately ? "   N.B.—
He could not bear her.   But my troubles were not
over, when the King and Queen, after going their
round, had returned to their places, for thanks to
where I was placed I was the last person to get
out of the room, which I had to do backwards along
two sides of the room, with my train on the floor

behind me. The Queen, when she saw how frightened I was, sent me word I had done so most beautifully.

I think those Courts abroad much more alarming than English Drawing Rooms, as you have to place yourselves in full view of the Royalties, and then wait until they come round to address you individually.

We had a very gay winter—gala, theatres and state balls at the King's and the Princes of Orange and Frederic, as at most of the Legations, several at the Dutch houses and at the Casino, all attended by the Court. Many of the balls were given for Princess Sophie, the King's only daughter, and a very great favourite with everybody. She was afterwards Grand Duchess of Saxe-Weimar. On the occasion of the King's ball we were always expected to be in our places in the Throne Room before 8.30, and had a good hour to stand before we followed the Royal Family into the ball-room. Many found the custom very tiring, and eager dancers thought it very tiresome, but I belonged to neither of those weary ones. I was always great at standing, thanks to my early training, and even now I can do so for a time that tires many better walkers than myself. Talking of standing, we young ones had a great deal of that to do, not only at Court, but in general society. We never spoke to an elderly lady except standing, unless she bid us sit down. There certainly was more respect for age in those days than exists now in England, and on that point I think those good old times very superior to ours. Again in that winter the report came that the King was going to marry the Comtesse d'Oultremont, and Prince Frédéric rushed off to Berlin to try to stop the marriage.

One fine day came a letter from the Comtesse to Lady Christina de Ginkell, a very well-known and remarkable person in the Hague society, to tell her she had no idea of marrying the King. Lady Christina, overjoyed at such good news, drove round the town to repeat the information. It turned out that on the very day the letter was written the wily countess got into her carriage and drove off (I think) to Aix-la-Chapelle, and was married morganatically to his Majesty on the 16th of February, 1841. Of course she became more unpopular than ever, and public feeling rose high.

When the King signified his intention of bringing his bride to the Hague everyone was furious, and no one knew how he would be received, but once more he listened to his son's remonstrance and stayed at Berlin ; not for long, however, for one dark night a carriage drove up to the palace, and the King and his new wife stepped out unannounced.

There was no one there to receive them excepting the women of the fish-market. It was said that two stalwart females lifted him out of the carriage and embraced him, saying in Dutch, " It is our old William." After that I think H.M. the Count of Nassau gave some family dinner-parties, but he did not entertain otherwise. Husband and wife were constantly to be seen walking out together, generally on the road to Scheveningen, which had a broad

T

pathway; she tall and erect, he short and bent, always holding his hat in both hands behind his back. I never saw him with his hat on his head. His Majesty wore a blue coat with brass buttons, and his gloves were almost invariably green. A chariot and four horses always followed along the road close behind them. The old King died in December 1843, I believe, at Berlin. I never heard much more of the Countess of Nassau, as she was styled, for she did not return to Holland. I do not remember in what year she died, only that it was before we left the Hague that we were told she had left a large fortune to her brother. I have no doubt she profited largely by the fortune the King had accumulated, as he died enormously rich. He was the first of his race who attained the age of seventy.

It must have been in 1840 that we went to three fancy dress balls in honour of Princess Sophie. The Princess had a quadrille of her own for the girls who had just made their *début*. I was one, and we were all dressed in costumes taken from "*Le lac des Fées*," an opera which had just come out, and was I believe by Auber. We wore very full white net dresses with several skirts, belts of gold, and wreaths of roses and stars. A special dance was invented, and led by M. Charles Selby, Danish Secretary, with Mademoiselle Barre. The Princess and her brother, Prince Henry, followed. Two Demoiselles de Nagell, Mademoiselle Arriens, and myself were the *débutantes*, and two Court ladies, Mesdemoiselles de Hagendorf and von Cappellen, made up the number. The gentlemen were dressed in black velvet, and represented students. The Princess was allowed as a great favour to have a table for her own quadrille instead of supping with the Royal Family. The other balls were repetitions of each other.

We received every evening when we were at home, excepting on Sunday, and on that day an exception was always made for the Duchess of Saxe-Weimar, Queen Adelaide's sister, who was the kindest and most gracious of friends to us. She dined most Sundays with the Court, and then spent the time between dinner and tea at our house. I have lately found an interesting account of the Duchess' most unpleasant adventure in 1838. She was on her way from the Hague to Rome to visit her eldest son, Prince William, who was very ill there, and who died not very long afterwards. She had with her, her youngest sons, Prince Hermann and Prince Gustavus, and her daughters, Princesses Anna and Amélie, both mere children, in addition to a tutor for the young Princes and Mademoiselle Houldi, governess to the Princesses, who wrote the account of the adventures to my mother. The party travelled in several carriages and had passed Besançon, when they were stopped by mounted *gendarmes* and bidden to return to the town, from which orders had been sent to arrest the Duchess, supposing her to be the Duchesse de Beira. The description of the two Duchesses was so different that at last the travellers were allowed to go on to Arbois, where they were to change horses and where a great consultation took place. It ended in their having to appear before the *Préfet*. An immense crowd had assembled rejoicing at the idea of the capture it was hoped had been made. The *gendarmes* treated the Duchess with much indignity, insisting on her leaving the carriage to appear before the *Préfet* alone, but her sons' tutor managed to follow her in spite of them. The discourteous official kept her Highness waiting for a long time as a prisoner, and even after he had recognised his mistake there was a further delay before he granted her a safe conduct as far as Lyons, to allow of her appearing before his colleague in that city and being honourably acquitted. The result was that the Duchess was very seriously ill when she reached Avignon, and unable to proceed. I found Mademoiselle Houldi's letter giving an account of all this a very short time ago and sent it to Prince Edward of Saxe-Weimar—now alas! no more—who told me he was glad to have it, and would forward it to his brother, Prince Hermann, to be placed with the family archives. I also learnt from him that the Duchesse de Beira was the wife of Don Carlos, the would-be king of Spain. I am glad to say Louis Philippe made an ample apology to the Duchess, and administered a very severe reprimand to the officious *Préfet*.

In 1842 we learnt that Princess Sophie's marriage with her first cousin, the Hereditary Prince of Saxe-Weimar, was arranged; another grief to Queen Anna Paulowna, who, as has been said, was much opposed to the marriage of first cousins.

We also heard that the Duke of Orleans had been

killed by a fall from his carriage. Strange to say the report was current at the Hague two days before it was known by the French Minister, who, when asked about it, denied the fact and said : " *Ce sont des bruits de bourse.*" The news was supposed to have been brought either by pigeon-post or semaphore, of which latter there was a line of communication between the Hague and Antwerp.

At the time of his accession or inauguration, William II. was most lavish of honours and decorations, and one evening we were much amused at the theatre by a well-known French actor stepping forward on the stage, coming as close as he could to the Royal box in which the King was seated, and saying, " *J'ai bien chanté une romance, et pourtant on ne m'a pas décoré.*" A roar of laughter sounded through the house, and I have little doubt that the King joined in it.

I cannot remember whether it was at that time or later that a terrible accident happened whilst a sea-wall was under repair. The sea rushed in, and most of the men employed in the work were drowned. The very shy wife of a newly-appointed Governor of the Province in which the disaster occurred went to the Queen with a petition for help for the survivors and said, " *Votre Majesté, il y a dixsept hommes de noyés, et ils ont laissé trente-six veuves.*"* I conclude the poor lady was covered with confusion, and the

* This recalls the story of one of the Kings of France on one occasion receiving the reply, " *Majesté votre cire est bien bonne,*" instead of " *Sire, Votre Majesté est bien bonne.*"— M.M.C.

Queen must have been clever if she kept her countenance.

Princess Sophie's marriage became an all-engrossing topic. She was the pet of not only the Royal Family but I may say of the whole society at the Hague, and of all who knew her. She was not pretty, but very graceful and pleasing. We seven ladies of her quadrille set to work on a sevenfold screen as a wedding present. It was made in cross-stitch on silk canvas, and I found it very hard to get my fold finished in time. I hope it was a success. At all events we received very kind and gracious thanks for it. The *trousseau* was exhibited to all the town, and was very beautiful.

The wedding took place on the 8th October, 1842. First the civil marriage was solemnized in the state ball-room, then the religious ceremony took place in the picture gallery, where we Diplomatists were assembled to await the bridal party. The happy pair came in first. The Princess wore cloth of silver with a small ducal crown of diamonds on her head, and her train was borne by six bridesmaids clad in white satin. The service was performed in the Dutch language by the Court Chaplain, who gave a long address, and it was arranged that as soon as this was ended the Princess should turn and embrace her father-in-law, and her husband was to kiss the Queen's hand and embrace the King. The dear little Princess however was much too overcome to attend to any orders of the Master of the Ceremonies, she simply threw herself into her mother's arms and sobbed aloud. The Queen coaxed, petted and patted her for

a long time before she would turn to the Grand Duke
of Weimar, who stood behind looking sorely puzzled
what to do.   Everyone present was deeply touched
by the pretty scene.   When the Princess had
recovered, the cortége left the church in the same
order as it had come, and we retired.   I was told that
when the time came for the young couple to leave
the King and Queen between them had to carry her
to the carriage, she clung so tightly to them.   I stood
on the balcony to see her pass, she knew me, and
waved her hand to me.   A house was bought for her
near ours, and called " *Le Palais Weimar.*"   Prince
Maurice, the Princess of Orange's second son, was
born in 1843, and the ex-King died in December of
the same year.

In 1844 we went to England and did not return
until the summer of 1845 ; my father having been ill,
was advised to winter at Bath.   On our return to the
Hague, we found the world much occupied by Princess
Marianne's affairs.   She was endeavouring to be
divorced from Prince Albert of Prussia.   To this the
King of Prussia would not give his consent, and her
children were taken from her and were brought up by
the King and Queen of Prussia.   The Princess
remained on at the Hague, her father having given
her an apartment in his palace.   She walked about
the wood and all public places (even in the depth
of winter), dressed in white from head to foot, to
prove her innocence.   She looked most peculiar in
the snow ; a tall woman with a sallow complexion.
Her own family, and especially the Queen, did not at
all patronise her, and in course of time the King of
Prussia withdrew all her Court.

It must I think have been in January 1846 that the New Year's ball, generally given about the middle of the month at the Palace, took place a week earlier than usual. No reason was given, but it was known that Princess Marianne was ill, and it was surmised that as the Queen did not wish her to be present she had hurried it on, whilst H.R.H. was safe in bed. The ball took place, and in the middle of it the Princess entered, covered with small-pox. She walked straight up to the Queen, who put her hands behind her back, the King shook hands with her, and the general consternation was great. My mother told me, as I believe most other mothers told their daughters, to run as fast as possible to the farthest room that could be reached. The Princess noticing the general stampede followed, and shook hands with as many girls as she could find, myself among the number. Fourteen hundred people caught small-pox, including the King and several Princesses, but mercifully there were no deaths and very few serious cases.

Later on H.R.H. went to the Holy Land, accompanied by the old pastor who had prepared her for Confirmation. She lived to an extreme old age, and died on the Lake of Como in the Villa Carlotta, which was so called after her eldest daughter, who married a Prince of Saxe-Meiningen, and died young. It was always said that after the divorce her husband, Prince Albert of Prussia, married Fanny Essler, the famous ballet-dancer, but I have not been able to authenticate that fact. I know that he distinguished himself among the many brave soldiers of the Franco-German War.

A fresh trouble was hanging over the Royal Family. Prince Alexander, the King's second son, a very fine young man, born in 1818, was evidently failing in health. Whether he had been injured in any way by the tree that fell on him, or whether he had done harm to himself by trying to reduce himself to jockey weight, I know not, but as he was six feet four inches in height, the latter experience would have needed most vigorous treatment. Often when dancing with him I had noticed how breathless he was, and how the perspiration stood out in beads on his forehead, and I wished I had the courage to beg him to stop. He got rapidly worse, and it was settled that he was to be sent to Madeira. We had a most touching account of the last sad gathering of the Royal Family to take leave of him. They all assembled in prayer, the Court Chaplain delivered a short discourse and blessed him, and then, supported on the arm of his brother, the Prince of Orange, afterwards William III., he was taken to the carriage to drive to Rotterdam and embarked, never to return. Queen Adelaide was at Madeira at the same time, and was as kind as possible to him and a great comfort, and Sir David Davies, her physician, attended him when he became worse. The Dutch Court physician was sent out to him, but could do nothing more. The poor young Prince was so happy to see his old friend and threw himself into his arms like a child.

CHAPTER X.

THE YEAR OF REVOLUTIONS.

MADAME ADELAIDE DE FRANCE, Louis Philippe's sister, died on the 31st December, 1847 ; and as soon as the event became known everyone feared real troubles for the Orleans Family, if not for all France. Madame Adelaide was known to have a great and wise influence over her brother ; indeed, was styled the " Man " of the family, and it was supposed afterwards that had she survived the disturbance of February 1848, would have gone very differently.

For some time in February we heard of the great state of uneasiness in France, but whenever the *Chargé d'Affaires*, Comte de Breteuil, was asked about the disturbances he invariably said, " *Ce sont des-bruits de bourse, tout va bien.*" He said so to me at a dinner-party one Saturday evening, and at five o'clock on the Sunday morning a carriage drew up at our door, and M. de Breteuil stepped out to call up my father and tell him that Louis Philippe and all the Royal Family had fled, and Paris was given up to mob rule, fire, and sword.

Madame de Bussièsse, wife of the French Minister at the Hague, who had himself already started to

take up a new appointment at Naples, had left for
Paris ere the bad news came, or I think my father
would have tried to persuade her to remain at the
Hague. Lord and Lady Ely who were there had
left their little girl, Lady Marion Loftus, at Brussels,
and my father advised Lord Ely to fetch her, as it
was feared the French evil doings would at once be
copied by Brussels. Every one was disturbed in mind
and anxious. Holland suffered less than most other
continental nations, but even at the Hague we had
several alarms from the mob that paraded the streets
on many successive nights. One evening we were at
a large party at Baron von Doorn's, President of the
Council, a strong Conservative, and therefore
obnoxious to the mob. He was a great friend of
ours, and as he did not think it right to put off his
party, we of course thought it right to attend. We
did our best to appear happy and comfortable, but all
ears were strained to hear if a stone were thrown at
the window, which would have been the signal that
the house was to be attacked. Mercifully however
the mob took another line of march, although they
came very near. I believe it was that night they
entered all the bakers' shops, seized all the loaves of
bread, and left the money for what they took on the
counters of the shops they had ransacked. Another
night my sister and I went to the theatre with
Comtesse Bille Brahe, daughter of Baron Selby, the
ex-Danish Minister, the wife of his successor. We
had not been at the theatre very long when a young
man belonging to the Diplomacy came in and said to
Comtesse Bille Brahe, " I suppose you will not stay

for the second piece, you will not like it." She
answered, " My young friends and I seldom come out
together, so we mean to enjoy ourselves and stay to
the end." Count Sievers then said, "You cannot
stay, the mob is assembling in the street, and you
must get home as fast as you can." Of course we
acted on his advice and got into the carriage as soon
as it came. It was our carriage, but no one had told
my father and mother of the disturbance, for when
they saw us arrive sooner than they expected they
were much astonished. It was well that we got home
safely. Within another half-hour the mob rushed
past our house in all sorts of attire, with torches and
lanterns, and yelling and screaming, but they passed
us by and did no harm anywhere.

The following night a concert was going on a very
few doors from our house, when the mob broke in
and demanded that the musicians should accompany
them round, the town. The leader, or *Maitre de
Chapelle*, as he was called (M. Lübeck), wisely assented
at once, saying that the gentlemen with wind instru-
ments would be very happy to go with them on
two conditions, one, that they should only serenade
the Royal Family, the other that he should lead
them. Of course, having such a well-known,
highly respected man to head them was a great
gratification.

It was from M. Lübeck himself that we received
this account next morning, when he came to give my
sister her music-lesson. He said he saw at once that
the only safe proceeding was to act promptly, so
giving the musicians directions to make as much

noise as they could regardless of time and tune, he put himself at their head waving a white pocket-handkerchief on his *bâton*. The mob was thus led through the narrowest streets (and some were mere passages), which made it difficult for them to follow. They were chairing the editor of a newspaper whose weight of body was greater than that of his virtues. In the struggle to follow the band they let him fall, and as M. Lübeck took care to give them no time to pick him up he was left in the mud to get up as best he could.   M. Lübeck told us he felt sure that had he given the mob time to stop and to take breath they would have begun to throw stones at the windows, and then it would have been well-nigh impossible to have controlled them and to have prevented the work of destruction.

The next day it was believed that another demonstration had been planned by King Mob, but the news came of the death of Prince Alexander, the favourite son of the King, at Madeira.   The burgomaster put up placards containing the news, and the populace said, "Our King is in such grief, we will keep the town quiet," and not a soul stirred that evening.   How well it spoke both for King and people!   The burgomaster told us later that he had been very much alarmed.   He thought the aspect of the mob so threatening, being largely composed of women, but felt reassured as to the personal safety of the Royal Family on seeing a considerable body of "*Turftregars*"* amongst the crowd.

* Turf carriers.

This trade was hereditary, and as a body the " *Turf-tregars* " had been known throughout history to be devoted adherents of the House of Orange.

It was a great comfort to all to feel that for a time at least we were safe from mob rule. Later on, it was whispered that everything had been prepared for the flight of the Royal Family, horses and carriages being kept ready night and day. I think many alterations were made in the constitution at that time. The King also made many concessions. All the old Ministers retired, and quite a different class of men came forward. Our particular friends, the good old Dutch families, retired in a great measure from society, and we had to put up with far less congenial company.

We were very thankful that our friends from Russia and Prussia were at least left to us. When M. de Liebe was sent to the Hague by the Frankfort Diet, Comtesse Königsmark said, " *Ç'est notre maître a tous.*" The said M. de Liebe on being presented to the King showed either his independence or impudence by going to his audience in plain clothes and dirty boots. I wonder what good or harm that Diet of Frankfort did. In some way or other it prepared the way for the aggrandizement of Prussia. Probably the surrender of the command of the small armies of the minor states was either discussed or settled by the Diet. I believe the prime mover of that cession was Duke Ernest of Saxe-Coburg, Prince Albert's eldest brother.

Heinrich von Gagern was a great man for a time. His brother, General von Gagern, I have often seen ;

he was in the army of the King of the Netherlands,
and William II. was fond of him, as an old brother-in-
arms. One day in 1848, when all Germany was still in
a very disturbed state, I sat next to him at a dinner-
party at M. Borel de Hegeland's. My father had
gout and could not be present. After. asking after
him and inquiring why he was not there, the General
said, " Will you give him a message from me ? " I
answered, " Certainly." " Then tell him that within a
very short time he will hear strange things about me."
When I told my father he did not attach much
importance to the message, as he, the General, was
such an odd, absent-minded man ; but the next day
there was a hue-and-cry throughout the town as to
what had happened to General Gagern. The King
was most unhappy, and all the more so when it was
found that from that very dinner-party he had started
for Heidelberg, where he had joined the rebels, *die
Freiwilligen*, as they were called, or volunteers.
These volunteers were insurgents, and the General
was killed in an encounter with the regular army. I
believe the King was rather relieved than otherwise
on hearing of his sad fate, for had he been caught
and brought back he must have been shot as a
deserter.

One of my mother's younger sisters lived at
Heidelberg ; her husband was superintendent of
some part of the Baden railways which belonged to
the State. Baron von Weiler had assisted the flight
of the Grand Ducal family, and thus made himself
obnoxious to the populace. He happened to be out
one day when the rebels came to his house and

demanded his person. My aunt, a brave little woman, stood on the staircase and assured them he was not at home. The armed men then said they would search the house. She answered, " The leaders may do so." Ten men then stepped forward, and said they were leaders. " That cannot be," she answered, " who ever heard of ten leaders to such a small troop. Two of you may search the house in which there are only women ; if more attempt to do so you will be branded as cowards for the rest of your days." My aunt gained her point through her courage and two men satisfied themselves that the Baron was not there. When he came home in the evening and heard the tale, he did not think it safe for his wife to remain at home that night, fearing the mob might return to revenge themselves on her. So she was sent off to Frankfort to her friends,* the Von Orlichs, to wait until things became quieter. That same day there were disturbances at Frankfort and Baron von Orlich sent his wife for safety to his friends, the Von Weilers, at Heidelberg. It was some time before either lady was able to return to her own husband and home.

Germany was for long in a very disturbed state, some grandees flying when none pursued ; but the two old Kings of Würtemberg and Hanover stood firm, and the young Emperor of Austria showed great courage, whilst in Belgium, King Leopold

* Baroness von Weiler eventually took refuge at Frankfort at the house of Lord Cowley, the British Minister. I have from her a tiny egg-cup, marked " from Freddie Wellesley, 1848." Lady Cowley's little son had given her this useful present on her flight !—M.M.C.

proved himself as wise as ever. The first German Emperor, then Prince of Prussia, came to the Hague as a fugitive. It was the only time I ever saw him. I believe he returned very soon to his native land to become Regent for his eldest brother, the King, who was failing in mind and body. The fugitives in whom I took most personal interest were Prince and Princess Metternich. They stayed with Count Esterhazy, the Austrian Minister, who, being a bachelor, asked my mother to do the honours for him on most evenings. I used to accompany her and make tea.

The Prince and Princess had terrible experiences in their flight, having travelled sometimes in a horse-box, at other times in a carriage all packed in matting to make it look as if freshly dispatched from a carriage maker's, at other times in a horse-box, marked " empty." The Princess, who gave us the account, said she never felt safe until she got into Holland, and at their first halting-place over the frontier, the waiter while serving them at dinner said, "You have come from Germany. Have you seen anything of that monster Metternich ? I wish I could catch him and kill him!" Very pleasant hearing it must have been for them. The Princess was in a state of wrath and excitement not to be described. She never ceased talking of her husband's wrongs and the ingratitude of his country. The Prince on the contrary was perfectly calm and said nothing on the subject. I was much struck by his likeness to the Duke of Wellington, only he was on a rather larger scale. It was meet they should resemble each other,

U

for they were called Napoleon's antidotes, and certainly those two great men combined to confound the other's knavish tricks and help if not cause his downfall. When we were visiting Brussels in 1850, we went to call on Prince and Princess Metternich, who were then living there. The Princess on receiving us said the Prince will soon be with us, but was engaged in writing to the Duke of Wellington to introduce Marshal Haynau, and the Princess added : "*J'espère bien que l'on ne s'imagine pas en Angleterre qu'il a maltraité les femmes en Hongrie ce n'est pas lui.*" It was not many months later that General Haynau was insulted and assaulted by brewers' draymen in London in the belief that he had been responsible for the flogging of Hungarian women. I can but look on Prince Metternich as a good authority, in spite of what was said on the subject by Lord Malmesbury.

The next time I saw Prince and Princess Metternich was at Blackwall, on board the Chinese junk, in 1849. I had gone there as a sightseer with the Bishop of Worcester and Mrs. Pepys, who were anxious to see the illustrious strangers. I ventured therefore to claim acquaintance and was most graciously recognised and introduced to Princess Mélanie Metternich, who had not been at the Hague. Prince Richard and Baron Hügel had accompanied them there. Princess Metternich was the old statesman's third wife (*née* Comtesse Zichy) and Princess Mélanie was her own child. Prince Richard was the Prince's son by his second wife, Comtesse Beulwitz.

CHAPTER XI.

I AM writing on regardless of times and seasons as to what happened, for I have to rely on my memory, having no notes. I should like to say how thankful we were when we got a church in which to hold our English Service. For a long time we had been dependent on the clergy from Rotterdam giving us a service when and where they could. My father placed our large dining-room every Sunday at the disposal of any clergyman who could come to us, and when this was impossible, read the prayers and a sermon to the household and to any of the Legation who wished to attend.

Many people in these stricter days would be very shocked to hear that when he was tired I read the Lessons, and on one occasion I misbehaved terribly. Just as I was about to read the Second Lesson my father began to cough and sneeze so loudly that I felt I should not be heard. I waited a little and then began to read Acts xx. commencing, " And after the uproar had ceased." This struck my sense of the ridiculous so forcibly, that I really did not know how to go on, and our nurse added to my difficulty by concluding that my little brother had played me a trick and rushing at him with her fist.

But to return to our dear little church. The money was collected and the Society for the Propagation of the Gospel came to our help, and we secured the services of our kind friend, Mr. Beresford. The King granted us a site in the Royal Library Gardens, on condition that the church should have no foundation, so that it might be moved if necessary. All things considered it looked very well, being built of wood and raised from the ground. It had a small chancel, pulpit, and reading desk, and an organ-loft in which we had a harmonium, and in which a little Sunday school was held, first by Mr. Beresford's daughter, and when he died and Mr. Brine succeeded, who had only small children, I undertook it. I found it no easy matter to carry it on, as I had to teach in two languages. The pupils being mostly the children of the King's English grooms, their language was very mixed, half Dutch, half English. In after years Mr. Tinnè, whose family was of Dutch origin, built an English church on the Boschkant. This he did on inheriting a considerable fortune on the death of his step-mother and sister, who had lived at the Hague. When I heard of it, I wrote to Mr. Brine, the chaplain, to beg he would let me know the date of the consecration, telling him I should like to be present. He, however, forgot all about my wish, and only when all was done, sent me a local paper describing the proceedings. I was much disappointed, as I had thought it would have been such a nice reason for revisiting the scene of my happy home of so many years.   I shall never do so now.   My travelling days are done.

Some time ago I read some travels in Holland in which the writer described the way Sunday was kept there as being as bad as in France and Germany. Things may have changed since I left in 1851, but my own impression is that Holland is only second to England in the true keeping of the Day of Rest. During the sixteen years we lived there I never heard of a ball, or opera, play or concert, or anything but a family gathering or dinner on Sundays.   The one exception made to the rule in the way of amusement was skating, and that principally by the working classes, who could hardly find any other time.   I think I may venture to say that as a nation the Dutch are true to their religion, and good, honest Protestants.   I well remember the great stir that was made when Halévy's Opera "La Juive" was to be produced on the stage.   I do not remember the opera well enough to state the exact objection made, but I think the idea was that a scriptural subject ought not to be introduced on the stage.   One of the most strenuous objectors was the minister of the Walloon Church, supported by a large number of his congregation, both Dutch and extraneous, and more especially by the colony of Swiss governesses, of which there was a regular *clique*.   The objectors, however, did not carry their point, and the opera was given.   A caricature appeared on the walls of the theatre representing scales, and M. Secretan, the Walloon minister, with all the Swiss governesses hanging on to his coat-tails, trying in vain to drag down "La Juive."

Under this picture was written: "*Malgré le cafard Suisse et sa digne cohorte, la voix publique s'elève et la Juive l'emporte.*" "Cafard" is an old word meaning a hypocrite, especially in reference to religious matters. Halévy, the composer of "La Juive," was born 1799, and died 1862.

In 1849 a sad misfortune happened to the country. King William II. was taken ill at Tilburg, near the Belgian frontier, where he had gone to visit his troops, who were encamped there, and he died on the 17th March, after a very short illness. All the Royal Family went in turns to see him, travelling all night, staying one day, and then returning home because no room could be found for them. The Queen was kept back by the doctor's orders, and when at last they yielded to her earnest entreaties, she did not see him alive, or at least she was not recognised.

Her Majesty arrived late at night, and the King hearing the carriage arrive, said: "I know that is the Queen; she was sure to come, and I must see her." His entreaties were in vain, and the poor Queen heard all that was said standing outside the door, not daring to enter. Within an hour or so she was called in only to see him die, and was almost beside herself. It was said she never forgave the cruel doctors. William II. was born in 1792, thus his death added to the long list of Orange-Nassaus, who had not lived to the allotted age of 70. He was much beloved, and was very good to England. He liked to remember that he had been at Christchurch, Oxford, and had fought with Wellington at Waterloo. Lord Raglan, then Lord Fitzroy Somerset, his brother-in-arms, represented the British Army at his funeral, and dined next day with us.

The heir, the Prince of Orange, had gone to England before the King was taken ill, and when the illness became serious it was not exactly known where to find him, and great was the horror expressed by the ladies of the Court when he told them there was no post in London on Sunday, and that that might cause some delay.

I think it must have been the day before the last sad news came that M. de Lightenfeld, the Minister for Foreign Affairs, ran after me and asked for my father, saying that I must find him at once, and tell no one else that the King was dying. He added, " I am going to England to fetch the Prince of Orange." I suggested that my father might be in the club, where he indeed was found after I had had a fruitless search both at home and elsewhere.

The Prince of Orange returned to the Hague as soon as possible, and was met by almost all the Royal Family at Rotterdam. It was said that on seeing the Queen he said, " I have two Queens to take care of now, my mother and *ma bonne Sophie.*" Of course we all went into the deepest mourning—cloth dresses, long crape veils, and so on.

The Inauguration took place on the 12th of May at Amsterdam. Black gowns were replaced on that occasion by grey or white, according to the age of the wearer, and excepting the public entry and a state dinner or so, there were no festivities. The new King rode as his father had done, and the Queen made her entry in a state coach, accompanied by her two little

sons, the Prince of Orange and Prince Maurice. She
looked very well as she walked up the church, tall
and fair, and all in white with a little son on each
side. All the Royal Family were present excepting
the widowed Queen. The King was very calm. He
was a much bigger man than his father, but had by
no means the same chivalrous appearance. I believe
he walked under a canopy, but we were waiting in
the church and did not see that. Among the visitors
was Alexandre Dumas, the French author. It was
said that he was invited by the King to give an
account of the Inauguration. Dumas was a peculiar-
looking man, very tall and big, with curly hair, giving
one the idea of a white negro. I believe he was a
Creôle. I allude of course to Dumas *père*.

The Queen-Mother, as Queen Anna Paulowna
elected to be called, went in the first instance to live
in a house that had belonged to her late son, Prince
Alexander, and was just outside the Hague ; and in
the course of the summer she took a small country
place near Arnheim, where we were asked to visit her
and dine with her. She was in a rather peculiar
widow's mourning—a close-fitting white muslin cap,
over which was one of black crape; her veil, white
weepers and collars were much like what were worn
in England. Her Majesty was most kind, and talked
very freely to my mother about her sorrows, and gave
her prints of herself and also of the late King and
Prince Alexander. We remained the next night at
Arnheim, and went from thence to the Loo, to which
we were invited by the King and Queen, who were
staying there for the hawking season. I thought the

place very pretty, and it was a treat to see running water, a thing quite unknown at the Hague.

The *Corps Diplomatique* were all invited week by week. My father being the doyen or senior minister, we had the first turn. We ladies were provided with black, grey and white dresses, to be worn according to daily orders sent to us. Queen Sophie disliked black so much, she was always finding out unknown birthdays or *fête* days of some kind as an excuse for either going out of black or into slight mourning. We lodged in a small hotel, and were fetched every day by royal carriages for a full dress three o'clock dinner. One day, whilst we were dressing, three different orders were sent to us, as to what degree of mourning we were to don, and after all we did wrong. The Queen appeared in grey and we in black. As soon as dinner was over we hurried back to our hotel to get ready as usual for a drive or ride with the Royalties. I generally rode with the Queen, who was a very timid rider. She had an equerry at each side, and mostly one or other of them had a hand on her rein. I was constantly told to keep back lest I should frighten her Majesty, and as my horse was an eager one it was not easy to obey. We used to ride to the top of a sand-hill, where the ladies dismounted. Cushions and rugs were placed on the ground, and we sat down to watch the hawking, while the gentlemen followed the sport. The time was always chosen when the herons went home with food for their young. The down-wind riders and up-wind riders as they were called loosed the hawks, and then followed at tremendous speed to save the herons' lives. They

took a particular feather from the birds' heads, placed
a ring marked with the name of place and date on
their legs, and let them fly. The hawks were hooded
to prevent them following their prey. Herons with
the Loo ring have been found at Naples.

We always had to make great haste on our return
from hawking to dress and be in time for the Queen's
tea ; and on the evening of the memorable day when
we had dressed in the wrong colour for dinner we
were later than usual. Her Majesty was already at
tea when we arrived in grey, to find that she had put
us at our ease by wearing black, as we had worn
black by mistake at dinner !

The young princesses staying at the Loo at the
time were Princess Louise, daughter of Prince
Frederic of the Netherlands, afterwards Queen of
Sweden ; and Princess Helen of Nassau, who married
the Prince of Waldeck, and was mother of the
Duchess of Albany. It pleased their Royal
Highnesses to have a game of whist, and they
chose my sister and myself as partners. As none of
us knew anything of the game, a chamberlain was
deputed to run round the table, look into each hand,
and tell each in turn what card to put down. It was
a most original game and the Queen was very much
amused.

Many old Dutch customs passed away in our day.
The fair at the Hague lost much of its importance
after the reign of King William II., who was I
believe the last King who gave a *fête* for it. He
used to issue invitations to all on the Court list to
meet at the Palace, and walk round the fair two and

two after himself and the Royal Family.   Generally
he stopped at some of the booths to make small
purchases and give presents to a favoured few.   I
remember his giving my mother a small china figure,
and telling her it was Baron Verstolk, the then
Minister of Foreign Affairs.   On leaving the fair we
returned to the Palace for our early dinner—dressing-
rooms were prepared for the guests—and we ended
the day by a dance.

A woman known by the name of Constantia,
remarkable both for her size and loquacity, came to
sell Saxon lace at the Hague most years.   She told
us it was chiefly made by miners, her husband and
sons making much of it in the winter evenings.   It
was very good lace, a great deal being copied from
Chantilly patterns, and was almost as fine as the
latter.   The woman made her journeys chiefly on
foot, with her pack on her back, but occasionally got
a lift on the Rhine boats.   If she was tired, her
tongue was not, for she never ceased talking.   She
recounted to us, amongst other things, that her eldest
son was a gentleman, that she had sold him as a
baby to a baron in Tyrol, who had no son, and that
when she went to see him he was told that she
was his old nurse.   I did not think much of the tale
at the time, but years afterwards I remembered it on
seeing an account in a Leamington paper of a
" Sensational Story in Tyrol."   I think that was the
heading.   The only daughter of an ancient Austrian
family was about to be married to the supposed only
son of the neighbouring baron, when it was discovered that he was not his son, but a peasant boy

whom he had adopted and brought up. I could but
connect the lace-seller's tale and the newspaper story
in my mind, and conclude that the old woman's
gossip was the cause of the discovery.

Another person who paid us a yearly visit was
a M. Etiennè, from Nancy, who brought some of the
most beautiful embroidery I have ever seen. One
year he arrived later than usual, and when I told him
I was sorry as he had missed on opportunity of
selling his wares to Madame de Tüyll for her
daughter's *trousseau*, he excused himself by saying,
"*J'ai eu un accident assez désagréable, j'ai perdu ma
femme.*"

The first arrival of the herring fleet was considered
a great event. The boats flew to the shore as fast as
the wind would blow them, and as high up on the
beach as the waves would take them, and unloading
was done as speedily as possible. Bright carts of a
peculiar shape, called *swane wagen*, were in waiting,
and the drivers all in their best clothes, often accompanied by their wives in full peasant costume, raced
from the landing-place, Scheveningen, to the Palace
at the Hague, to be the first to present fresh herrings
to the King. The man fortunate enough to win the
race received a present in money, which was well
worth having. In our time the same man had been
the happy winner for several years. It was amusing
to watch this race. Flags were flying from many
parts of the light carts, which were painted up for the
occasion with curious devices ; I have the impression
that one ornament was always a swan. Raw and
smoked herrings were very much appreciated in

Holland, and our friend, Madame Hergèles used to give us an annual invitation to her country house, Marlot, a few miles out of the Hague, and feast us on raw herrings and green peas, [and I really liked the mixture. Talking of green peas, very small Dutch babies from three to four years old are often fed on green peas and young carrots with plenty of brown sugar, and they seem to thrive on that food.

A great deal of food is grown in Holland for the London market. The vegetables are very fine, and meat, or rather the animals, are brought over in considerable quantities. I remember once crossing to England with a large number of very small calves, and wondering how many there were. In a few days my curiosity wes satisfied by seeing in the paper that Sir William and Lady de Tüyll, Miss Disbrowe, and two hundred and forty calves were landed at Blackwall on Thursday from the Rotterdam steamer.

Sheep are brought over in great numbers, and curiously enough, mutton is not considered whole-some meat in Holland. Our doctor said the meat was feverish, because the sheep were usually fed on marshy ground; but I have no doubt that a great deal of that mutton is eaten in England without causing fever, possibly a case of "where ignorance is bliss." Our doctor, Wachter by name, made an expedition to England in our day, and on his return my mother asked him what his impressions were. His answer was that he did not think much of our beef and veal, but that the mutton was superb, and if

he could get any like it in Holland he would
recommend it to all his patients. Of course we were
amused, and wondered whether the mutton in question might not have come from his own native land.
Potatoes were certainly very good ; my father sent a
large quantity to Ireland at the time of the potato
famine in 1847. They were grown in large quantities as the first crop on land reclaimed from the
sea. It is possible that the salt in the soil improved
them. I cannot help thinking that the same may be
the case with Dutch hyacinths, which are grown
principally in large fields near Haarlem, and the
sand, which is very light coloured, looks like that on
the shore at Scheveningen.

People in England always talk about Dutch tulips,
but I think the natives are much more proud of their
hyacinths. When a new one is produced, the owner
invites some person of note to come and name it,
who then brings a party with him for the occasion.
We were invited by Prince Alexander to accompany
him on such an errand, and H.R.H. gave us a
luncheon at Haarlem, where we were treated to some
very nasty little cakes, peculiar to the town, and
made and called after it, " *Harlemje Rooze-Letter,*"
they being made to represent a letter.

Whilst we were in Holland the great works for
draining the Lake of Haarlem were begun, and we
went several times to watch the progress of the
undertaking. A large circular canal was made to
surround the lake, with one outlet to the old Rhine
at Katwyk, the other into the Zuider-Zee. The
gigantic engines were worked by Cornish miners.

The work was not nearly completed when we left in 1851, but was finished a few years later, and the land is under cultivation. The depth was not very great, but the lake was fourteen miles long. A large quantity of stag horns were found and some remains belonging to a long-buried past.

Holland was and still may be famous for several secret remedies, of which perhaps the most remarkable was the remedy for epilepsy, known by the name of "*Sloet Powden.*" The secret possessed by the families of Sloet and Schimmelpenich; and during our residence in the country, old Baron Sloet, who had himself watched, treated, and cured many cases, thought it would be right and humane to make the recipe public and so let the doctors know all about it. We heard of many cures effected both before and at the time of our sojourn in the country, but I believe all the cures that had succeeded were those that had been watched by doctors of the country. Of course I speak of more than fifty years ago. I have been told that Mr. Bouldon, a chemist in Edinburgh, has the recipe and makes it up better than other chemists, but I cannot answer for that. My mother often talked the matter over with our doctor when he was treating a young lad in whom we were much interested. He said very few medical men recognised the extreme caution needed to carry out the cure. The medicine was so strong that sometimes it could only be given twice a week, lest the brain should suffer. The governess in charge of the boy said at first she thought Doctor Wachter a terrible fidget, making a fuss about trifles, but as she watched the treatment she saw a meaning in each apparently trifling precaution. She was to describe to the doctor how the patient held his thumbs during each attack, whether they turned in or out as he clenched his hands, and he showed her how to hold him during the fits, a matter to which he attached great importance. The poor fellow became wonderfully better during his stay at the Hague, but most unfortunately his father insisted on his return to England, and treated all special care in small things as nonsense. The result was fatal to the lad's brain.

In 1850 we spent some very pleasant days with the Queen-Mother. She was always specially kind and gracious to us. She was living at Soesdyk, an old residence of the House of Orange, which the King had left to her, and she in turn left it to her youngest son, Prince Henry. Her Majesty told us about the Princess Anne of England, eldest daughter of George II., who had lived there. She was Regent for her son, the Stadtholder, and died in 1759. Anna Paulowna spoke of her in high terms as a most useful woman when Regent, but that is not the impression given in some modern memoirs. Her's was the last alliance between the House of England and Holland royal.

The Prince of Orange's youngest son, Prince Henry, greatly admired Princess May of Cambridge, afterwards Duchess of Teck. And I myself heard the Duchess of Cambridge ask my father what he thought of Princess Sophie of the Netherlands, who married the Grand Duke of Weimar, adding, " I did think of her for George."

In later years the Prince of Orange, son of William III., came over to be inspected by Queen Victoria, I feel sure to find out if he would suit Princess Alice, but with no success. My sister and I were in London at the time, when an old friend, who accompanied the Prince, came to see us, and said, "What a wonderful woman your Queen is ; she drew from me in ten minutes all I did not mean to tell her." We were invited one evening to meet the Prince, who was very gracious and pleasant. I thought him like his grandfather, William II., both in figure and manner. He spent much of his short life away from his own country ; was a great deal in Paris, where he used to be called "*le citron*," and died there. His next brother, Prince Maurice, born in 1843, died either in 1850 or 1851. There were sad differences between the King and Queen during his illness, the King wishing him to be attended by the Court physician, the Queen by a favourite doctor of her own, a man of no reputation at all. At last General Boreel, who was attached to the Court, persuaded the Queen to yield to the King's wishes. The child, however, died. On his death, Princess Frederic, who was always the peacemaker in the Royal Family, persuaded the King to forgive the Queen. The three stood by the dead child's bed, and the King said, " As the loss of a child of that age is far greater to a mother than to a father, I will try to comfort her." He made one condition which, alas ! he soon found was not fulfilled. X

Prince Alexander, the youngest son, was born in
1851. He was an invalid from his youth. Both
these sons survived their mother, Queen Sophie,
and they, as well as the King, were present at her
death, which took place at the House-in-the-Wood,
near the Hague, during the seventies. Both Princes
died before their father, who married Princess Emma
of Waldeck in 1879, and died in 1890, leaving by
her the present Queen Wilhelmina. Prince Frederic,
the late king's uncle, had also lost both his sons in
their infancy. Of his daughters, the elder, Princess
Louise, married the Prince Royal of Sweden, afterwards King Charles XV. She died in 1871, leaving
one daughter, the Princess Royal of Denmark. The
younger sister, Princess Marie, married the Prince
of Wied, and is the only member of the House of
Orange, whom we knew, who is still living. Prince
Henry, the late King's last brother, was married
twice; first, to Princess Amèlie of Saxe-Weimar,
who died, I believe, in 1872; then to a Prussian
Princess, who left no children.

Not long after Prince Alexander's birth the old
King of Würtemberg came to see his daughter, it
was said to try to arrange matters between her and
the King. But, however, no real conciliation could
be effected ; so he arranged that they should remain
in the same palace, but in different wings, and once
a month they were to dine together with their
Court, on which occasion the King was to fetch
the Queen from her apartment, and lead her in
before the assembled company. The King then
gave her the choice of several of his houses, should

she prefer to live there, only hinting that he would like to keep the Loo for himself. It was said that he even bought a place near Arnheim, in case she liked that part of the country best. She, however, chose the House-in-the-Wood, and on arriving there found the conservatory filled with her favourite flowers. The arrangement for the Palace at the Hague was only kept for the season, and for State occasions. I think that King William III. deserved some credit for the way he behaved under these trying circumstances. It was also known that when the Queen was travelling all over Europe the King remained at his post, and never would allow a word to be said against her. She was a clever woman, a great politician, and much devoted to the Emperor Napoleon. Perhaps if she had had a more extended sphere for her talents than the little country where her married life was cast she might have been a happier woman. Yet she had many friends and admirers. I once had an audience with her when she was at Claridge's Hotel. She came to England not long after Princess Beatrice was born, and said she saw much for which to envy the Queen of England ; and mostly she envied her lovely baby. This last was not said to me. The next time we saw any of the Dutch Royal Family was when Princess Frederic and her daughter, Princess Marie, came to Torquay in search of health, and my sister and I went to pay our respects, and were most graciously received.

But to return to the Hague, where our days were ending most sadly. My dear father fell ill in

September, and although for some time we had
hopes that he might be spared to us, we soon saw
how his sufferings must end. The last time we
attended any function was when Prince Alexander
was christened. My father could not be present;
only my mother and we two sisters were able to
go. The Prince was a very puny baby. He was
carried in on a cushion of cloth of silver, with a
train of the same material attached to it; and the
"*Dame du Palais*," who carried him, said that it was
most difficult to keep the poor little thing from
being jerked off the cushion, especially as the
chamberlain who bore the train did not keep
step.

After that day our anxieties increased. As the
doctor gave no hope, my dear young brothers were
sent for from England; but neither they nor my
father's eldest sister, Lady Taylor (who came as fast
as she could in spite of her own weak health), nor
my Kennedy grandmother and aunt were in time to
see him. My mother, my sister, and myself, our
kind chaplain, Mr. Brine, and good old Page, our
housekeeper, were the privileged ones who witnessed
the most peaceful and happy death on the 29th
October, 1851.

We experienced the greatest kindness from all
who knew our dear one, and it was indeed a comfort
to receive the assurance of how he was valued and
appreciated by high and low, rich and poor. On
the last day of his life my father bid us send for
his friend, Sir William de Tüyll, who was near
Arnheim at the time, and came as fast as his

horse could bring him.   He was a great help to my mother.

The English Government sent the " Lightning," the same vessel in which we had been so nearly lost coming home from Sweden, and in which we had gone there, to take the dear remains back to England.

The King of the Netherlands sent an escort of cavalry to follow to Rotterdam ; and Sir William de Tüyll and Mr. Mark, the chaplain at Rotterdam, accompanied my young brothers to England.   My dear father was laid in the family vault at Walton-on-Trent, by the side of his father and mother. Then began the trying preparations for breaking up our home of sixteen years.   It was hard work, for my mother wished that no time should be lost, and everybody we had known wished to see us.   My father's old servant, Eggert,* who had been with him in his early wanderings, came all the way from Frankfort to know if he could be of use, and remained after we left to pack up and see to the sale.   My aunt, Lady Taylor, stayed with us to the last.

We started in the old coach at four o'clock one December morning to catch the steamer at Rotterdam, and on arriving on board found that we had been followed by an omnibus full of old servants come to bid us a last farewell.

On reaching England we went in the first instance to my aunt Lady Taylor's house, St. Catherine's, in the Regent's Park, but did not settle anywhere

* *See* Eggert's Letter.   Part I.

till Michaelmas, 1853, when my mother took a house in London, because my brother Edward had exchanged from the 85th Foot to the Coldstream Guards. She thought it wise to give him a home, but it was not of use to him for long. The Crimean War broke out, and the Coldstream Guards were some of the earliest troops to be sent to the seat of war. The dear fellow, who had carried the colours safely through the Alma, fell, as has been already said, at Inkermann, November 5th, 1854, a never-to-be-forgotten day to us.

My mother's health never recovered from that terrible loss, and what made it still more trying was that the same day that she learnt of it she also heard from her younger son William that his regiment was ordered to the Crimea, and that he was to go with the first detachment. My mother saw him once more in 1855. When her case was pronounced hopeless by the doctors, Lord Raglan kindly expressed a wish that my brother should be granted leave, that he might be with her. He stayed with us until after her death in October, 1855, then returned to the Crimea, and from thence went with his regiment to Canada, where he became adjutant, one of the youngest in the army.

I wrote after he had been some time in Canada to ask if he could not come home, as he was of age, and I believed our agent was failing in health. My brother replied that, being regimental adjutant, he could not leave until the summer drills were over, but would try to come later on. The next letter brought the news that he had been named aide-de-camp to Sir William Eyre, then commanding the forces in Canada; and in a few weeks from that time we learnt that he had been taken from us after a very short illness. He died at Sir William's house at Sorel, nursed by Lady Eyre as if he had been her own son. The details she gave us of his last days showed how deservedly he had been loved by all who knew him. He was only twenty-three years old, and we had not seen him for three years.

My sister married Mr. Wise, of Woodcote, M.P. for South Warwickshire, in 1868. I bore my solitude as best I could; and in her widowhood she returned to me and to the old home in which she had been born. She brought with her her dear young son and daughter, who remained with us until they married.

Days are dark and friends drop off with the lapse of time, and I had better drop my pen and wonder who will care to read the rambling recollections of the octogenarian daughter of an old Diplomatist.

THE END.

LIST OF SUBSCRIBERS TO THE
ORIGINAL EDITION.

Mrs. Charles Bagot
The Lady Burton
Sir Robert and Lady Frances Gresley. *(2 copies)*
Miss Gresley
Miss Gisborne. *(3 copies)*
Mrs. Mapplebeck
Miss Deedes
The Misses Wilbraham. *(2 copies)*
Honble. Mrs. Richard Boyle. *(2 copies)*
Mrs. C. Elphinstone Dalrymple *(2 copies)*
Miss Nadin
Colonel Thomas Innes of Learney
Mr. and Mrs. Robert Levett. *(2 copies)*
Mrs. Levett-Prinsep
Miss Patten *(2 copies)*
Miss Lyon
Henry Nadin, Esq.
Miss Arden
The Lady Jane Levett
Honble. Mrs. Alexander
Mrs. Bridges Taylor
Honble. Mrs. Griffiths. *(10 copies)*
Basil Levett, Esq.
Mrs. Grafton
The Misses Fisher. *(2 copies)*
Miss Ratcliff
Mrs. Beard
Mrs. Milligan
Mrs. Selwyn. *(2 copies)*
Mrs. Charles Wise
H. E. D. Wise, Esq. *(2 copies)*
Gilbert Kennedy, Esq.

John Gretton, Esq., M.P.
Honble. Mrs. Gretton
Rev. H. Skipwith
Miss E. Skipwith
Miss Louisa Hobart. *(4 copies)*
Mrs. Charles Gresley
Sir Reginald and Lady Hardy *(2 copies)*
Mrs. Anson-Horton
Mrs. W. Ross King
The Lady Knightley of Fawsley
Admiral Sir William and Lady Kennedy. *(2 copies)*
E. H. Leycester-Penrhyn, Esq. *(2 copies)*
Lady Clerke. *(2 copies)*
Colonel Hobart
Rev. H. M. Oswald
Mrs. Meach
Mrs. Brown
H. Anson-Horton, Esq. *(2 copies)*
Miss Campbell
Miss Montgomery-Campbell. *(2 copies)*
Arthur Legge, Esq.
The Marquis of Ripon, K.G. *(3 copies)*
The Marchioness of Ripon. *(3 copies)*
Honble. Elinor Wilson Patten. *(3 copies)*
Miss Gisborne. *(2 copies)*
The Lord Bishop of Bristol
Honble. Mrs. Meynell-Ingram *(3 copies)*
Miss Disbrowe. *(8 copies)*
The Lady Florence King King
Mrs. W. A. Traill

www.ingramcontent.com/pod-product-compliance
Lightning Source LLC
Chambersburg PA
CBHW031941080426
42735CB00007B/213